Provisional Authority

Provisional Authority

Police, Order, and Security in India

BEATRICE JAUREGUI

The University of Chicago Press
Chicago and London

The University of Chicago Press, Chicago 60637
The University of Chicago Press, Ltd., London
© 2016 by The University of Chicago
All rights reserved. Published 2016.
Printed in the United States of America

25 24 23 22 21 20 19 18 17 16   1 2 3 4 5

ISBN-13: 978-0-226-40367-0 (cloth)
ISBN-13: 978-0-226-40370-0 (paper)
ISBN-13: 978-0-226-40384-7 (e-book)
DOI: 10.7208/chicago/9780226403847.001.0001

Publication of this book has been aided by a grant from the Bevington Fund.

Library of Congress Cataloging-in-Publication Data

Names: Jauregui, Beatrice, author.
Title: Provisional authority : police, order, and security in India /
    Beatrice Jauregui.
Description: Chicago : The University of Chicago Press, 2016. | Includes
    bibliographical references and index.
Identifiers: LCCN 2016022229 | ISBN 9780226403670 (cloth : alk. paper) |
    ISBN 9780226403700 (pbk. : alk. paper) | ISBN 9780226403847 (e-book)
Subjects: LCSH: Police—India—Lucknow. | Justice, Administration of—Social
    aspects—India—Lucknow. | Uttar Pradesh (India). Police Department. |
    Police corruption—India—Lucknow.
Classification: LCC HV8250.L8 J38 2016 | DDC 363.20954/2—dc23 LC record
    available at https://lccn.loc.gov/2016022229

♾ This paper meets the requirements of ANZI/NISO Z39.48-1992 (Permanence of Paper).

Contents

Acknowledgments vii

1 **Police and Provisionality** 1

2 **Corruptible Virtue** 33

3 **Orderly Ethics** 60

4 **Expendable Servants** 83

5 **Bureaucratic Politics** 113

6 **States of Insecurity** 138

Appendix 159
Notes 161
References 177
Index 193

Acknowledgments

First and foremost, I would like to thank the many Uttar Pradesh Police officers who have shared their thoughts and experiences with me over the years. Each of you has made a vital contribution to this study, and my appreciation for your openness about your life and work can never be adequately expressed. I hope that you may be able to read and reflect on some part of your own story here. Special thanks to "Y. K. Yadav" and the staff at "Chakkar Rasta Thana" for sharing their lives with me.

I must also thank the many people in Lucknow and New Delhi who extended their hospitality, assistance, and friendship to me as I conducted my research over the years, especially Ram Advani, Fazal Iqbal Ahmed, Suniti Kumar, and the staff at the local outposts of the American Institute of Indian Studies. My gratitude to my research assistant, colleague, and friend, Virendra Pratap Yadav, extends far beyond words. Without his formidable ethnographic skills, indefatigable scholarly spirit, generous sense of humor, and his enhanced ability to do *jugaad*, much of the analysis presented here never would have been possible. I am forever grateful to him and his wonderful family for all they have done for me.

Financial support for research was provided by the American Institute of Indian Studies, the Andrew W. Mellon Foundation, the American Council of Learned Societies, the Committee on Southern Asian Studies at the University of Chicago, the Jacob K. Javits Program of the US Department of Education, and the Social Science Research Council. Further support and the invaluable resource of time for writing in a collegial and inspiring intellectual milieu were provided by the Center for the Advanced Study of India, Emmanuel College at the University of Cambridge, and the Humanities Forum at the University of Pennsylvania. I thank them all for their incredible generosity.

Portions of the manuscript were presented to audiences at the University of Chicago, University of Pennsylvania, University of Cambridge, University of Toronto, and several other institutions of higher learning in Asia, Europe, and North America, as well as at the annual meetings of the American Anthropological Association, American Ethnological Society, Annual Conference on South Asia at Madison, Asian Association of Police Studies, and the Association of Asian Studies. I extend my sincere thanks to everyone who attended these presentations and engaged critically with my work.

I am very grateful to all of those who commented on various portions of the manuscript and offered support in other ways over the course of this project. Since the research and writing spanned more than a decade, there are too many people to name here, but I especially wish to acknowledge Jacqui Baker, Debjani Bhattacharyya, Lisa Bjorkman, Betsey Brada, Khadija Zinnenburg Carroll, Jessica Cattelino, Dipesh Chakrabarty, Balraj Chauhan, Richard Delacy, William Elison, Jessica Falcone, Didier Fassin, Alexander Flynn, Francine Frankel, Chris Fuller, William Garriott, Eric Haanstaad, Thomas Blom Hansen, Nadeem Hasnain, Julia Hornberger, Brian Horne, Matthew Hull, Craig Jeffrey, Devesh Kapur, Kevin Karpiak, Sudipta Kaviraj, Nita Kumar, Joel Lee, William Lutz, McKim Marriott, Jeffrey Martin, William Mazzarella, Sean T. Mitchell, Rahul Mukherji, C. M. Naim, Olly Owen, Anastasia Piliavsky, Erika Robb Larkins, Anasuya Sengupta, Lawrence Sherman, Michael Silverstein, Lisa Simeone, Jonathan Spencer, Meg Stalcup, Michelle Stewart, Heather Strang, Nathan Tabor, Justice Tankebe, Mariana Valverde, Sylvia Vatuk, Jeremy Walton, Steven Wilkinson, and D. N. S. Yadav. Special thanks to Linda Kim and Jenny Carlson for providing invaluable feedback on earlier drafts of the full manuscript. Heartfelt thanks to my *atma behen* Thangam Ravindranathan for the eternal dialogue in search of understanding, and to my dearly missed friend and mentor Steven Rubenstein for inspiring me to become an anthropologist and showing me the provocative power of popular films, especially *Cop Land*. I owe an immeasurable debt of gratitude to John D. Kelly, John L. Comaroff, and Joseph Masco, who offered support over the course of this entire project. Our dialogues have been an ongoing source of encouragement and insight, and I can never thank them enough.

David Brent, Ellen Kladky, and their colleagues at the University of Chicago Press have helped in innumerable ways with the preparation of this book. I would like to extend my gratitude to them and to two anonymous reviewers, whose constructive questions and comments helped me to clarify and improve the analysis considerably.

Parts of this book were first published in other venues. An earlier version of chapter 2 was published in *American Ethnologist* as "Provisional Agency in India: *Jugaad* and Legitimation of Corruption," and an earlier version of chapter 4 was published in *Conflict and Society* as "Just War: The Metaphysics of Police Vigilantism in India."

None of this would have been possible without the love and support of my family. My parents, Helen and Stephen, have been an unending font of inspiration and encouragement for me from the beginning; and my siblings, Ellen, Stephen, and Kitty, have backed me up in so many ways throughout the years. Anasuya, Mukund, and Hillary have also been illuminating sources of support. Special thanks to Kitty and Helen for being there weekly to help with child care over the months it took to complete the manuscript (especially to Kitty for the home-cooked meals peppered with provocative discussions about, among other things, police and society). And finally, as the spouses and children of writers contribute more to a manuscript than can ever be acknowledged: Anand, you have been my rock and my home through all of this, our life *sangam* born just as this project began to find its beating heart. Kiran, our rapidly growing ray of light, you and the culmination of this book simultaneously emerged into the world as your own inspired beings. My loves, thank you.

Police and Provisionality

Police in the Field

It is June 2007, and a typical summer evening patrol for Uttar Pradesh Police (UPP) constables Arvind Sharma and Ashish Tiwari; typical, except that an American anthropologist and her research assistant, a PhD student at a local university, are accompanying them on their journey through their *halka* (beat) in the northern rural areas of Lucknow district. Sharma and Tiwari have been assigned two main tasks today by their boss, the station chief of Chakkar Rasta Thana (circling path police station), or what they abbreviate to CRT in English.[1] First, ensure that all is peaceful near the Ma Devi Mandir (temple of the mother goddess), since there have been some reports of possible "tensions" of a political-religious nature. Second, gather some information about the whereabouts and activities of some nearby farm owners who seem to be generally absent from their landholdings.

Tiwari, a balding moustachioed constable who has been with the UPP for almost twenty years, drives his own motorbike. Sharma, a younger constable with about thirteen years in service, sits behind Tiwari as passenger, an old .303 rifle from the CRT armory slung over his bony shoulder. A few kilometers before reaching the temple, we all stop at a small stand selling various wares near the local cold storage unit, which is surrounded by open crop fields. The stand is little more than a hutch resting on sticks, crudely assembled with wood and cloth coverings. A bare lightbulb is strung on a wire, but is mum for lack of working electricity.

Upon our arrival, the *dukandar* (shopkeeper) promptly leaps up to offer us a seat and has a boy fetch chai for us. But the constables make known that they are here to take in more than a hot beverage. They would like to learn or confirm the family names, phone numbers, and alternative addresses of some area landowners. When I ask them about why their boss wants this information—is it not public record?—Sharma and Tiwari say that they are helping to track a very common process of money laundering. They inform me further that they are usually able to get this type of information from people like this humble *dukandar*, or from house servants or tenant farmers who work the land.

They proceed to describe in great detail how wealthier people buy up property in these villages to hide their excesses of *kaalaa daan* (black money) by claiming that it is farm income, which is nontaxable by law, and thus cannot be audited.[2] The constables chuckle about the fact that Bollywood film megastar Amitabh Bachchan and his wife, Jaya Bachchan—who is a Member of Parliament representing Uttar Pradesh (UP) in New Delhi for the Samajwadi, or Socialist, Party—are on trial for this very crime, having some time ago acquired farm property in Barabanki, a district just east of the UP state capital of Lucknow.

"The Big B, calling himself a farmer, ha!" they laugh.[3]

Their laughter disappears into a hot dark night that plays host to few sounds besides the nattering of mosquitos and other insects. After a few minutes, a thunderous engine and high beams pierce the black dusty air, and a truck overloaded with lumber rattles past us. Tiwari elbows Sharma and gesticulates.

"*Chalo chalo!*" (Go, go get it!), Tiwari urges.

Sharma seems reluctant.

"*Tumhara hai, bas, chalo*" (This one is yours, that's it, you go).

Tiwari sighs and jumps up to dash after the truck. Unable to find the key to his own motorcycle (which he later learns is locked in the side box), he takes another two wheeler from one of the village youth, a small group of whom have gathered to stare at the curious scene of two uniformed police constables accompanied by a visibly foreign fair-skinned woman who speaks Hindi and wears a *salwar kameez* (lady's suit).

Less than five minutes later, Tiwari returns. In response to Sharma's expectant nod, he shakes his head with what appears to be glum resignation.

"*Voh jaan pehechaan ka hai*" (He is known to us).

This is clearly the death knell to a glimmer of hope; the quashing of a chase of chance. After my assistant and I do some careful prodding, Sharma and Tiwari admit that upon seeing the overloaded vehicle they had been hoping to extract a bit of money from the driver, perhaps Rs. 50–100 (US $1–2) to split between them. But something beyond their visible authority as police has denied them *ghuus khaanaa* (to take, literally "to eat," a bribe).

We ask them on what basis they would have been able to take money.

"Was he doing something illegal?"

They respond that yes, he was driving an obviously overloaded vehicle and, Tiwari learned during the stop, without a license. They had thought he might also be transporting illegally cut wood, a common crime in this area (turns out he was not). So, the constables could have received a bribe from the truck driver in exchange for letting him go without a fine for the overload and lack of license, a common practice.

"We don't even have to ask for money, people just offer," Sharma notes.

My assistant makes a provocative "joke" about how they also could have beat it out of him, "*hai na?*" (right?). They snicker and admit they could have, and perhaps would have . . . but when we inquire as to why they did not harass this truck driver further and demand money, Sharma repeats his partner's utterance.

"He is known to us."

Upon being asked if they know him personally as an acquaintance, they explain that they do not but the driver had dropped the name of their boss, the CRT chief station officer (SO), and indicated that there is already an agreement between them. We learn that the truck driver gives a regular protection payment glossed as "monthly" (the English word)[4] to the *dalaal* (fixer or broker) of the SO. The driver's categorization as "known to us" (i.e., known to "the police" at large) thus points to an existing set of relationships and exchanges that trumps what might otherwise be their coercive capability to extract a payoff.

Tiwari sighs and sits down on the *thakt* (wooden cot) with Sharma. We are several kilometers from the main highway, and the evening *puja* (prayer gathering) at the Ma Devi Mandir ended a while ago; so there is little traffic on this village road. Apparently confident that there is not much need for vigilance at the *mandir*—though we do drop by later, so that the two men can greet the priest and take *darshan*, the common ritual of devotees glimpsing deities in Hindu temples—Sharma and Tiwari sit back and we continue to chat.

One of the top local news items of the day for these police is the fact that they have a new boss. The SO who gave them today's investigative orders has been in his post as chief for only a couple of weeks. The prior SO, Y. K. Yadav—whom I know quite well since I have by now been conducting fieldwork at CRT for many months—has been transferred out of the post with some controversy. UP state legislative assembly elections have recently finished, and one of the candidates, a high-caste person, had complained that Mr. Yadav was engaging in illicit practices on behalf of the previously ruling Samajwadi Party, which is led by members of his caste, considered "lower" and officially classified as an "Other Backward Class" or OBC. Yadav denied the charges of bias in favor of his caste or the Samajwadi Party, but was removed from his post anyway.

Many CRT-based constables and sub-inspectors have by this time offered various theories about why Yadav was "really" removed: perhaps he did not pay the district superintendent a good enough bribe to keep the post; perhaps he upset one of the local elected MLAs (Members of Legislative Assembly); perhaps someone else with influence charged him with corruption (for Yadav's own explanation, see chap. 5). Sharma and Tiwari offer another possibility: SO Yadav had offended, and therefore been recommended for removal by, his immediate superior in the local police hierarchy, a circle officer named Valmiki. Valmiki is a Dalit, or untouchable, legally known as SC/ST (Scheduled Caste/Scheduled Tribe), and locally known to be affiliated with the Dalit-led Bahujan Samaj Party, the primary rival of the OBC-led Samajwadi Party.

Sharma and Tiwari, who are both of Brahmin castes, think that Valmiki resented that Yadav seemed to enjoy more power than he, even though Yadav ranked lower in the police hierarchy. They say Valmiki believed that Yadav did not always follow orders because the latter would be protected by his political connections with the ruling party if he was reported to higher authorities. But Tiwari seems to defend Yadav, insisting that if he did not always follow orders, it was only because, "Yadav is much more experienced . . . he knows the system better than Valmiki, who has fewer years in the service and is a newcomer to this area, having been transferred here himself only a few months ago."

Sharma chimes in, "You know, Yadav remained at CRT as station chief for some thirteen months. That means he is honest, because if he were dishonest, there would have been complaints against him by local villagers, and he would have been removed much sooner."

Tiwari continues, "Yadav is a good man, a good officer. He is the kind of boss who supports and takes care of his men. They are not all like that."

Sharma agrees vigorously, "Yes, I have had some terrible bosses!" and launches into a story about how he was once badly beaten by some men in a family of wealthy media moguls, after intervening in their assault on one of their youngest brothers.[5] When Sharma first reported the incident to his then boss, the sub-inspector laughed at him. But he makes it a point to say that the next day, the sub-inspector went ahead and accompanied Sharma to the house of the men who had beaten him, and stood watch while Sharma gave several of them a thrashing of his own.

"I took out all of my frustration, and beat three men single handedly. This is the importance of officer support. If your boss is with you, then you can do the work of four men. If he is not with you, even four men cannot do the work of one."

When I ask Sharma whether beating his assailants had any productive effect besides giving him satisfaction in vengeance, Tiwari jumps back in, comparing Sharma's situation to other fellow police who have recently been criticized in the media for using excessive force and mismanaging crowd violence among protesting Gujjars (another OBC group) in the neighboring state of Rajasthan.

"Imagine a situation in which there are very few cops and thousands of people. Police have no choice—they have to *lathi-charge* [beat with batons] or fire on the crowd, or instead be killed. Everyone focuses on deaths of civilians at the hands of police, but they never think of how a mob will also kill police."

He then points to a farmhouse across the way.

"Now, imagine some criminals in this farmhouse, running from a mob of villagers who want to kill them. Our first duty is to protect the criminals, because it is for the court to decide what happens to them, not us. But then the next day's newspaper headline says, 'Police Save the Criminals.'"

Sharma chuckles at this, and adds another hypothetical scenario to the list of complaints alleging public misapprehensions leading to a poor police image.

> Suppose I am doing *picket duty* [security guard] on the road, and there is an accident nearby. My first duty is to help the injured man, send him to the hospital, and I have to take him myself if I have my motorcycle or ask a *tempo* [group taxi] to take him [because there is no public ambulance service immediately available], and pay the doctor out of my own pocket if he doesn't have any money. When I report back to my SO, he is angry that I have not secured the victim's mobile phone or some other item that has been reported missing from the scene . . . then the police are blamed for pocketing peoples' valuables.

At this point in the conversation, almost as if fate were having a bit of fun, a young man approaches the constables and says that an accident has happened up ahead on the road. We all go to the scene, finding there another young man with a bloody gash next to his right eye, an old woman standing by listlessly and a cow grazing in the grass nearby. The two youths say they skidded on the road to avoid hitting the cow that the woman was prodding down the dark road. They want money for medicine, and when she offers Rs. 20 they scoff. Tiwari negotiates a compromise, telling the woman she should help out, since they saved her cow by having the accident; but he also notes that they were not wearing helmets, and suspects they were speeding, so he tells the young men they need to pay the remainder out of their own pocket.

Everyone agrees to the compromise, more or less begrudgingly; the woman gives the youth Rs. 50, and we all move along.

As we ride our motorbikes back to CRT, I see the truck overloaded with wood that Tiwari had chased earlier stopped on the side of the road. Some of the timber has fallen, and the driver is loping around surveying the situation, presumably trying to figure out what to do. Sharma and Tiwari speed by without stopping to help, and I follow them.

Chalta hai: Police Authority in India

At the heart of this book is the puzzle of police authority and its relationship to social order, democratic politics, and security in postcolonial India. What exactly constitutes police authority? How does it manifest differently depending on the context and the actors involved? Where, when, and how is it exercised? By, for, and against whom? Where, when, and how is it limited; and again by, for, and against whom?

The seeds of these research questions were planted the moment I set foot on Indian soil for the very first time on a trip to study intercommunity marriage in 2000. A senior officer with the Indian Administrative Service (IAS) that I knew had made some arrangements on my behalf with his associates in New Delhi, expressing hope that my arrival would be "hassle-free." When I deplaned, two uniformed police constables greeted me with a name placard, then led me past the long queues of tired passengers awaiting immigration approval to an officer in a private room who quickly stamped my passport. I was then shepherded into a white government ambassador car topped with a red beacon and taken to the office of a deputy superintendent of police (DySP), an amicable man who spoke as if he could grant my every wish. He told me to call him directly if I ever had a problem, and he would fix it right away. Over the next few months, he helped me set up interviews for my research and even arranged for me to visit the Taj Mahal and other historic sites all free of charge.

It was all quite impressive and I thought to myself, "So this is how it works in India when you are a police officer—or when such an official is your friend." It felt like all doors were open to me, that access to people and resources was total and free. Based on this experience, I designed an ethnographic study of police power with the idea that I would be conducting a textbook case of what Laura Nader (1972) called "studying up." When I returned to India to conduct preliminary field research in 2004, I began by interviewing more than a dozen senior police officers appointed to the Indian Police Service (IPS) who were either retired or serving in various departments like the Criminal

Investigation Division, Anti-Corruption Wing, Economic Offenses Wing and the Commission on Human Rights, among others.[6] I hoped to learn how authority worked "on the ground" in everyday police work, and soon discovered that the realities of police authority were far more complex that I thought, wrought with gray areas and apparent inversions or shifts in power that were often incredibly puzzling.

A large puzzle piece emerged toward the end of my four months of studying Urdu and doing pilot research in Lucknow, UP. I had met with the district senior superintendent of police (SSP) several times, and he had agreed to allow me to observe police work in situ, first at his central office, and then at another police station. I was excited about my first opportunity to follow police "in the field" or "on the street." But after calling him repeatedly on the appointed day, and finally reaching him on his mobile phone after a couple of hours of busy signals, I was alarmed when he said in a rather frantic tone of voice that there was a "big, big problem . . . great trouble, a breakdown of law and order." I could hear a lot of noise in the background as we spoke, but at that time he did not specify what the problem was; he simply said that he was sorry, but he would not be able to show me around that day as planned. Half-disappointed and half-relieved that I had apparently missed being caught in the middle of one of India's notorious ethnopolitical riots, I initially assumed that the SSP had had to deal with some sort of flare up between caste or religious groups, or that a political protest of some sort had gotten out of hand. I was astonished to learn later that day that, in fact, the incident had involved a clash between hundreds of police officers and public prosecutors.

A riot involving state officials who are supposed to be on the same side of enforcing law and order? What was this?

According to news and police reports, following a minor accident involving the car of a lawyer arriving at the UP High Court, the police intervened in his altercation with the other driver, and when other lawyers gathered in support of their colleague, the two groups came to blows. As more people joined the fray—the police in khaki uniforms, the lawyers in black robes—the violence spread via moving bodies and mobile phone text messages to various parts of the city over the course of the day, disrupting traffic and resulting in scores of critical injuries and severe damage to government property, with fires set to vehicles and broken windows in some buildings.

News media represented police in what we might call the usual way: visiting unwarranted and unjust brutality on a crowd of civilians. Even the former prime minister of India, Atal Behari Vajpayee, chimed in, reportedly remarking that "all he saw [in media reports] was the lawyers being chased with 'lathis' [batons]" (TNS 2004). But ironically, police also appeared quite feeble, ultimately unable to subdue a mob of irate and arrogant lawyers. Their authority to intervene and maintain order seemed questionable at best. Images printed in local newspapers and shown on television demonstrated clearly that lawyers were chasing and harming police as much as the reverse (see fig. 1). When I asked various local acquaintances what they thought of this bizarre incident, I was surprised when most of them shrugged, citing it as simply the latest example of "corruption" and the "general breakdown of law and order" in India, using colloquial phrases like *chalta hai*.[7]

The Hindi idiom of *chalta hai* presents a host of translational challenges, but I will try to make it legible since the phrase arises routinely across northern India in discourse about the ineptitudes and iniquities of everyday governance. The phrase literally means "it moves," and tends to be invoked when something goes wrong, or when some act or event is read as having a more negative than positive moral valence and set of consequences. People often deploy the phrase somewhat dismissively to indicate something like "so it goes, what can you do." Social critics extrapolate from utterances of *chalta hai* the presumption of a widely shared attitude of cynical acceptance of something antisocial or inferior as being "just the way it is" or "how the system works" (Thakur 2013). People often use the phrase with specific reference to abuse of government office: "the police harass and oppress the public with impunity . . . *chalta hai*."

But in the case of this police-lawyer clash, the police certainly were not wielding their coercive force with impunity. They were not metaphorically "making law" with their violence as might be suggested by some critics (Das 2004). Instead, the purportedly universal authority of police to deploy what Egon Bittner has famously described as "*non-negotiably coercive force employed in accordance with the dictates of an intuitive grasp of situational exigencies*" (1970, 46, original emphasis), was being roundly questioned and, in this case at least, ostensibly overrun. When I returned to India in 2006–2007 to continue and deepen my fieldwork with police in UP, I found more and more that their authority to intervene with coercion in various "situational exigencies" was actively negotiated, forcefully doubted, and regularly defied among a variety of actors, many of whom did not necessarily have the "public good" in mind (cf. Geuss 2003). For example, in May 2006, a DySP was almost killed when five young brothers claiming to be relatives of powerful politicians disobeyed the officer's attempt to halt their vehicle at a traffic check point and tried to run over him (Jauregui 2013a).

I regularly witnessed, and was also told numerous stories about, police trying to investigate a crime or inquire into some problem situation, only to beat a hasty retreat in the face of a challenge to their authority by a wide range of citizens, sometimes crowds of villagers, sometimes known criminals,

FIGURE 1. Front page headlines and photos from *Hindustan Times*, Lucknow ed., September 4, 2004, representing police-lawyer clashes in Lucknow. Note the symmetrical representation of a bloodied lawyer and police officer under the "Protests Spread" section, and how the lawyer's title and name are distinguished in contrast to the unnamed "a cop." © *Hindustan Times*. Reproduced with permission.

Lawyer-police tiff leads to violence

ALL AGGRESSION: Lawyers pelt stones at lathi-welding policemen (not in the picture) near Parivartan Chowk in Lucknow on Friday.
ASHOK DUTTA, TRILOCHAN SINGH, RUPESH KUMAR / HT PHOTOS

CITY ON THE BOIL

Cops cane a group of lawyers as they take shelter on a traffic island in Hazratganj.

Protests Spread
- Punjab, Haryana lawyers skip court
- Delhi lawyers to strike work on Saturday
- Congress condemns 'attack' on lawyers
- Lawyers block roads in Allahabad

DM demonstrates Courage

(Left) Avadh Bar Association president Ashok Nigam and a cop were among the injured

She faced a violent mob of over 800 lawyers who hurled expletives at her, yet District Magistrate Anuradha Shukla did not lose her cool and handled the situation with courage

- Mulayam Singh Yadav orders inquiry
- Allahabad High Court, Lucknow Bench, summons Principal Secy (Home) and DGP

P3

CHRISSEY STATS

The duration: Violence occurred between 11am & 7:15 pm

The suspension: SJ AK Dwivedi suspended for 'not having patience while dealing with the crowd'

The injured: 33 lawyers, 28 policemen were hurt in the incident

The arson: Four vehicles set ablaze, six others damaged. Vehicles belonging to Attorney-General, a Cabinet minister, home secretary Deepti Vilas also damaged

The probe: State Government has ordered a judicial inquiry. It would request the SC to nominate a judge

HT Correspondent
Lucknow, September 3

LAWYERS AND police fought a pitched battle in the State capital for hours leaving several people including senior lawyers, cops and commoners seriously injured. Heavy damage to government property and vehicles including those of AG Virendra Bhatia and senior police officials has been reported.

Agitated lawyers also set two government vehicles on fire. Heavy brick batting between lawyers and the police continued for several hours at different places in the city.

Several senior lawyers including former Avadh Bar Association president LP Mishra, present bar association president Ashok Nigam besides senior cops including CO, Hazrat-gang Rakesh Jolly, KD Singh Babu Stadium police outpost in-charge Arun Kumar Dwivedi were among several people who were seriously injured in the incidents.

The High Court has taken a strong view of the incident and summoned UP chief secretary's secretary, Home and DGP to the court. Till the time of filing this report the chief secretary reached the court.

Chief Minister Mulayam Singh Yadav has ordered an inquiry by a retired Supreme Court judge into the issue. Entire working in the city courts has come to a standstill. One cop has been placed under suspension.

Trouble started soon after LP Mishra's Honda City — on which the senior lawyer was driving from home to the court in Kaiserbagh here — suffered a minor damage after it was hit by an Atyyut truck from the right side at 10.25 a.m. An angry Mishra reportedly jumped out of his vehicle and took the erring military driver to task.

As the Stadium Police outpost was nearby, the outpost in-charge Arun Kumar Dwivedi tried to intervene. Eyewitness accounts suggest that Mishra was trying to take the driver of the vehicle to court while Dwivedi felt that if Mishra's car has been damaged then he should lodge an FIR against the truck driver at the police station.

There are two different versions on what happened afterwards that sparked off the violent clashes across the city.

The first version suggests that since several lawyers, who were on
Continued on P5

sometimes wealthy youth who could call on relatives with *pahunch* (local influence, or "reach"). Headlines like "Cops Are Unsafe in State Capital" and "Goons Run Amuck, Cops Run for Cover" and "Policemen Live in Fear in Akhilesh Yadav's Uttar Pradesh" appear not infrequently in English-language and vernacular newspapers (TNN 2006a and 2006b; Srivastava 2015). Many such incidents that I witnessed in the field were not even reported in official legal records or the news media.

Of course, it is vital to acknowledge that the opposite was also true. As police do elsewhere, police in UP and across India often display vicious hyper-empowerment in a variety of forms: illegally detaining and torturing suspects; raining down intensive organized violence on peaceful protestors; engaging in discriminatory treatment of persons from minority groups; planning or participating in extrajudicial killings, and neglecting or even harming people in need of immediate help, like medical aid or legal assistance. These and other types of abuse of authority are neither deniable nor excusable, and should be publicly questioned and vocally challenged. But just as frequently and systemically, police authority in India counterintuitively coheres as confusion and impotence. Police authority is neither absent nor absolute. Rather, it seems to come in and out of focus, sometimes bludgeoning one in the face full force, sometimes finding itself crushed under the weight of some greater force, often casting a mere shadow of itself, always a moving target. Police authority moves, literally and figuratively. Police authority *chalta hai*.

While politicians running for office routinely blame police (alongside opposition parties and candidates) for a generalized "breakdown of law and order," and grass roots activists wage campaigns for police reform based on principles of transparency and accountability, police stand by and shake their heads cynically, making remarks like, "It is all just a *tamasha* (spectacular show) . . . most people have no idea how the system works, and those who do know make it work for themselves only." Police aver that many people do not want to follow the law, or have ways of evading or manipulating it. Moreover, they complain that they do not always know how to enforce the law, because their jobs keep changing and the rules keep changing according to whomever happens to be the governing "master" of the moment. As a sign of this indeterminacy, one senior officer quipped, "Show me the man, and I'll show you the rule."

Such indeterminacy indexes a social order of interconnected official governance and unofficial power relations that is not just continually in motion, but mutating in both content and form. On the negative side, the amorphousness of this order renders a detractive instability in everyday life, making people feel insecure. But on the positive side, it signals the attractive possibility of productive transformation. Theorizing such an incessantly shifting order

by triangulating the expressed views of police, critical ethnographic observations of police practice, and public perceptions and experiences of police, allows us to consider state authority as something that is not simply coercive
but also provisional.

Provisional Authority

In the ideal typical liberal democracy deriving from colonial European models,
public police authority is structured by a legal bureaucracy that is supposed to
be rational and impersonal, beholden to clearly codified rules and free of politics (Silver 1967; Weber 1978 [1919]). Such rational authority has never been a re-
ality in pure form, but it remains a normative principle. As a corollary, theories
of policing generally assume a categorical imperative for the exercise of control
over police authority, in the sense of both directing and restraining it, through
institutions of governance established to limit excessive conduct and generate
accountability to the public (Bayley 2006; Pino and Waitrowski 2006; Gold-
smith and Sheptycki 2007; Sklansky 2007). Such a scheme assumes a bright line
between the idea of "the state" and the rest of "society"; and by association "the
police" as institutional representative of the state are thus conceptualized as a
kind of distinct sociocultural sphere of human actors and action that is, if not
fully enclosed, then largely divorced from "the people" (Chan 1997).

The state is here conceived as a set of institutional ideals and interactive
practices around governance and order embodied in authoritative office. Much
conceptual work has been done to highlight the ways in which the presumed
division between the state and society is a symbolic and historical construction
with real and often problematic consequences (Abrams 1988; Mitchell 1999;
Scott 1999). Further work toward understanding how various communities relate to official governing institutions, and effect transformations in them, has
led to the production and application of integrative heuristic categories like the
bourgeoisie-based "public sphere" and "civil society" (Habermas 1991 [1962]),
or the purportedly more pluralistic or inclusive ideas of "counterpublics" (Warner 2002) and "political society" (P. Chatterjee 2006; cf. Gramsci 1971). Even
amid these insights, the imagined state-society dividing line remains implicit
in most critical discourses of governance, politics and social change, including
in fields of critical inquiry like the anthropology of the state (cf. Sharma and
Gupta 2006). Indeed, there is no corresponding or distinct subdiscipline called
the anthropology of society (qua society), which might seem an absurd redun-
dancy. In short, the state remains a conceptual externality, as does its authority
as a set of social processes and practices, as do its agents associated with the
public police institution.[8]

The types of defiance, negotiation, and entreating of police authority to intervene in everyday life that I observed and heard about from the likes of constables Sharma and Tiwari unsettle conceptions of state externality, not least through their demonstrations of the inextricability of "official" and "unofficial" spheres of influence and authoritative action.[9] The constables' inability to extract a bribe from the truck driver who indicated he already had an unofficial exchange relationship with their boss is a particularly striking example. These grounded realities raise questions about other prevailing theoretical assumptions and framings relating to public police and state authority, particularly those around their mandates and capabilities to deploy coercion by violence. Ideally, police are understood to embody the famous Weberian maxim that legal and legitimate "coercion by violence is the monopoly of the state."[10] As many scholars have already noted, there has rarely if ever been a monopoly on rightful control of the means of coercion, by the state or by anyone else, at least not for very long.[11] But more importantly for the purposes of this analysis, the conception of coercion itself seems to have a monopoly on theorizations of police authority (see chap.3).

Scholars at the helm of policing studies—an area of inquiry that initially emerged among sociologists, and more recently has become a subfield of criminology—have put forward mostly functionalist accounts of coercion as constituting the core of the social role of police, an assumption that still holds sway today (Bittner 1970 and 1990; Muir 1977). For many social theorists and humanists in other fields, police appear to have virtually unchecked power to intervene in everyday life with violent coercion, legal or otherwise (see, for example, Arendt 1951 and 1998; Benjamin 1978 [1922]; Derrida 2002; Rancière 2001). Since the post-structuralist turn in cultural studies, most of these thinkers and the social scientists they inspire link the coercive authority of police more or less directly with processes of normalizing discipline promulgated through institutionalized structures of "governmentality" and "biopower" (Foucault 1991 and 2003 [1976]; Pasquino 1991), or with forces and relations of sovereignty as a claim to the capacity to produce and enforce social order through violence (Diphoorn 2015; Goldstein 2008; Hansen and Stepputat 2006 and 2005; Das and Poole 2004).

The theoretical framework constructed here for understanding and explaining police authority in contemporary India—a framework which may also apply in other times and places—departs from master narratives of power, sovereignty and the originary violence of law that have come to dominate contemporary scholarly and popular discourses about police. Coercion by potential or actual violence is undoubtedly a crucial and problematic component of police authority the world over—one need only attend to ongoing

and ubiquitous outcries against systemic police brutality and injustice, especially in their treatment of many social minority communities. Put another
way, everyday police practice is saturated with coercive authority. However,
coercive violence and police authority are not isomorphic. As demonstrated
throughout this text, violence is hardly the sole constituent or effect of police
authority, which is also configured by qualities of specialized knowledges,
capabilities, positionalities, and exchange networks. Thus, police coercive
authority is not simply an essential mechanism of domination, nor a mere
cog in the wheel of ideological "hegemony" allowing elites to maintain social
control through cultural constructions of "common sense" producing a kind
of coerced consent of the governed or the subjected classes (Gramsci 1971;
cf. Guha 1997; P. Chatterjee 2006). It is not just a technique of productive
"power" as a contestable "moving substrate of force relations" that is "constantly engender[ed] . . . always local and unstable" (Foucault 1990 [1976],
93; see also 2003 [1976], 29). And it is not, in the framework utilized here, the
singular origin point of police or the ultimate determinist "big bang" from
which every problem emanates or may be explained. Police coercive authority *qua* violence is rather one vital (and sometimes fatal) means to various
ends that, like other means—from unofficial gifts to legal decisions—hang in
the air as a potential force that may be applied or denied contingently and exi-
gently. It is a relation and provision of sociocultural order making that is co-
constituted with configurations of moral right and instrumental exchange.
Police authority in toto, including but not limited to coercive authority, is a
contextual and conditional social resource variously demanded, drawn upon,
and deployed to help realize human needs and desires.

After more than a decade of research on the political and legal history of
South Asia—including more than two years of ethnographic fieldwork with
police in UP, the largest subnational state of the world's largest democratic
nation-state—I have found that police authority as an everyday practice is
recognized and valued as an amorphous and multidimensional social field. In
this field of authority, various actors in particular positions in specific time-
spaces may express more or less "virtuosity" in navigating and utilizing the
knowledges they share, the capacities they have, and the networks in which
they find or place themselves, as a means to accomplish tasks that apparently
provide some moral or instrumental good for themselves and their associates. Virtuosity in English entails qualities of both moral good and ingenious
technical skill, both of which apply here. Several key elements of this field are
continually shifting, including but not limited to the types and forms of status
conferring prestige and respect; the individual and group subjects inhabiting
roles that embody and enact such status; individual and group capabilities to

access and offer resources, wield influence, and achieve particular goals; and the moral boundaries configuring what goals ought to be accomplished. This shiftiness generates among police, and arguably among other state officials, what I call *provisional authority*.

The polysemy of the modifier "provisional" for police authority seems most apt as an index of contingency in spatio-temporal, resource allocational, and moral-instrumental fields of human life and modes of social practice.[12] First, it refers to possibilities and occurrences of authoritative interaction bound by time and space—for example, when a provisional government of a specific territory serves in the interim until an ideally more "permanent" or "stable" government may come into power. In this sense, police authority may be considered chronotopic, expressing variance across different time-spaces (Bakhtin 1981; cf. Valverde 2015). Second, it refers to conditions of supply and demand, and exchanges of resources, material or otherwise, as in provisions that may be expected, offered, distributed, traded, or taken among multiple interested parties. Police authority is linked with the provision of specific kinds of resources, including and especially coercion, which may be constructive or destructive, legal or extralegal. Finally, it refers to a partial (in both senses of biased and fragmentary) and integral component of a socio-cultural code characterized by binding interdependence of actors and acts, such as a statutory provision of a bylaw that declares something may or may not happen only if another thing has or has not already happened. In short, police authority is fundamentally interdependent with the demands of various others who may express provisional authority themselves.

The interdependence of authority and demand is vital to this analysis. Max Weber makes it a point to distinguish authority from power (*Macht*), the latter of which he defines as "the probability that one actor within a social relationship will be in a position to carry out his own will despite resistance, regardless of the basis on which this probability rests," a definition that connotes a vectoral imposition of will by one subject vis-à-vis its others (Weber 1978 [1919], 53; cf. Foucault 1990 [1976]). By contrast, he conceives authority (*Herrschaft*)[13] as a relationship involving a confluence of plural subjective wills and a fluctuating "probability that a command with a given specific content will be obeyed by a given group of persons" (ibid.). The interactional fluidity inherent in this concept of authority provides some elbow room for the multiplicity and inconsistency in police expressions of authority that I witnessed in the field. But rather than conceptualizing authority simply as a function of probable obedience to command, I conceive it here as a relational force configured by compounded and competing *demands*, broadly defined as a multiplicity of pressures, requests, or claims.

Distinguishing command and demand in this way may seem like semantic hairsplitting between two Latin-derived terms with occasionally converging connotations and diverging denotations. However, I submit that we may find it analytically useful to conceive the two terms as having a subtle but significant difference in meaning. I understand the verb "to command" to mean giving a discrete order or forcibly directing action, with the implication that "a command" given emanates from a specific subject—often one with an "official" status position—whose authority may be presumed (if by no one other than the subject itself) as an extant thing, a fait accompli.[14] There is something very "top-down" about command. From wherever a command may come—be it an individual actor (e.g., a military general), a collective subject (e.g., a supreme court), or a social institution (e.g., a law)—it assumes its own unquestionability or, to invoke Egon Bittner regarding police coercive authority (1970), its own non-negotiability. One may certainly identify a multitude of moments and modes in which police express authority as command that is, if not non-negotiable, then still highly likely to be obeyed: traffic direction is but one example.

That said, in my fieldwork with the UPP, I routinely observed expressions of police authority that were in dialogue, and often in direct competition, with both commands and demands from various sources and subjects. In this vein, I understand the verb "to demand" to indicate a forceful request or call for something that may come from an authoritative source or be linked with legal right. But a demand may also be made by anyone or anything, and it leaves space for questioning and negotiation. Though a demanding subject may hope for acquiescence, it does not always expect obedience. It does expect work and expenditure of resources. A demand performs force as aspiration, but in the final analysis it demonstratively asks rather than declares itself an absolute. Command is a declarative, demand is an interrogative. Understood as such, while command aims only to reproduce its own sui generis authority, demand serves as a flexible tool that may generate, question, retract, or even abolish its own authority in concert with the authority of others. This more pluralistic and indeterminate sense of demand seems much more well-suited to explaining many of the questionable, negotiable, and inconsistent expressions of authority among police in India that I have observed, and which seem to run counter to widely held assumptions about "the police power" (cf. Dubber and Valverde 2006) and the sources and meanings thereof.

Provisional authority as deployed analytically here thus indexes ongoing shifts in knowledge, influence, capability, resource exchange, and rules of interaction across time and space. Its multiplicity and indeterminacy reflect and reproduce collective insecurity and compel subjects engaging it directly to be continually creative and reactive as they speculate and strategize their actions (cf. Ortner 1996). It works through networks of actors who exhibit forms of subjectivity that depend not only on their social position vis-à-vis others', but also on changing evaluations of their *position's* moral and instrumental value. This form of authority entails the promised delivery of a social "good" as a morally charged resource, and is thus potentially virtuous; but the capability to provide the good is limited and variable, as are the type, tenure, and quality of the good itself, all of which render the authority potentially corruptible. Moreover, that which is considered to be a "social good" is itself continually contested.

It follows that if police authority specifically, and state authority generally, are provisional in all the senses suggested here—that is, providing resources with contingent and contestable virtues and values—then the processual legitimation of this authority is provisional as well. This conception of legitimation as a provisional process works against the assumption that legitimacy is a condition that is either present or absent (Jauregui 2013a). This assumption has long permeated critical theories of state authority, whether they are framed in terms of a dialogue of claims-making recognition between "powerholders" and "audiences" (Bottoms and Tankebe 2012) or in terms of "domination" divorced from actual belief in legitimacy (e.g., Wedeen 1999; see also Guha 1997). Such frames seem to reinforce the problematic conception of the state as a fundamentally coercive externality, as well as the idea that "power," however mobile or productive, is a priori to the instantiation of legitimacy itself. As authority is provisional, legitimation is processual.

I give close attention here to the ways in which police authority in UP and India more broadly may be constantly delegitimated and relegitimated (cf. Reiner 2010), and also to the ways in which it continually shifts between counterintuitive disempowerment and counterproductive hyper-empowerment. To better understand these ongoing shifts, I ask: What cultural, historical, and legal forces and relations both reproduce and result from this continually transmuting form of authority? And how do the understandings and expressions of this authority in everyday police practice both configure and explain broader understandings of sociocultural order, democratic politics, and security? Based on my fieldwork with the UPP, authority is less about a Weberian probability of obedience to command, or a routinized belief in its legitimacy, and more about shifting capabilities and evaluations of the provision of "the good" and "the goods" (cf. Robbins 2013).

Contextualizing Police Authority in India

India is internationally touted as the world's largest democracy, with more than a billion inhabitants spread across twenty-nine states and seven union

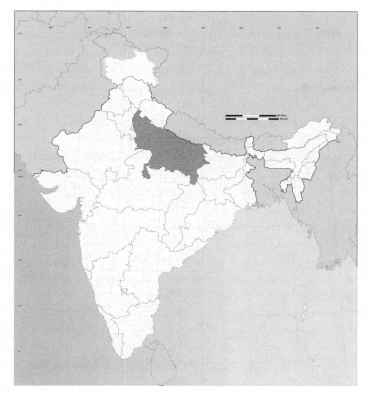

FIGURE 2. Map of Location of Uttar Pradesh in India. CC-by-sa Planemad/Wikipedia. Reproduced with permission.

territories (UT) who speak hundreds of dialects related to at least twenty-two officially recognized languages. Not surprisingly, in this context one may expect there to be great regional variation in how governance works on many registers including that of policing and public order, which by constitutional decree is a power delegated to the governments of individual states.[15] I chose to do fieldwork with police in UP because governance in this particular state seems to represent a microcosm of how everyday local policing intersects with the fragmentation and fractiousness of sociocultural order and democratic politics in the country more generally.

UP is a regional mammoth within a global mammoth (see fig. 2). It is India's most populous state, claiming approximately two hundred million inhabitants as of the 2011 census, more than the combined populations of Russia and Canada, the world's two largest national land masses. If UP were itself a sovereign nation-state, it would be the sixth most populous country in the world, slightly smaller than Brazil, slightly larger than Pakistan, all encompassed in a land mass approximately the size of the US state of Michigan, which houses less than ten million people. While UP has the second-largest state economy in India after Maharashtra, which is home to the country's financial capital of Bombay,[16] almost 80 percent of UP residents live and work in rural areas, and it remains one of the nation-state's most economically depressed regions, with low growth and per capita income rates.

While many people in India, especially denizens of large urban centers like Bangalore, Bombay, Calcutta, and Delhi, may judge UP negatively as being a "backward" or "feudal" place, a vast number of people also consider it a national heartland (Kudaisya 2006). The state is a vital political power center of extraordinary significance. Many people say, "The road to New Delhi detours through Lucknow," the UP state capital. Historically, and even following several post-independence state partitions (Tillin 2012), UP state politics have had an enormous impact on the trajectory of national level politics. The state has been home to more than half of India's post-independence prime ministers and boasts eighty Members of Parliament in the Lok Sabha (lower house) in New Delhi out of a total of 543 constituencies—this is almost twice as many MPs as the next-largest state, Maharashtra, which has forty-eight.

UP is also a hotbed of ethnoreligious tension and caste-based conflict. It is cosmologically important to many Hindus as the locus of myriad pilgrimage sites and home to the greater part of the holy Ganga (Ganges) and Yamuna Rivers. As a former center of Mughal rule, UP is also of great significance to India's enormous Muslim population, which comprises approximately 15 percent of the national total. Thus, communal tensions between Hindus and Muslims constitute a significant political fault line in UP.[17] In addition to this ethnoreligious strife and concomitant violence—which is often exacerbated by the fact that less than 5 percent of police in UP identify as Muslim—there is the continual quaking of caste politics inflecting everyday life as much as electoral outcomes. The two primary political parties vying for parliamentary seats at the national level, the Bharatiya Janata Party (BJP) and Congress Party, have historically been led by persons of "higher" caste groups (e.g., Brahmins and Rajputs), also known as "general castes," and used to be powerful in UP. But since the early 1990s, the Congress and BJP have weakened in UP following the rise of two regional parties associated with castes and other social groups (including some Muslims) considered to be of "lower" status and historically disenfranchised.[18] As previously mentioned, the Samajwadi Party is spearheaded by OBCs, especially the dominant Yadav caste; and the Bahujan Samaj Party (BSP) is led by Dalits (former untouchables).

Many caste distinctions and categorizations are listed in national and state constitutions, and importantly some of them are legally recognized differently among the states. These legal listings may also be—and in many cases have been—amended over time. Persons belonging to OBC and Dalit groups (the latter of which are legally classified as "Scheduled Castes/Scheduled Tribes" or SC/ST) are respectively entitled to approximately 27 percent and 23 percent reservation quotas in all public posts, including the police. But crucially, the inflection of policing by caste politics is not limited to these official "affirmative action" type quotas. Above and beyond reservation quotas, the ruling party of a state government may also have a major influence on who gets recruited to the police and other government services and placed in *unreserved* posts; and all political parties have been known to favor persons from caste or religious groups that comprise their major constituencies. Moreover, since there is not a clear vertical symmetry between caste, class, and official rank hierarchies,[19] there are ongoing contests among all groups to hook into provisional authority networks that will allow them to take advantage of reservations and other resources of *sarkar* (government).

Altogether, these sociolegal classifications and their concomitant contestations have configured the machinations of bureaucratic politics to a great degree (see esp. chap. 5). This was one of the main reasons that I wanted to study district policing in the UP state capital of Lucknow. Lucknow is a provincial city at the center of a district with a population of more than 4.5 million people[20] including many and sundry authority figures, not least the top police officer in the state, the director general of police (DGP). Lucknow is also a city of historical significance for any scholar of Indian policing specifically, and state governance generally, since it comprised a key site of the (in)famous 1857 uprising of thousands of indigenous soldiers (sepoy) from the British colonial Indian Army, an event known variously as the Sepoy Rebellion, the Mutiny, and, in postcolonial South Asia, the First War of Independence. Following this moment of terror for the foreign colonists, the Crown took over colonial administration from the British East India Company, and a host of commissions were formed to reorganize legal governance resulting in the Indian Code of Civil Procedure (1859), the Indian Penal Code (1860), and the Indian Code of Criminal Procedure and the Indian Police Act (1861). All of these codes and acts remain in effect today with only minor modifications and amendments.

Many senior police officers would say to me things like, "We did not inherit the British Bobby, who is a civilized officer walking the beat. The Indian police was modeled after the Royal Irish Constabulary, which was very violent and oppressive." There is some truth to this claim, following from multidirectional traffic in ideas, practices and large numbers of administrative officers among Great Britain's various colonies in the eighteenth to the twentieth centuries (Brown and Brown 1973; Hussin 2014; Hussain 2003; Anderson and Killingray

1991; Singha 2000; Alavi 1995; Gupta 1974 and 1979; Owen 2016).[21] And many scholarly studies of police in India have echoed this claim by demonstrating how continuities between colonial and postcolonial forms of knowledge and legal administration have constituted a police composed of persons largely cordoned off from the community it serves and oriented toward forms of "law and order" that protect elite or "VIP" interests rather than one that promotes liberal democratic criminal justice or community policing (Arnold 1985 and 1986; Campion 2003; Cohn 1987 [1956], 1987 [1966], and 1996 [1989]; Dhillon 1998 and 2005; Verma 2005; see also Rawlings 2002; Skolnick and Bayley 1988; Mastrofski et al. 1998; Skogan 2003). This organization and orientation manifest not only in legal codes, but also in spaces like district "police lines," which are not stations serving the public so much as large compounds that serve as central sites for police recruitment, administrative offices, temporary living quarters, parade grounds, and even horse stables.[22]

While various attributes of police organization in India—from laws and regulations to practical habits—exhibit clear continuities with an oppressive and discriminatory British colonial administration, it is crucial to understand that they are also integrated with social forms that both predate and postdate the official period of colonization by Europeans. In addition to having limited control over the continuation of centuries old systems of justice meted out by counsels of village elders—which to this day may include harsh punishments like public shame, ostracism, even rape as a criminal "sentence" (Pestano 2015)—British administrators integrated into their legal practice Mughal and Sultanate modes of policing, especially things like the practice of station chiefs sitting as extra-legal "judge" (see chap. 3); the colloquial titles of police stations and officers (*kotwal, chowki, darogha, sepoy*), and the continuing institution of *chowkidar* (village watchmen) reporting to local police on a routine basis.[23] Indeed, there remain many echoes from past eras. However, contemporary policing in India is also configured by developments that followed national independence on August 15, 1947, particularly the ways in which the official police rank structure has become imbricated with other types of social inequality like socioeconomic class.

The Indian police organizational hierarchy is a direct descendent of the British Raj and has four lateral levels of recruitment, which from the top down are (1) the IPS; (2) the Provincial Police Service (PPS); (3) sub-inspectors; and (4) constables (see appendix). While a small fraction of police at each of the three lower levels may eventually be promoted to the next level up,[24] historically entrenched structures of practice mean that the masses of constables that comprise more than 90 percent of the total force never even rise to the level of assistant sub-inspector before mandatory retirement at age sixty. Even

FIGURE 3. In the Uttar Pradesh Police headquarters of the director general of police in Lucknow, the official photographs of every (colonial) provincial and (postcolonial) state police chief are posted in order of succession, beginning with L. M. Kaye (1919–1923). Note here the changeover on October 26, 1947, from S. G. Pearce to B. N. Lahari. Photo by author.

so, since authority and influence are not necessarily congruent with official rank, as we shall see throughout this book, obtaining a job with the police is still idealized by many people as a path for social mobility.

While IPS officers tend to have been well-educated in English medium schools and are members of wealthy or otherwise influential families, police in the subordinate ranks have usually attended regional-language schools and come from more humble socioeconomic backgrounds, often hailing from rural areas or small towns. The merger of these unofficial class distinctions with official rank make for a vast gulf between the worlds of the senior officers, from whom official orders come down, and the masses of subordinates that are supposed to execute said orders. The senior officers and the subaltern rank-and-file are patently and sometimes violently alienated from one another, as evidenced in disciplinary proceedings like "orderly room" and a history continuing into the present of union movements and uprisings among the subordinate ranks.[25]

Many of the senior police officers I met expressed a kind of ancestral pride in their continuing British policing traditions, even as they made critical statements about "colonial hangovers" plaguing the police institution. This proud lineage was particularly evident at places like the DGP Headquarters in Lucknow, where the line of police chiefs officially commemorated in portraits extends back to the pre-Independence period (see fig. 3). And yet, interestingly, one of the IGs I met at this office also made it a point to say, "We IPS are just symbolic. We all had to do field training early on in our careers, but our job is mostly supervisory and administrative. Most of us have never spent much time at the *thana* [district police station]." Many of his colleagues implicitly agreed, saying (in English) things like, "Yes, you must see cutting-edge police in action to understand how it really works."

In this context, "cutting-edge" does not refer specifically to something innovative or avant-garde. Rather, it indexes police who work at the coalface or, in their terms, "in the field" doing everyday criminal investigation and "law and order" maintenance, especially things like case inquiries, crowd control, traffic management, and emergency first response.[26] While some IPS and PPS officers in a few specific postings—like district SSP or circle officer (CO)—may be considered to do cutting-edge police work, the term generally refers to the masses of constables and their immediate bosses, sub-inspectors, who are posted at local police stations and serve as the public "face" of the police to local inhabitants and anyone passing through their area of jurisdiction. As one sub-inspector put it, "We are the edge of where 'the state' meets 'the society.'" Thus, the somewhat fluid connotations of cutting-edge policing relate partly to the subaltern ranks, partly to the specific duties that they are authorized and ordered to do, and partly to an idealized confluence of state and society. I agreed completely with the senior officers who suggested that I needed to observe the world of cutting-edge police in order to "understand how it really works," and anticipated that it would take time, luck, and perhaps some ingenuity to enter their world. What I did not anticipate was how the winding track that I took to enter this world would tell me about how their authority "really works."

Accessing and Analyzing the World of Cutting-Edge Police

When I returned to Lucknow to begin my most extensive period of fieldwork in early 2006, I still thought that going top-down through the official police chain of command would be the key to conducting sustained observation of everyday police interactions with the public. In short, this strategy failed. Every time I tried to meet with the "top dog," as many called the UP DGP, I was told that he was too busy. After several weeks of phone calls and personal visits to the DGP headquarters, one senior officer with whom I had by now become quite familiar over the course of several meetings, finally admitted to me that his boss was "not keen to chat." I asked if there was a problem with the framing of my project, which I had outlined in a letter, and he snorted, "No, he doesn't even know what your project is." Not to be defeated, when I asked him again to help me set up a meeting so that I could show the DGP my hard-won research visa, letter from the US embassy and other supporting documents listing my credentials, this officer said that no one in Lucknow cares about approvals from New Delhi or the US, especially the DGP—what matters is the approval of the "real boss," the UP chief minister. Most of my other contacts agreed, one of them saying, "What you really need to do is find a party man," meaning that I needed to connect with an officer who had unofficial affiliations with the Samajwadi Party, which had a majority in the state Vidhan Sabha (legislative

POLICE AND PROVISIONALITY

assembly) at the time. In the end, I never met this particular DGP before he was removed from office for "political reasons" (see chap. 5).[27]

In the meantime, I managed to meet with dozens of other senior police officers as well as with several civil servants and politicians. While some greeted me with suspicion or disinterest, most seemed welcoming and expressed a willingness to help with my project. Several seemed to be remarkably open to discussing everything from government corruption to the discriminatory treatment of minority groups by police. Our conversations usually took place across a huge desk in an air-conditioned office guarded by one or more rifle-toting constables. The speech genre tended to follow a pattern of officers pontificating about "how the system works, or more accurately doesn't work," and I began to refer to these sessions as "officer hours," a play on the idea of professorial office hours at a university. These opining and informative conversations provided a critical starting point for my research, helping me to understand general things about police history and hierarchy, the functions and relationships of various offices and officers, and the ways in which most senior officers felt brow-beaten by politicians and cynical about "the system." But as I had more and more of these "official" meetings, I felt like a well-prepared runner at the start line of a race, waiting intently for a shot that would not come. I began to feel weary and "stuck behind a desk" rather than "in the field" myself (cf. Karpiak 2010; Fassin 2013).

One site that I considered a key starting point for my research was police training; but as with meeting the DGP, my initial requests to visit the central UPP training academies in Moradabad met with repeated roadblocks.[28] I received multiple but frustratingly vague promises of help from senior officers working in the training division, which ultimately turned out to be empty. Again, persistently showing my credentials, making repeated office visits and phone calls, and even asking serving or retired senior police officers with whom I was already acquainted to try to call in favors simply did not help. What did help was when I mentioned the problem to an acquaintance of mine whose family happened to have a long history of direct involvement in electoral politics and government. This person called on a relative who was an active Member of Parliament for many years, who then called an IPS officer who was posted with the Training Establishment. Within a couple of days, I was at the Bhim Rao Ambedkar Police Academy attending a graduation ceremony for newly minted constables (see fig. 4), observing training exercises and interviewing cadets (see chap. 4). The IPS officer who served as my guide was amazingly obliging compared with his colleagues who had been stonewalling me for more than a month. To discern the probable cause of his noblesse oblige, read chapter 5.

FIGURE 4. Passing out parade for newly minted constables graduating from training school in Moradabad, Uttar Pradesh, May 2006. In the foreground a newly sworn-in constable faces his superiors, senior IPS officers, to await an award. Hundreds of other new constables stand in formation in the background. Photo by author.

Several other serving and retired IPS officers helped me by arranging introductions and field trips to other key sites of the police organization, including visits to the police lines in Faizabad district, where I observed a highly competitive constable recruitment drive (see Jauregui 2014a), and to the UPP Headquarters (PHQ) in Allahabad, not to be confused with the DGP Headquarters in Lucknow.[29] On a couple of occasions, I was also able to make day trips to several functioning police stations and ride along in patrol cars in Lucknow district. All of this legwork crossing about a dozen policing districts in the state allowed me to map and navigate the behemoth bureaucracy of the UPP, an organization that boasts itself as the largest subnational police force under a unified command in the entire world. There is a relatively small "armed police" branch as well as a paramilitary reserve wing called the Provincial Armed Constabulary (PAC). But the vast majority of "civil police" include more than 130,000 personnel spread across seventy-five districts, each headed by an SSP.[30] Large as these numbers are, the UPP still has one of the lowest ratios of police per general population in the country, the latest reported measure being seventy-eight officers per one hundred thousand people (NCRB 2013, 164).

The organizational mapping I completed on these field trips and in interviews with senior officers laid a strong foundation for understanding many of the official-legal structures of police work. But after several months, these trips and meetings began to feel disjointed and superficial, like I was only able to engage with spokespersons as tour guides and look at policing through binoculars from a distance, safari style, instead of becoming deeply immersed in observing routine police practices and forming long-term relationships with interlocutors, anthropology style. I still felt like I did not really understand the dynamics of everyday policing, or how the organization itself actually worked or held together, especially since I kept receiving different and sometimes conflicting answers to basic questions about who is in charge of what, who makes decisions about things like investigations and personnel postings, and where one may find records and reports about these types of things. I became increasingly anxious that my wish to observe cutting-edge police work in situ still seemed far out of reach. And the variations and fluctuations in senior officers' apparent willingness and, as or more importantly, their apparent ability to help me advance to the next level suggested that I would have to work via more "unofficial" pathways in order to push my fieldwork to the next level.

Clifford Geertz (1977) wrote about gaining cultural insights and access to the world of his interlocutors as a result of accidentally being present when police raided an illegal cockfight in Bali that he attended, following which he built rapport with some of the local people when he collaborated with them in refusing to inform on the gambling suspects. Such a moment would be impossible for me, not least because I was trying to enter the world of the raiders more than the raided. Still, like Geertz, I did eventually and accidentally manage to "break in" with cutting-edge police, and did not require official credentials or even connections in the senior ranks. Instead, I met a scholarly colleague who happened to have an elder relative that was an SO of a police outpost on the edge of Lucknow district. Within one day of meeting this SO's relative, and with just one phone call, I made my first excursion to CRT, which ultimately became my ethnographic base of operations, where I eventually met Sharma and Tiwari, the constables I was accompanying on patrol in the vignette opening this introduction.

Without showing any documents or receiving permission from a more senior officer or politician, I was invited by the CRT SO, Y. K. Yadav, to observe daily life at the station. After a few weeks, I became a regular presence at CRT and could come and go as I pleased. This went on for many months without disruption. Was this because the UPP bureaucracy is so huge that I could somehow fall between the cracks? This explanation might seem plausible but for the fact that as a visibly foreign young woman from the US, I was such an exceptional presence that most police I met for the first time already had heard something about me.[31] Was the reason for my access rather that no one cared much about an "outsider" observing police work from "inside," or that, as one acquaintance suggested, people feared my American passport as a sign of associations with international "power"? I think the answer to both of these questions is also a resounding no, not least because my application for research clearance was initially challenged at a high level, delaying my field-work and compelling me to relinquish a generous research grant from the American Fulbright foundation. This unfortunate moment in my research trajectory, along with a variety of other obstacles to my work and fraught engagements in the field, made it clear that many government officials might have a strong interest in barring my research, and also that apparent connec-tions with global power sources were not nearly as important as having the *right type* of *local* connections and resources in a particular time and place.[32]

The key to explaining my access to the world of cutting-edge police and their everyday practice in UP is the concept of provisional authority itself, a concept that I submit only could have developed in dialogue with an eth-nographic methodology of insinuating oneself in the social field of police authority over a vast expanse of time and space.[33] A constable named Praveen said to me that even to get a job with the UPP, "you have to get to know people" and that everybody "is just looking for the right connection" (see chap. 2). As an anthropologist, I had to do this, too. CRT station chief Y. K. Yadav's authority to offer me access to his world was itself provisional. As will become clear, his official posting at this particular police station was tempo-rary and tenuous, and theoretically he could have revoked my invitation to observe daily life there at any time, either of his own accord, by official order of a superior, or by unofficial demand generated by the influence of someone with provisionally greater authority than himself.[34] He had to answer to the official police chain of command as well as a variety of other authority figures, not least persons connected with the then ruling Yadav caste-led Samajwadi Party, one member of whom, the SO later revealed to me, had unofficially helped him to obtain his post as station chief of CRT (see chap. 5).

CRT is a medium-sized police outpost located about one hour's drive out-side the Lucknow city center, just off of a major arterial expressway on the rural outskirts of the district (see fig. 5). It is situated near a *mandi* (market) town, covering a jurisdictional area of approximately one hundred square ki-lometers that encompasses about sixty villages with a recorded population of well over 100,000 people. Like most police stations in UP, it is severely under-resourced, allocated only one government-issued jeep and about a dozen very old .303 rifles for the armory.[35] Confiscated vehicles and other material

FIGURE 5. The Chakkar Rasta Thana (CRT) building. The large number of bicycles and other vehicles neatly lined up in front of the station were confiscated the previous week during a police raid on an illegal cock fighting ring. Faces and other identifying markers have been obscured for purposes of publication here. Photo by author.

"evidence" are sprawled across the surrounding yard, many items rotting away or seemingly forgotten and blending into the landscape (see figs. 6 and 7). The station building has seven small enclosed areas in which to conduct police business: (1) an open waiting room area with rickety table and chairs; (2) the SO's minimally furnished office; (3) a tiny back office where the *diwan,* or register-keeper, sits with the radio and all the station records; (4) the *maal khaanaa,* or evidence room; (5) one small holding cell for male detainees; (6) one small holding cell for female detainees (which is used for storage of things like evidence that won't fit in the *maal khaana*); and (7) a cramped enclosure for a hole-in-the-ground toilet that does not flush mechanically.

Since the electricity is not working much of the time, a significant amount of CRT police work is conducted in the large yard outside (see fig. 8). Behind the station are barracks where scores of constables who are unmarried or living apart from their families, based elsewhere, sleep on hard cots assembled in a couple of large rooms. The SO has his own quarters, a Type 3 (three-room) "en suite" arrangement where he can cook, bathe, and rest privately. There are also a large number of Type 1 (one-room), and a few Type 2 (two-room) units

FIGURE 6. Confiscated property in the CRT front yard. Several of these vehicles were reportedly intended as evidence for trial prosecutions, while others were seized from persons who did not "cooperate" with police in some spontaneous interaction (see chap. 2). Still others were recovered stolen vehicles that never made their way back to the owner (see chap. 5). Most of these items remained in the yard for the entire duration of my fieldwork, and beyond. Photo by author.

FIGURE 7. More confiscated property in the CRT back yard. None of the CRT staff claimed to know how long this tractor (left foreground) and ambassador car (right foreground) had been sitting here, but clearly it was long enough for the vehicles to begin melding with the overgrown and untended landscape. The CRT "mess" (kitchen) and subsidized housing are visible in the background. Photo by author.

FIGURE 8. A sub-inspector does paperwork in the CRT front yard on a sunny winter morning. A local *chowkidar* walks under the tree in the background. Faces have been obscured for purposes of publication here. Photo by author.

of police family housing where almost one hundred people live in a kind of police station village. On any given day, one may see children playing on the CRT grounds, sometimes engaging in a pick-up game of cricket right in front of the station (see fig. 9).[36]

The sanctioned number of staff posted to CRT and available for service is supposed to be more than forty sworn officers including the station chief. But in my experience, less than half the sanctioned number of both sub-inspectors and constables were assigned duties within the thana jurisdiction on any given day; and there were almost never more than four or five police personnel at a time present at the station, if anyone at all.[37] CRT staff were often assigned to duty in Lucknow city, with its large crowds requiring "control" and its burgeoning population of politically connected VIPs demanding "protection" (Jauregui 2013a).[38] The SO was often away from the station, and if no other sub-inspector was available when someone would arrive requesting police assistance, then the complainant would be told to wait or come back later (see chap. 3). Although the UPP Rules and Regulations officially stipulate that a head constable may take the place of a sub-inspector "in a case of extreme urgency" (Kabir 2005, 29), they generally bar constables from

FIGURE 9. Children from police families play cricket in the CRT front yard. Subsidized family housing for police personnel is visible in the background. Faces have been obscured for purposes of publication here. Photo by author.

intervening in a situation without orders from above.[39] This in part explains why Sharma's boss laughed at him when he was beaten up at the media mogul family's house, as mentioned earlier.

CRT was not always a bustling police station. On many days, it was rather quiet, with only the occasional complainant requesting police inquiry into a case. On some days, however, CRT would be very busy, with multiple parties simultaneously appealing to the SO or his designated officer in charge (OIC), while one or more persons were being detained for questioning, or injured and seeking aid, or sitting around waiting for assistance while police prioritized paperwork, which took up an enormous portion of the CRT staff's time and resources in relation to things like renewing gun licenses, making entries in one of the registers, gathering evidence for cases, or writing First Information Reports (FIRs) that initiate the process of police investigation (see chap. 3 and Jauregui forthcoming). Often CRT police would not even conduct evening patrol because they were bogged down with other work and under-supervised.

Under such conditions of scarce and deficient resources, as well as partial knowledge of the local scene (again, "partial" in both senses of fragmented and biased), conflicting demands from multiple authoritative sources (including

the law itself), and pressures generated by both official and unofficial relationships, it begins to become more clear how provisional authority as a function
of continually shifting capabilities, influences, exchanges, and access routes
may render a host of ethical problems for police themselves as well as for the
anthropologist conducting participant-observation in their world. Many of
the dilemmas I encountered in the field will be familiar to other ethnographers, including things like maintaining distinct "emic" and "etic" perspectives, my presence affecting my interlocutors' behavior, our having awkward
miscommunications and frequent misunderstandings (see esp. chap. 5), and
my being misidentified as sympathetic with all police practices, or even as being a police officer myself (cf. Hornberger forthcoming).

Such dilemmas are particularly challenging for the ethnographer in the
field working with subjects who are uniquely authorized to deploy violence
on behalf of the state against its own citizens, inspiring as much fear and
loathing as awe and admiration.[40] These dilemmas also have an indelible impact on the analysis conducted herein. The writing of this book, and of the
articles and essays that have led up to it, has involved a continual struggle to
triangulate the perspectives of "the police" themselves with my own observations of their practice and those of third parties in a way that reveals some set
of truths, many of which may be inconvenient or unpalatable. Some readers
may feel that I rely too heavily on the expressed views of police at the expense
of others. In response to such a charge, I would first note that the core concern of this analysis is how the social lives, practices, and narratives of police
are configured by the complex sociocultural, political, and legal bureaucratic
worlds with which they are deeply entangled. Foregrounding police expressions is fundamental to the project of critically analyzing the motivations and
meanings of their quotidian practices. I would further note that foregrounding police worldviews does not equate to apologizing for, agreeing with, or
prescribing them. Instead, I consciously engage in what I call "strategic complicity" (Jauregui 2013b): that is, I acknowledge that my ethnographic involvement with police unquestionably implicates me in the violence and inequality that they often reproduce, and I concurrently strive to maintain a critical
sensibility that continuously questions, and occasionally perhaps even con-
travenes, such reproduction, both in the field and in the written analysis (cf.
Marcus 1997). Like my police interlocutors themselves, I work with an ethical
sensibility made possible and reasonable by the conditions in which I find
and place myself, but I can never be a morally pure subject. This is the work
of "dirty anthropology" (Jauregui 2013b).

This analysis presents many of the most commonly expressed moral, ethical, and practical principles and problems of police life and work in India

today, and explains their foundations in both official and unofficial forces and relations of provisionality as conditional access, capability, morality and positionality. Chapter 2 looks at how police "doing *jugaad*"—that is, using unofficial social networks or substitutive materials to "get the job done"—disrupts a clear line between corruption and virtue, revealing a social order in which both instrumental power relationships and moral distinctions are interdependent and shifty. Chapter 3 examines how routinized illicit police practices like manipulating case evidence and unofficially arbitrating disputes follow what I call an "orderly ethics" founded on an endless multiplicity of moral-instrumental demands placed on police combined with the indeterminacy of the law itself in defining their authority to intervene. Chapter 4 delves into the paradoxes of how police are figured as expendable servants through ambivalent public calls for, and interpretations of, their authoritative violence as a kind of service. Chapter 5 continues exploring police subjectivization by theorizing how the politics of bureaucratic postings shapes common structures of feeling and strategies of professional life. Finally, chapter 6 assesses how the conceptual framework of provisional authority may elucidate our understanding of police, order, security, and state authority in contemporary India and beyond.

Reframing police authority in terms of provisionality and decentering violence as the foundation of the police allows, indeed compels, rethinking some of our most basic assumptions about long-standing and ubiquitous problems of police brutality, corruption, cronyism, discrimination, and various other systemic excesses and inadequacies. I have sought to examine how quotidian police practices and expressions in contemporary northern India offer a lens to view policing as a shifting field of resource exchanges and subjectivizing forces that may be simultaneously productive and stagnant, helpful and harmful, impotent and oppressive. Understanding police authority as a contingent social resource demanded to realize various human needs and desires may open new vistas for interrogating and explaining many hybridizing and emergent local, statist, and transnational modes of producing and enforcing order and security.

Corruptible Virtue

Corruption, or What?

In May 2006, I find myself sitting in front of a class of LLB students at Lucknow University Law School, presenting to them my plan to conduct fieldwork with the Uttar Pradesh Police (UPP) and eliciting their thoughts on the project, all in a mixture of Hindi and English. Reflecting a widely noted tendency of people to impute ubiquitous corruption to the Indian state (Gupta 1995 and 2005; Mathur 2012; Parry 2000; Wade 1982a, 1982b, and 1985; Webb 2012), the students' statements immediately turn to the problem of police venality:

> "Police in India are completely corrupt."
> "They work for criminals and politicians, not common people."
> "Police collect weekly protection money from hardworking shopkeepers."
> "They find any opportunity to take a bribe."

One young man relates how a police sub-inspector recently demanded a bribe from him for parking illegally, in lieu of charging him the (more expensive) legal fine. "He used abusive language . . . and said he would charge the full amount of the fine next time if I didn't pay up now." The student does not disclose whether he paid the bribe but proudly claims that he later made a phone call to a senior police officer friendly with his family, who then made sure that the sub-inspector was "punished."

A young woman says in English, "But see, you are corrupt too, no better than the police . . . you are using your personal contacts instead of the law."

He replies in Hindi, "*Nahin, main ne jugaad kiyaa hai, bas*" (No, I just did *jugaad*, that's all).

Parts of this chapter were previously published in Jauregui 2014a.

Some students in the class chuckle or nod apparent agreement, while others look skeptical.

The critical young woman is not convinced and replies: "*Nahin, voh bhrashtaachaar hai*" (No, that is corruption).

The students erupt into a din of argument until the professor stands up and yells at them to quiet down and remember they have a "special guest" (me). After a halting decrescendo, someone asks me if I know the meaning of the Hindi word just used by the first student—*jugaad*. When I admit that I do not, the class again becomes very animated, the students talking over one another while trying to explain it to the foreigner:

"It means you know a lot of people who can do you favors."
"No no, it's not how many people you know, it's *who* you know."
"It's the regular way of doing business in India."
"Actually, it's the common man's way of making sure his rights are protected."

Soon they are again arguing among themselves, and the professor looks on wearing an amused expression.

When I ask him after class to explain the term, the law professor says that *jugaad* means many things and is difficult to translate into English. He says that many people associate the word with corruption but that, more generally, it connotes actions that involve "quick and dirty" fixes or problem solving through improvisation, especially in a context of scarce resources. I inquire about the term's origins, and he says he is not sure, but he thinks it may be linked with the eponymous automobile that is put together with old spare parts from various vehicles or other mechanical apparatuses (like water pumps), which is regularly used by poorer villagers across India as a form of low-cost transport (see fig. 10; Mitra 2006; Nikelani 2010).

"Really," the LU law professor explains, "*jugaad* is best translated as something like 'approach' or 'source,'" as in the ability to get close to and combine forces with other subjects who can help make a specific goal attainable (cf. Parry 2000, 32). Thus, Hindi speakers not only say *jugaad karna* (to do *jugaad*) but also "*jugaad lagaana*," which means "to make *jugaad* attach" or "to apply *jugaad* (to oneself or the situation)." It seems that those who can apply *jugaad* in the most timely and effective way will tend to succeed even over others who may have a greater legal claim or legitimate right to a different desired outcome. This tendency toward measurable success via social action appropriate to a specific situation is part of solving the puzzle presented in the students' disagreement over whether an act characterized as *jugaad*

FIGURE 10. A man and a young boy drive a *jugaad* vehicle made from spare parts in a village near Jaipur, Rajasthan, November 25, 2005. Photo by Sanjay Kattimani. Reproduced with permission.

may be categorically isomorphic with, or distinct from and even opposed to, corruption.

Later, I look up *jugaad* in my Hindi-English dictionary and see that it is translated as "provision, means of providing" (McGregor 2002). Over time, as I hear it used by more and more of my interlocutors, especially police, I learn that *jugaad* is a highly polysemic term that connotes qualities of resourcefulness as well as recombination, similar to the French concept of "bricolage" (Lévi-Strauss 1962). But crucially, and as already suggested by the LU students' debate, *jugaad* does not necessarily refer to the combination and production of working physical objects only; it also characterizes patterns and possibilities of social relationships and interactions that may or may not lead to material gains or a kind of protection.[1] It is thus a *social* practice of *provision*, not simply a display of individual creativity and innovation. Moreover, *jugaad*'s connotations of ingenuity inflect the practice with qualities beyond pragmatic, instrumentalist value. As a social expression of capability that may lead to the realization of some kind of good in the world, doing *jugaad* also takes on a moral charge; virtuosity becomes virtue.

Jugaad, Corruption and Virtue

This analysis is centered on how doing *jugaad* mobilizes relationships to conduct everyday exchanges that work to allocate or provide a social good, thereby constituting a (potentially) virtuous practice. This is what may distinguish it from sheer "corruption," which is associated with (collective or individual) selfishness and unfair apportionment of goods. Notably, doing *jugaad* does not guarantee a successful outcome (howsoever "success" may be determined); and even if it is successful, the effects tend to be quite ephemeral and contingent on a host of other factors that are not necessarily under the control of the subject expressing the virtuosity (known as a *jugaadu*). These social facts alter *jugaad*'s quality of "provisionality," adding to its allocational quality associations with temporal and moral-legal flux. Through this qualitative change, evaluations of doing *jugaad* as both a discrete event and a more general mode of practice may shift into the realm of corruption. In the analysis that follows, I will show how this transformation in interpretation may happen in practice in order to demonstrate how many common exchanges glossed as *jugaad* work to do at least two things: (1) they disrupt clear and stable distinctions between corruption and virtue, as hinted at in the debate among the LU law students, and (2) they serve as the foundation for provisional authority when state agents like "the police," who often are as under-resourced and socially dependent as "the policed," are involved in the exchange relationship.

In the independent documentary film *The Great Indian Jugaad* (Kapur 2009), people report conflicting common wisdoms. One man holding his child says of *jugaad*, "It can be corruption, but most of the time, it is not." Another man and a woman disagree with each other:

MAN: *Jugaad* is more of corruption.
WOMAN: No, it is more of innovation . . . you need *dimaag* (brains, smarts) to have *jugaad* (pointing to her temple).[2]

The filmmaker herself is quoted as saying, "There are many Jugaads: One is for the privileged city-slicker who uses it to *bend laws or work around his problems;* and the other, more importantly, for the less privileged where Jugaad is the *means to their survival*" (Molekhiet 2010, emphasis added).[3] This statement is congruent with the dividing line in the Lucknowi students' debate: Either doing *jugaad* is a reprehensible form of corruption among "privileged city-slicker" types or, among "the less privileged," it is necessary in the face of adversity and may even be read as taking the moral high road *against* corruption performed by an immoral powerful "other."

The symmetry presumed by the filmmaker between opposing moral charges and presumed status inequalities (i.e., *jugaad* is legitimate for those of lower status, but illegitimate for those of higher status) reveals one way in which perceived moral virtue may be mapped onto perceived power, in the Weberian sense of *Macht* (see chap. 1), or the probability that one actor within a social relationship will be able to impose his or her own will despite resistance. According to this diametric map, the more that one is perceived as able to impose his or her will, the more likely it is that one will be perceived as corrupt, or at least corruptible. This well-trod assumption is globally reflected in transhistorical wisdoms, including but not limited to Lord Acton's famed maxim that "power tends to corrupt, and absolute power corrupts absolutely." One of the LU Law students actually quotes this phrase in the classroom debate. But if we follow Michel Foucault far enough to concede that power is always already dispersed, relational, and contestable across time and space—and add to that the insight that power has a complex and unstable relationship with agency, as the ability to realize a desired goal—then we may find ways to refigure concepts of corruption and their apparent legitimation or delegitimation.

Scholarly theories of corruption have historically evolved primarily from fields like political science, legal sociology, and development economics. Theorists in these fields have generally conceived corruption as an extant problem that, even if contextually variant, should be universally understood as a "there there" and ultimately eradicated (Bayart et al. 1999; Brass 1997; Nye 1967; Rose-Ackerman 1999; Wade 1982b and 1985). Theorists with more normative inclinations often deploy definitions of corruption revolving around interpersonal or institutional exchanges that violate idealized (and Westerncentric) boundaries between public and private spheres, legal and illegal acts, procedural and arbitrary decisions. Some have interrogated or inverted the negative moral valence of corruption by arguing that it allows less powerful people to penetrate or navigate unequal and inefficient social systems (Huntington 1968). Some have even argued that corruption may "grease the wheel" of economic development and technological innovation, suggesting that it is inherent to political-economic progress more generally (Bardhan 1997; Mahagaonkar 2008; Méon and Sekkat 2005). But even in giving it a utilitarian pass as something potentially progressive, rather than essentially decadent, there remains an assumption that corruption as immoral practice is somehow fundamentally tied to positional and institutional power—whether it flows through "public" or "private" channels—and that it is tied especially to the state authority to govern.

Anthropologists have pioneered an understanding of corruption as culturally and historically produced and productive in everyday practice.

Ethnographic studies have highlighted the categorical instability of corruption as a practiced social concept by emphasizing issues like the role of corruption discourse and performativity in imagining the state into being (Gupta 1995), and by analyzing the plasticity of social meaning in transgressions of public-private boundaries (Ruud 2000). The analysis performed here builds on this previous work by examining how the legitimation of corruption among police in Uttar Pradesh (UP)—through its conflation with terms like *jugaad* as an index of coproduction and creativity—allows for reconsideration of the motivations, moralities, and abilities of presumably powerful actors in terms of provision and possibility.

Ethnography of police, who are broadly conceived as always already powerful and (thus) corruptible (Wade 1982a), constitutes a particularly fruitful field for examining these dynamics. Exploring the ways in which *jugaad* works in everyday police practice reveals how a diametric conceptual distinction between powerful elites using euphemisms for their corruption and powerless subalterns virtuously trying to survive does not reflect the complex realities of social life in contemporary India and, arguably, elsewhere. Doing *jugaad* often entails multiple subjects and types of interactions working over time, with varying circumstances and intentions and continual shifting of positions (cf. Price 1999, 64, regarding fluidity of social rank and status and personal contingencies in relation to bureaucratic functioning). Doing *jugaad* may or may not involve the quintessential embodiment of corruption: the supposedly dyadic exchange of "the bribe." The realities of *jugaad*-cum-corruption in police practice allow rethinking of simplistic lopsided judgments about authoritative actors always committing extortion.

In the analysis that follows, I relate several ethnographic vignettes demonstrating how *jugaad* is conceived and practiced among police in UP, to draw out the practice's contronymic character as simultaneously isomorphic with, and opposed to, corruption. I then discuss the contradictory discursive spread of the concept of "*jugaad*" over time, among Indian national and, increasingly, international publics. Comparing and contrasting the ways that *jugaad* has come to be understood by social groups as diverse as multinational corporate executives, Indian state officials, and Sanskritologists, I develop a context-derived analytical concept, "provisional agency," to explain what appears to be routinized legitimation of corruption among a wide swath of people inhabiting variegated social positions.

Focusing on the ways in which police express provisional agency in their everyday practice, and the ways in which these expressions of agency construct police as state authority figures, I show how the foundations for what I have described in chapter 1 as provisional authority rest in a shared concept of agency or capability as a social good. Building on previous anthropological analyses of the complexities of corruption in everyday practice, I deploy the concept of provisional agency in a way that compels us to turn away from conventional questions about how immoral activity serves as a means to realize power, and to turn instead toward understanding how expressions of agency help to realize shifts in, and contestations over, social positions of authority, the ability to provide for others, and the moral boundaries associated with these positions and abilities.

Bribes and Free Rides

It is a sunny October morning, and my research assistant and I arrive at Chakkar Rasta Thana (CRT) to find a young man crouching in a corner of the record keeping room at the back of the station. A young female sub-inspector (SI), who is still under training, and two male constables are yelling at the squatting man. Through listening and inquiring to another constable named Prithvi, who is also standing by watching, we learn that the man has been detained overnight at the *thana* (station) because the CRT police had wanted him to drive them around yesterday in his *tempo* (a three-wheel taxi that holds about six people safely) so that they could conduct their *gasht* (patrol); but he had refused. For this, the constables are hurling verbal abuses at him, opining that they must *shikshan* (discipline) him.

As we watch, the *tempo* driver becomes emboldened (perhaps due in part to the presence of two of us not wearing khaki uniforms?) and begins to yell back at the police. He says to them that if they continue to harass him, then he will tell the senior superintendent of police (SSP) of Lucknow District that they are trying to extract a bribe from him. The threat visibly upsets the CRT police, who yell back at him using expletives indicating that he is a liar and a coward who will be sorry if he tries to go to the SSP. In the end, all they can do is draw out a vulgar shouting match and then grudgingly let the *tempo* driver go free.

After he leaves, we delicately try to inquire about what happened. The under-training SI and constables, still clearly agitated, explain that the day before, the chief station officer (SO), Y. K. Yadav, had ordered them to patrol some local villages where informants had reported questionable activities. Because Yadav had to leave CRT for duty in Lucknow city, and took the station jeep with him, the remaining SIs and constables did not have any vehicles to take them where they needed to go. (Prithvi usually drives his own motorcycle, but he was away on other business.) So they decided to employ their usual adaptive solution to this problem: find a private driver to transport them.

The constables say that they walked to the main road and flagged down the *tempo* driver. When he stopped, the police basically told him, "We need to use your truck for some work, so let us in and drive us around." They clarify that they did not demand a bribe in the sense of a monetary payoff; but the clear implication to the *tempo* drive was that he must forego his usual business of charging passengers for taxi services and instead act as chauffer for the police without receiving any compensation. So the demand amounted to a different type of attempted coercive extraction, but an extraction nonetheless.

Notably, the *tempo* driver did not have any preexisting "arrangement" with these local police, as did the wood truck driver stopped by constables Sharma and Tiwari in chapter 1—so he could not appeal to a preexisting relationship as a shield against their attempted extraction. But also unlike the other truck driver, this *tempo* driver had all of his licenses and registration papers in order; and at the time of being stopped, he was not carrying more than the maximum allowable number of passengers. This meant that he was not acting outside the law, and thus had no clear incentive to do the officials any favors without compensation. So, legally at least, he was in a position to refuse to give in to their demands.

Constable Prithvi says:

> You see, this is what happens to us [police]: when we are in an emergency situation, or when we need to do a raid, we are without equipment, and cannot do our job. And now this driver is blackmailing us by saying he's going to spoil our name [by claiming that we were demanding a bribe]. What are we supposed to do? If we don't patrol and something happens, we are blamed for neglecting our duty; people will even say we are helping the criminals. If we try to do our job, we are threatened with a bad name. We have to make them help us.

Make them help us . . . The other police present nod their agreement. Momentarily leaving aside questions about the oddity of coercing people to help an under-resourced police, we ask Prithvi and the others why they fear this threat of a bad name—would the current Lucknow SSP not listen to their side of the story? Would he unquestioningly believe the driver's accusation of attempted bribery? Prithvi responds that the recently appointed district SSP was given the job because he has a reputation for being "tough on crime," and he is also known to be harsh in disciplining his subordinates and punishing them for infractions. There is no way to prove anything one way or the other, from the driver's side or from the police's side. But Constable Prithvi expresses a belief that since so many police are "just known" to take bribes, both by demand and as voluntary "gifts," then it is likely that the SSP would believe the worst of them, and that they would then fall out of favor with him and perhaps experience negative repercussions, now or in the future. He does not verbalize it explicitly, but I gather from other comments by him and his colleagues present that it is also the case that even if the SSP were open to hearing the police's explanations of what had happened, their admission of what had transpired would be quite embarrassing. They would appear incompetent and ineffective, and their already low morale would worsen.

Like their colleagues Sharma and Tiwari, the CRT police here fail in their attempt to extract a provision from a driver. But, in each case, the provision demanded and the resulting failure are different, and the contrast is instructive. Sharma and Tiwari fail to extract a bribe because they demand it from someone who already has an existing unofficial relationship with their boss, which involves an agreement to engage in illegal activity that is mutually beneficial to both the police, who gain protection money, and the driver, who gains from being able to drive oversized loads without a license. In the case of the *tempo* driver, the CRT police fail to extract provision of a free ride because they demand it from someone who believes the law is on his side and does not have an immediate interest in an unofficial relationship with these police at this time. Sharma and Tiwari fail because they have the social "wisdom" to voluntarily self-limit in the face of an authoritative system greater than themselves—they do not attempt to use coercion to get what they want because they know it would work against the systemic arrangement already in place, and thus would probably work against them somehow. But the (much less experienced) sub-inspector trainee and constables fail because they try to unilaterally coerce the *tempo* driver into giving them a free ride, rather than exhibit provisional authority by working within a system of exchange in which both parties may benefit.

Crucially, this incident with the *tempo* driver is not a unique example of punitive and excessive force meted out by police in response to citizens rejecting police attempts to coerce assistance without offering compensation. Several weeks prior, Prithvi told me that he and some other CRT police found a deceased woman on the road, apparently from a vehicular accident, and when they hailed two men passing by in a car and made a "request" that they help transport the corpse to the hospital the men refused. In retaliation, the CRT police seized the driver's license and registration papers, and I observed the two men come to the *thana* and fail to retrieve them. (I could not get a straight answer from anyone on whether and how many times they came, or whether they eventually received their papers.) In another incident Prithvi recounted, he tried to convince a *tempo* driver to take him to pick up some gas cylinders for cooking in the CRT "mess" (kitchen), but was rebuffed. Prithvi became so frustrated that he said to the driver that he would burn his *tempo* when he got the gas; but the *tempo* driver just sped off dismissively.

Such interactions are common because the UP state government provides police with relatively few resources, such that they have to rely on other sources of provision. That said, it must be understood that these exchanges also happen in a context where people express dismay that many police try to abuse their authority by expecting that they can unilaterally "take" without giving anything back. The image of the fat-bellied police officer taking chai or food at local restaurants and shops without paying is notorious, and resonates with a broader set of assumptions that most state officials at all levels make excessive demands (as bribes or otherwise) before they will perform their public functions. Many people feel helpless in the face of extractive demands that they must meet in order to get even the most basic tasks performed, be it obtaining a license, a paycheck, a land title, or any number of other resources provided by the state.

On the other side, however, the same systemic fluidity and flexibility that allows some state agents to abuse their official position of authority may also be put to work in such a way that people will find it useful to form a relationship with police that allows for mutual benefit. This was the case with the truck driver stopped by Tiwari in chapter 1, who did not have to pay off the police constables at that moment because he was already in an exchange relationship with their boss, the SO of CRT. While this kind of relationship is often viewed from the outside as purely extortionate, part of a "protection racket" unilaterally imposed by police (read: "power" as *Macht*) in practice, it often involves pragmatic and even mutually beneficial exchanges of provision between an official authority figure and a member of the public. There are many other instances that I observed reflecting the existence of such relationships. One of these instances occurred just three days prior to the incident with the *tempo* driver.

Following another early morning arrival at CRT, I am invited to accompany SO Yadav and some constables on a *dabish* (raid) in a village in which illegal cutting down of mango trees has been reported (see fig. 11). Yet again, CRT's single government-issued jeep is unavailable, having been usurped by the Lucknow city division for use at the Vidhan Sabha (State Legislature) for the day. Only this time, the station chief did not have to report to duty in the city; so now, along with his subordinates he too is stuck without transport to the sites they need to investigate.

But Yadav has a plan. Several minutes after he makes a phone call, a large off-road utility vehicle arrives to take us to the scene of the reported crime. I

FIGURE 11. Tree that has been illegally cut down in a village near CRT. Photo by author.

mistakenly think that it is an official car that has been sent by some other police
station, and say as much.

"No, this is a private car," the SO corrects me.

"Oh, so you hired it?"

Yadav smirks, "No, we don't pay . . . we have an arrangement."

We pile into the truck and drive to the village where the illegal tree-
cutting activity has been reported. Constable Prithvi, who called in the report, is waiting for us. After stopping to examine the evidence—recently cut
wood piled in a couple of fields—we all proceed to the nearby inhabited areas,
where the police file down dirt paths to search people's huts while residents
stand by and stare in eerie silence (see fig. 12).

We leave the village, and our oversized vehicle galumphs along the uneven
dirt roads through thick brush. We suddenly halt next to a thatched-roof hut
that I probably never would have seen had we continued moving. A couple
of thin, weathered-looking men come out and speak in hushed voices with
constable Prithvi. The men disappear into their hut, and a few seconds later
reemerge. One is holding a large saw, and the other is holding an axe, both of
which are handed over to the SO.

"Is this also evidence?" I ask innocently.

FIGURE 12. CRT police investigate a report of illegal tree cutting in a village under their jurisdiction. Constable Prithvi leads (in white sneakers), followed by SO Y. K. Yadav (in plain clothes), and a Home Guard carrying a rifle in the rear. Photo by author.

I receive a curt "no" from Yadav. Then the driver restarts the engine, and we begin again to make our way through the tangled foliage arching into the roadway.

We stop at a residential area in another nearby village, and the police ask a couple of women some questions and perform more searches in several huts. They eventually find a man whom they begin reprimanding in public for cutting the wood. He stares at his feet without saying anything, and then we return to the vehicle without him—so apparently he is not under arrest. We continue driving a bit farther down the road, then stop again at another hut, where the SO gives the saw and axe that we picked up to a couple of other of men with whom he has a few quick words, which I do not hear because they are out of earshot.

By the time Yadav returns to his front passenger seat, I am thoroughly mystified and so ask him what is going on. He says casually that he provided these last two men with the saw and axe that he borrowed, and asked that they gather some of the already cut wood from the crime scene, cut it up into smaller pieces, and transport it back to the station so that the police can put it on file as evidence. They are then to take some of that evidence to the court, which will be presented to a judicial magistrate alongside an official charge sheet drawn up by police, listing the name of the man whom they were admonishing.

"So you just order these guys to gather up the wood, and they do it because you are police and they are afraid of you?"

"No," says the SO, "we will give them some money."

I learn later that this money will come out of the CRT "kitty," a small fund collected mainly through one-off petty bribes at traffic checkpoints, or through periodic protection payments to police, such as that paid by the truck driver from whom Sharma and Tiwari failed to extort their own bribe. Apparently, the kitty was empty when the CRT police needed a ride a few days later, which was part of the reason they had nothing to offer the *tempo* driver as compensation to forego his trade and transport them instead.

One element of police corruption in India—an element that generally has been neglected in studies of South Asia but discussed in ethnographies of policing and organized crime in the West (Chambliss 1988; Hobbs 1988; Rubinstein 1973)—is that a significant portion of the material resources gathered through petty bribes and protection payments is used not for private gain by individual officers (cf. Nye 1967) but to contribute to mundane work expenses that are inadequately provided for by the state government, such as office supplies or petrol to power vehicles, as well as for expenses like occasionally or regularly paying police *mukhbir* (informants). This money may also be used by subordinate officers to pay bribes for postings and transfers that may be demanded of them by some of their seniors (see chap. 5), in what Robert Wade (1985) has called an "internal labor market."

The point is that the geography of exchange is far more complex and uneven than can be accounted for with binary economic models of rational-legal trade on the one hand, and illicit bribes and corruption on the other hand. The social field in which material and relational currencies are exchanged is continually shifting with time, circumstance, and the contingent positions of actors involved. Provisions move horizontally for both "official" and "unofficial" work-related expenses and go "down" to crime victims requiring assistance like immediate medical attention about as often as they go "up" the chain of command, out to politicians funding their campaigns, or into individuals' pockets for personal consumption (Jauregui 2010; cf. Gupta 1995; Wade 1982a, 1982b, and 1985).

Continuing my inquiry to the SO about the wood cutting case, I ask Yadav, "Why do you have other people gather evidence instead of doing it yourself?"

Prithvi pipes up, "Well, we don't have our own tools, and there's not enough room in this car to transport the wood. . . . Those guys have the necessary equipment and skills because woodcutting is their line of work. So they help us out."

"We also don't have enough time to do it all ourselves," the SO chimes in, "because we have too many other jobs to do today, and we have to submit the case materials within twenty-four hours of framing the charges in an FIR [First Information Report] according to the rules of evidence."

"So, do you always pay people to do work for you?" I ask.

"No, not necessarily," the SO answers. "For example, we are not paying this driver anything."

When I ask why not, he smiles, "Like I said before, we have an arrangement."

Mimicking the SO's smile, with the addition of a cheek bulging with *paan* (chewing tobacco wrapped in betel nut leaf), another sub-inspector on the team says, "*Jugaad kartha hai*" (*Jugaad* is being or must be done).

Later in the day, when we are eating lunch at a local *dhaba* (truck stop) and the SO is not present, I ask the driver of the private vehicle why he chauffeurs the police around in his car without any monetary recompense. He first clarifies that he is not the owner of the vehicle but, rather, drives it on behalf of his *malik* (boss), who pays him on a set scale. Then he tells me that the *malik* has an unofficial agreement with these local police. If he occasionally provides them the service of driving them around when they need it, then they in turn allow him to use the truck as a "public transport" vehicle—that is, as a group taxi that gives people rides for a small fee—even though he does not carry the proper licenses and registration papers to legally do so. This allows the *malik* to keep more of his profits and to avoid the time and trouble (and yes, bribes) required to obtain the legal documents to run such a business. Like the truck driver in chapter 1, the *malik* has an "arrangement" or personal relationship with police that fosters goal-oriented exchange (cf. Hornberger 2013).

These kinds of symbiotic arrangements reflect a sociocultural order in which activities that many would readily categorize as corruption are collectively legitimated in everyday practice. In this particular case, evidence in a criminal case is potentially compromised, and a businessman profits without having the legal permits to do so. And yet there is a mutual recognition of both need and desire among all parties involved, leading to the formation of a web of exchanges that allow police to proceed with an investigation, laborers to acquire paid work, and a vehicle owner to conduct a profitable business that, even if not fully licensed according to the black letter of the law, is relatively harmless and constitutes a kind of social provision of not only needed transport for local persons without other means of mobility but also a paying job for the driver. The "spirit of the law" may be compromised, but people also experience and express a sense of agency and responsibility as jobholders, householders, working citizens, "protectors of the peace," and state authority figures (see chap. 6). This means it is not just an instrumental interaction, fatalistically excused as merely surviving or "making do," but also a *virtuous* one expressing a hopeful and valuable "can do" mode of providing for both the self and others.

The virtue of doing *jugaad* is constantly contested in India, sometimes by opposing *jugaad* to corruption, sometimes by conflating the two. This results in multiple meanings and valuations of *jugaad* not merely as a static mode of getting by or making do but also, crucially, as a potentially transformative mode of sociality, a means of opening up possibilities through improvisation and creation of something new and effective, which may allow for thriving as well as surviving (cf. the distinction between routine action as habitus, on the one hand, and agency as intentionality, on the other, in Ortner 2006). This quality of *jugaad* as both "make do" and "can do" is well illustrated by another ethnographic moment, this time involving someone aspiring to obtain a full-time police job.

One morning, while accompanying CRT police guarding polling booths during *nagar nigam* (municipal council) elections in Lucknow, I strike up a conversation with Praveen, a twenty-year-old man who is on his first assignment with the UP Home Guard. Home Guard (HG) personnel are not sworn police officers but auxiliary day wage laborers who wear khaki uniforms identical to those worn by police constables, making them virtually indistinguishable from police except for a shoulder pin that says "UPHG" rather than "UPP" (see appendix). They could be analogized to adjunct professors rather than tenured or tenure track faculty.

Praveen's declaration that he is a neophyte seems odd to me, because the uniform he wears bears the three stripes of an HG sergeant, a rank analogous to that of head constable, which usually takes many years to achieve. I ask Praveen how he is able to wear the sergeant stripes on his first day, and he says as part of his reply, *"Jugaad kiya hain"* (We did *jugaad*). He explains that because he attained the job so recently, the stitching of his own official uniform (for which, he notes, he must pay out of his own pocket) still has not been completed by the tailor; so his uncle, who is also an HG employee, has lent Praveen one of his own uniforms. When I express surprise that this public misrepresentation of rank is permissible, he shrugs that it does not really matter since "no one checks," and, with a slight glint in his eye, he indicates that it is good "practice" for what he sees as a brighter future, when he has a higher official rank and more authority.

Praveen already exhibits a general disgust for the HG job itself, both identifying with and distancing himself from it, saying, "Nobody respects us." He looks forward to the day that he becomes a full-time police constable, saying, "Then I can earn more money." He makes clear that he means not merely commanding a higher wage and full government benefits but also being able to use his official status and authority to solicit more lucrative bribes and favors.

"The higher your rank, the more people will give you," he says, flicking his thumb under his index finger, a local gesture signifying a transaction of money.

Praveen's utterances reflect a widespread phenomena among police and HG officials of "impersonating up" the ranks, with subordinates purposely representing themselves as being more senior in rank, or better connected socially and politically, than they actually are as a means to command more substantial material or relational favors (Gurung 2011; HT 2011; TNN 2007 and 2008; UNI 2011). This social fact suggests a shared belief not that "power corrupts," absolutely or otherwise, but rather that greater quantities and qualities of provisions vary directly with social positions that are identifiable, representable, manipulable, or ultimately achievable over time.

The subaltern side of this sensibility is demonstrated on occasions when low-level police from a particular station together engage in counting and re-distributing their petty bribe collections for the day, a practice I witnessed at CRT several times (see Jauregui forthcoming). Constables would sometimes engage in this apparent "division of spoils" ritual because of a shared under-standing of the inherent contingency of the potential to earn *kaalaa daan* (black money) across different types of duties and different locations. Some as-signed duties, like working a traffic checkpoint along a major smuggling route, have relatively good black money earning potential; others, like sentry duty at the house of a VIP, will garner very little income, though there is the small possibility of forming a relationship with someone with *pahunch* (influence). Subordinate police have virtually no control over the duties they are assigned unless they pay a bribe themselves to a senior officer or happen to be among the senior officer's *hamraahi* (fellow traveler) constables.[4]

Praveen says he decided to join the HG before applying to the police be-cause his uncle informed him of a personnel quota requiring that a certain percentage of constable recruits have at least three years of experience with the HG—a subordinate-level analogy to the requirement that approximately one third of Indian Police Service (IPS) officers be promoted from the Pro-vincial Police Service (PPS) rather than directly recruited.[5] Praveen hopes to take advantage of this policy to obtain the job of constable and rise through the ranks more quickly and smoothly than average. When I press him a bit on how one normally gets a job and rises through the ranks, he says, "You have to get to know people . . . and, of course, you always must pay . . . everybody knows he has to give money to get this kind of job, and is just looking for the right connection . . . you have to be smart and persist." In addition to finding the right connection, he says, one must also learn how much the bribe will cost, to whom it should be given, and the right time and place to give it.[6]

Praveen then reiterates what I have already learned from some of his police colleagues: to have any chance of being recruited as a constable these days, one must usually pay a hefty bribe of Rs. 200,000–300,000 (approx. $4,000–6,000). The starting base salary for a UP constable at the time of writing is just over Rs. 5,000 (approx. $100) per month.[7] This means most new constables who obtain their jobs in this fashion must struggle for a long time to repay the enormous debts to their sponsors, even as they manage to collect extra money through petty bribes (emphasis on "petty"—recall that Sharma and Tiwari said they were hoping for about Rs. 50–100 in the interaction related in chap.1). These debts add to the already heavy weight of the ordinary pressures often placed on these men as providers for large joint families, in keeping with responsibilities linked with the second life stage for Hindu men: *grihastha*, or head of household.[8]

Even to become a mere Home Guard, the lowest of the low in the police hierarchy—not even really considered "police" but something more like an "out of caste" subaltern—I am told that one generally gives a bribe of about Rs. 25,000 ($500). However, with evident self-satisfaction, Praveen boasts that he only had to pay Rs. 5,000 (just over $100) to get his current job.

"That is a steep discount!" I say, "How did you manage to pay so little?"

"*Jugaad lagaaya*," he smiles enigmatically.

He eventually reveals that his uncle managed to fix a good deal using his social network.[9]

Like Praveen, many police claim that these types of activities are routine, simply the way people must operate if they want to gain or maintain the job security and access to resources that come with government employment. As drudging and difficult as a government job in India can be (as officials would almost constantly complain), competition for this particular type of position is intense and often overwhelming, something that I learned firsthand when I observed an official constable recruitment drive in Faizabad. The senior officer in charge at this drive told me that, by the end of the drive, more than twenty thousand youths had shown up in the hopes of obtaining one of fewer than six hundred spots on the recruitment rolls (see fig. 13).

Beyond sheer employment Darwinism, other cultural factors configure the positive rationalization and evaluation of *jugaad* as job attainment in which Praveen and so many others engage. One of the most significant factors is the centrality and strength of kinship relations to concepts of trust and

FIGURE 13. Aspirants for a post as constable with the Uttar Pradesh Police wait in line to submit their applications, September 17, 2006. Photo by author.

right in everyday sociality in India (cf. Smith 2001). Someone arranging employment for a relative or neighbor may draw not only on monetary capital but also on the currency of a shared understanding of obligations to provide for the family and the community, and on the durable webs of reciprocity and possibility built therein. Thus, the discriminatory and "unfair" network in which Praveen participates cannot be reduced only to a rational economic exchange of money, nor can it be reduced only to a sentimental familial bond engendering naked nepotism. Rather, it involves both kinds of relationships and their concomitant exchanges, and it works via creative combinations of variegated social currencies that are crucial for navigating the stark and stormy seas of finding employment and achieving promotion.

Social connectivity and other currencies co-configure each other in this context as part of an everyday order marked by valuation of collective provision. Some people express sadness or even shame about the social fact that entrance into a government job usually requires underhanded manipulation of such connectedness (cf. Jeffrey 2010, which deploys the idea of "intimate culture" (Herzfeld 2005) in describing how university student political leaders and fixers discuss and practice the application of *jugaad*). But many others, like Praveen, display not just neutral nonchalance but a positive pride in

their demonstrations of ingenuity and capability. They undergird moral evaluations of their practice with an emphasis on provision of some collective
good, as does a CRT constable, Aman, whom we will meet in chapter 3, who
says to me, "This the way it is . . . sometimes a little bit of dishonesty benefits
everyone . . . the victims, the judges, the police . . . sometimes even the criminals. Therefore, it is not wrong."

What this analysis of *jugaad* among police shows is that collective provision may be, and often must be, performed or utilized by people in just about
every social position imaginable, regardless of their class or caste, whether they
inhabit the countryside or the city, as state officials or as other types of subjects.
Of course, this does not mean that there is a level playing field. Individuals and
groups in authoritative status positions—including but by no means limited to
police officers of various ranks—will have a greater quantity or quality of access to social and material resources in particular time-spaces. Occupation of
official positions by persons with unofficial influence over long periods of time
may lead to deep entrenchment and ongoing reproduction of relationships of
dominance, which is reflected in charges of "creamy layer" or historically more
wealthy and influential "lower" caste groups (especially among those legally
classified as Other Backward Classes, or OBCs) snaffling up reservations and
other available resources for themselves while others in the same legal category
languish.

But since authority at the intersection of official and unofficial social categories and practices is provisional, structures of inequality and the dominance of certain social groups are very unstable, and this instability pumps
the heart of democratic politics in places like UP (cf. Michelutti 2009; Banerjee 2014). Moreover, there is a shared sense that individual agency in the
service of providing a social benefit is itself a moral good and that one should
use whatever capabilities and connections she or he has to do this. As such,
jugaad may be associated with practices and persons that are categorized by
some consensus as corrupt or clientelist. But, as the ethnographic examples
related here demonstrate, it may also be associated with agency as adaptation or innovation that could be better understood as mutually beneficial and
therefore virtuous production and progress.

The idiom of *jugaad* as virtuosity is a moral game changer, if also a moral
danger. It shifts the margins usually distinguishing the powerful from the powerless, those who have more from those who have less, and the takers from the
givers of material resources or future favors. Unlike the negatively charged category of "corruption," which connotes structurally static, and historically statist, illegitimacy in a context of power inequality (Ruud 2000, 283), *jugaad* ac-
knowledges the contingencies of social interactions and the shiftiness of social

positions. It entails not merely the transgressions of moral boundaries that produce ambivalence and ambiguity but inter alia the constant reconfigurations of the boundaries themselves through continual improvisation, recombination, and recreation in both senses of "play" and "remaking."

In making this claim for the positive moral evaluation of improvisation and social provision, I dispute cynical (and arguably neocolonial) claims that in northern India people simply manipulate the idiom of "the gift" for all it is worth because the socially connected " 'source' has been progressively replaced by 'note' (the bank variety of course) as the most important means of securing a job in public (and increasingly also private) sector employment" (Parry 2000, 33; cf. the problematic distinction between "parochial" and "market" corruption in Scott 1972). Along with the work of others (Anjaria 2011; Beek 2013; Jeffrey 2010; Smith 2007), my ethnographic observations suggest not that there has been a unilinear displacement of social connectedness by monetary exchange, but rather that these (and other) modes of getting things done may work in tandem.[10] In this way, corruption and virtue can often exchange places via doing *jugaad*.

A Cultural History of Virtue and Corruption in India

The contronymic moral character of *jugaad* as simultaneously corruption and virtue exploded on the world scene amid India's international embarrassment at appearing unready and inadequate to host the 2010 Commonwealth Games. Mere days before the games began, facilities being built for athletics and accommodation were shown to be in disrepair, compelling some contestants from other countries to cancel their participation, fearing for their health and safety, and prompting at least one Indian official to make a gaffe about Indians and foreigners having different "standards in hygiene and cleanliness" (Yardley 2010). At the same time that news coverage predictably turned to allegations of corruption in the public-private contracts made by organizers preparing for the competition, Indians began discussing the role of *jugaad* in ensuring that the games could proceed on schedule, which they ultimately did. While some people blamed a culture of *jugaad* (and *chalta hai* as mentioned in chap. 1) for problems that arose in preparing for the international event, condemning this culture as a key obstacle to India realizing its rightful place as a great world power, others celebrated *jugaad* as the best response to endemic corruption, as a kind of saving grace employed at the last minute that allowed India to shine (Daruwala 2010; Dasgupta 2010).

This puzzling popular display of opposing definitions of *jugaad*—as simultaneously the worst manifestation of corruption and the best means of salvation from corruption—reflects the broader debate around this practiced concept that has emerged over the past several years. Upon hearing UPP officers and others associate *jugaad* with corruption during my fieldwork in 2006 and 2007, I performed a keyword search in my university library catalog and found little to nothing in the way of scholarly writing on the subject. But an Internet search at the time showed that *jugaad* was beginning to crop up as a topic on international industry blogs, business news sources, and corporate websites. These online arenas served as virtual spaces for deliberations about the merits of *jugaad* that went well beyond what I had witnessed in the Lucknow University Law School classroom or in the field with the CRT police.

Reflecting what I would read later in several books and articles, online debates considered whether *jugaad* is an ability or skill, a tool or formula, an industrious ethic, an entrepreneurial spirit, a mentality or mindset, a tradition or value set, or even a "culture" in itself (Aiyar 2010; Cappelli et al. 2010; Chadha 2009; Philip et al. 2010; Singh et al. 2011). Some began to argue that while *jugaad* may be indigenous to India, it is potentially exportable to other parts of the world and may be especially useful in developing countries facing severe poverty, political disorder, and resource constraints (Gupta 2008; Radjou et al. 2012). Many would sing its praises as the secret to India's continuing rise as a global economic power. A former national minister of commerce and industry even claimed that *jugaad* forms the bedrock of Indian discovery and development, going so far as to "wonder whether *jugaad*, a form of scientific innovation, represents a suppressed Indian inventive gene" (Nath 2008, 4; cf. Chadha 2009).

Numerous actors in transnational political, business, and science and technology circles have been proclaiming *jugaad* a force for good and the definitive key to "the way India innovates" (Bhushan 2008).[11] But not everyone has been hopping onto the shaky *jugaad* bandwagon, and a number of critiques of the idea of extolling and exporting *jugaad* have emerged. Some are not satisfied with calling *jugaad* "innovative" and argue that it is at best an adaptive measure that serves as a temporary stage or evolutionary stepping stone on the way to truly "systematic" innovation (Krishnan 2010). Others feel compelled to find different terms to describe "Indian" modes of innovation, because doing or having *jugaad* seems to have associations with shoddy practices and "the connotation of compromising on quality" (Prahalad and Mashelkar 2010), placing at risk not only national citizens but also perhaps the world at large—for example, when doing *jugaad* while building a nuclear power plant (Elliott 2011). A sociologist asserts in dire tones that *jugaad* "exacerbates systemic risk" by forging or reinforcing detrimental "path dependencies" that maintain poor infrastructure, and that it represents nothing more than a dodgy coping mechanism, a form of ad hoc " 'skirting' around resource constraints" rather than a positive force for social mobility and political-economic transformation (Birtchnell 2011, 364–68; cf. Thakur 2013). These types of critiques point toward the writhing bedfellow relationship between *jugaad* and corruption by alluding to provisionality as a confluence of temporality (a temporary "fix"), allocational capability (getting something done, but with a kind of material insufficiency), and moral flux (the material insufficiency indexes metaphysical decadence).

However, in line with proponents in transnational business and science circles, both Praveen's long-term plan for job attainment and the Lucknow district police's adaptive methods of criminal investigation exhibit a praxis of *jugaad* as relational resourcefulness that engenders progressive advancement, or even forges *new* pathways and possibilities rather than detrimental "dependencies." Significantly, this concept of *jugaad* is much older and more entrenched than the term's current connotations of possible corruption. The word *jugaad* is etymologically related to the Sanskrit idea of *yukti*, which insinuates a clever stratagem or gambit as well dexterity and discovery, to wit virtuosity (McGregor 2002). *Yukti* has for millennia indexed evidence-based scientific advancement in the *siddhantic* traditions of Indian philosophy, as well as a broader cultural valuation of ingenuity and the probability—though not the inevitability—of invention through making connections (Narasimha 2007). Both *yukti* and *jugaad* emerge from the root word *yug,* which means "paired, joined, twin" and linguistically manifests a shared sense of the moral good of provision through combination (McGregor 2002). *Yug* also translates as "to unite" (Forbes 1866; Taliaferro and Griffiths 2003) and is known to be the Indo-European ancestor of words like *yoga, yoke, junction, adjust, juxtapose, rejoinder, jugular,* and *junta.* And recall my earlier statement that in the Oxford Hindi–English dictionary, the descendant term *jugaad* has been translated as "provision, means of providing" (McGregor 2002).

Knowledge of this etymology makes it understandable and unsurprising that *jugaad* as an everyday mode of sociality would be conceived as something constructive and opposed to corruption, the latter of which would be associated more with properties of isolation and individual interest, inability and impossibility. This semiotic valuation of combinatory provision also resonates with anthropological scholarship showing how, in western and southern India, local understandings of corruption tend to be associated less with misusing public office for private gain and more with selfish ingestion of good fortune or misdirection of favors as well as failure to repay debts, redistribute wealth, or otherwise demonstrate and share largesse in the community (Piliavsky 2014; Price 1999; for an example of a similar phenomenon in Papua New Guinea, see Pickles 2011).

Crucially, in addition to connoting provision through combination, *yug* or *jug* as unification and universal force also indexes a particular temporality with a circular morphology—specifically, a concept of four cosmic eras through which, many Hindus believe, the universe endlessly cycles: *satya, tretaa, dvaapara,* and *kali.* Multiple Hindu texts and oral traditions contend that the world is currently in the *kali yug,* or morally degenerate age of the demon, which immediately precedes and is intimately connected with the *satya yug,* the age of truth and virtue. One who believes in this cycle of ages would probably argue that doing *jugaad* is the only—or, at least, the most practical and feasible—way of managing the challenges and dilemmas of the *kali yug,* even if it means engaging in action that might be considered corrupt, since even the most morally upright beings are fighting destructive cosmic forces much larger than themselves.[12]

Reading everyday practice through this epochal cosmology, as virtuous provision abutting (and perhaps sometimes abetting) universal dark forces, may also help explain how *jugaad* has become conflated with corruption (*bhrashtaachaar*), or the general condition of being "fallen" or "polluted." Provision as an ability to furnish material and metaphysical goods for the future must contend with provisionality as a condition of impermanence, instability, and potential iniquity. In Eric Wolf's (1990) terms, the human good fight against superhuman destructive forces might be conceived as deploying "tactical power" against "structural power." But this conceptual binary of opposing powers seems to divorce individual or collective subjects as "tacticians" from the shifting statuses and multiple relationships with which they must contend, and the context in which such contentions occur. Moreover, it does not account for agency as a potentially transformative capability that takes on a positive moral valence.

In place of tactical power, and applying some *jugaad* of my own, I propose a concept of "provisional agency" that reflects qualities of temporary necessity, social-material capability and moral virtuosity. I add to Max Weber's useful distinction between *Macht* and *Herrschaft* (chap. 1) attention to Sherry Ortner's (2006) distinction between agency-as-power, or imposition of will, and agency-as-project, or the pursuit of goals. Ortner claims that these two forms of agency are distinct fields of meaning that may articulate with one another but remain categorically separate, with power "always in the service of projects" (p.153). I argue that provisional agency is a co-articulation of power and projects in dialogue with moral virtue constructed by the contingent capability to provide for the self and others, as collective beneficence. It often manifests as doing *jugaad* and, when exhibited by persons embodying social roles associated with the power to command obedience *on occasion*, like police, serves as the primary foundation of what I am calling provisional authority.

Attention to the integration of agency and authority with provisionality helps us to build on, and reconsider, previous ethnographic work on corruption in South Asia, and potentially elsewhere. Acknowledging the fluidity of social positions and the importance of social provisions in evaluations of corruption, two social scientists from India make the following critical points:

> The English word "corruption" conveys a sense of biology, of something negative, rotten, sickly, parasitic, smacking of decay, without the possibilities of composting. It suggests a culture being eaten up by nature. *Such a word blinds one to the inventiveness, the survival quality of corruption or even as a strategy of mobility* [sic]. *When you see corruption as service, an activity, you see it prosaically as a form of work.* (Visvanathan and Sethi 1998, 4, emphasis added; see also Roitman 2005).

These remarks resonate strongly with what the CRT police and many of their colleagues express to be "work." The suggestion that corruption exhibits "inventiveness . . . survival . . . a strategy of mobility" and therefore may be seen as "service" echoes the explanations provided by police of their actions as "*jugaad.*"[13] Such explanations are not unique to police in UP. They may also be found in India among un(der)employed youth who serve as "fixers" at local universities, routinely brokering backdoor student admissions, influencing teaching appointments, and arranging construction contracts with favored companies—practices well within the ambit of "corruption" (see also Berenschot 2014). Craig Jeffrey has noted how such youth conceive of themselves and their fixing practices in terms of waiting for real life to begin, or "timepass" (2010), and consider doing *jugaad* a morally positive form of service to others (Jeffrey and Young 2014).

Conceiving corruption as work, as service, as provisional agency can also be seen in realms like caste politics and street economies. Jeffrey Witsoe's (2011) ethnography of caste-based political parties in the UP neighboring state of Bihar shows how since the late 1980s persons in historically disenfranchised lower-caste groups—notably, though not exclusively, the Yadav caste of which the CRT station chief is a member—have adopted, tolerated, and even celebrated some forms of corruption as expressions of empowerment and upward mobility. This is the case because many of the persons who enact these forms of corruption are seen as both generous patrons and potential conduits of state provisions to underserved populations (see also Piliavsky 2014; cf. Martin 2013 regarding personalistic power and the rise of "outlaw legislators" in Taiwan). In a rather different South Asian scene, Jonathan Anjaria (2011) demonstrates how illicit exchanges of material goods and favors among street hawkers, police, and other municipal officials in Mumbai[14] constitute an "ordinary space of negotiation" that allows various types of journeymen to question and appropriate state power through claims to urban space.

In all of these analyses of everyday exchanges in contemporary India, actions and relations as seemingly disparate as repairing a building at the last minute, paying a bribe to become a police official, selling recycled material accessories to uplift the poor, and transforming a struggling corporation into a profitable business—perhaps, though not necessarily, through "creative accounting"—may all be conceived by a wide swath of people as manifesting essentially the same type of thing, and, moreover, a good type of thing: namely, provisional agency.[15] And this expression of agency may be evaluated as *both virtuous and corrupt.*

The Durkheimian social fact of the "provisionality" of virtue and corruption in contemporary India has profound implications for the ebbing and flowing national-level "anti-corruption movement" led by Anna Hazare that began in 2011, and also for the political party that grew out of it called the Aam Aadmi (Common Peoples') Party, as well as for analyses and enactments of transparency and accountability activism more generally. Such activism often buckles under the weight of equating the corrupt with the illegal (Nuijten and Anders 2008), or it becomes mired in the contradictions of framing corruption as a problem of an "unruly local state" that must be "disciplined" by rights-bearing citizens into following its own legal procedures and policies, sometimes reproducing or reinforcing the very "informal mediated connections" that seem to serve as the primary conduits for corruption in the first place (Webb 2012). But if we conceive of corruption as a shifting category of practice broadly configured by provisional agency, then we may also be able to build new theoretical frameworks that help us understand and explain a host of questionable practices, and to clarify which practices require reevaluation or eradication or reform through particular policy responses. The same is arguably true if we conceive of state and police authority as another shifting category of practice configured by provisional agency.

Provisional Agency and Police Authority

The everyday interactions analyzed here, and the provisional agency produced therein, may be conceived to some extent in terms of what Sherry Ortner refers to as culturally constructed "serious games," which she describes as "consisting of webs of relationship and interaction between multiple, shiftingly interrelated subject positions, none of which can be extracted as autonomous 'agents'; and yet at the same time there is 'agency,' that is, actors play with skill, intention, wit, knowledge, intelligence" (1996, 12). That said, while the mutating moral distinction between virtue and corruption remains epiphenomenal in Ortner's analysis (e.g., women who exhibit "too much" agency in a particular context are punished, whether they are considered to be good or bad), I place the shiftiness of moral boundaries in the center of my concept of provisional agency. And while Ortner is careful to consider agency in relation to (Foucauldian) power, my emphasis on provisionality moves away from power as a totalizing force and relation limiting agency, and shifts toward (Weberian) authority as a relational field constructed through moral and instrumental exchanges among transmographying actors with varying capabilities of and interests in giving and obeying commands (see chap. 1). In the context under discussion, the probability of obedience to authoritative command changes depending on a host of factors shaping the social field of exchange relationships. Vehicle drivers may refuse police commands to give bribes or free rides, or they may provide these resources depending on the conditions of the moment. In this shifting field, *all* subjects involved may have provisional agency; however, certain subjects will be imbued with the extra quality of provisional authority as well, by virtue of their official position or their capabilities and responses to pragmatic contingencies and moral contestations in a particular time-space.

Placing Praveen's two expressions of *jugaad*—familial expertise in bribe-fixing and the temporary misrepresentation of official rank (as making possible the command of greater favors)—in dialogue with the CRT police's more or less successful adaptive measures of criminal investigation, we may begin to theorize how provisional agency as a moral praxis shaped by social demands undergirds state authority, rendering the latter provisional as well. The social acts of mobilizing personal connections to fix a bribe for police employment, or to ensure the safe and timely transfer of evidence to court, demonstrate provisional agency as a capability to realize a goal more than an increased probability that command will be obeyed in the face of authority. That said, these two ethnographic examples, together with those of the failed coercion of the *tempo* driver and the failed extortion of the truck driver in chapter 1, also reveal how tenuous—or more positively, how provisional—the authority of police actually is. There is no guarantee that police commands will be obeyed, not even the fact that they may legally use coercion by violence. Pace Bittner (1970) and Weber (1978 [1919]), the police authority to use force is and always has been quite negotiable and contingent, as are the results of any specific command they may give. The probability that police will achieve their own goals—whether those goals involve arresting and charging a suspected criminal, controlling a crowd, presenting admissible evidence, or on the darker side taking a bribe or using unwarranted or excessive force—depend on a host of contingencies, which vary by context. In UP, this probability depends on things like who police know, what their official rank is, what they have to offer in exchange for some favor, the timing of their command, the resources they have at hand, and how well they negotiate with others, among other factors, not least, the question of which others may be negotiating with or commanding *them*.

In addition to the temporal and allocational flux indexed in the contingencies listed above, the provisionality of police authority also entails fluctuations of a moral-legal character, which are intimately linked with the ways in which police conceive of their duty to enforce law and maintain order. As we will see, police themselves recognize that their authority is negotiable and subject to the shifting boundaries of moral and legal practice that make "doing *jugaad*" sometimes isomorphic with corruption, sometimes in opposition to corruption, and most often a demand to do their duty in what they may consider to be an ethically consistent manner. Police ethics of practice are imbricated not only with the social fact of moral shiftiness, but also with one of the most crucial and global demands of police work: the fact that that police are routinely called upon to respond rapidly and with discretion to a host of unpredictable situations that require decisive action and adaptation (Van Maanen 1978; Bittner 1970 and 1990). This is a tall order and, not surprisingly, police rarely satisfy all parties involved with their responses, not least because they must work along a variety of irreconcilable social fault lines. The disjunct between expectations of police by various parties and the actual capabilities of police to act often leads not only to readings of police as incompetent, violent or corrupt, but also to police constructing for themselves an ethics of order-keeping practice that appears more transgressive than protective. I analyze this "orderly ethics" in terms of provisional legal authority, *jugaadi* legitimation, and dirty policing.

3

Orderly Ethics

Law and Order

On another bright October morning, my research assistant and I enter the portal to Chakkar Rasta Thana (CRT). We greet the two khaki-uniformed men sitting at the wooden table in the main front room, an Uttar Pradesh Police (UPP) constable named Prithvi (whom we met in chap. 2), and a recently transferred in UPP sub-inspector (SI) named Trivedi. Trivedi and Prithvi say their *namastes* to us, and then return to the First Information Report (FIR) they are cowriting, which Trivedi dictates while Prithvi scribes. Behind them, in the *hawallat* (holding cell), sits a man who they say has been detained since the previous afternoon. We are told that the man was arrested and detained after being caught in the act of illegally severing metal rods and wiring from a fence around a plot of land several kilometers from the police station, to steal and presumably sell as scrap. Y. K. Yadav, the CRT chief station officer (SO), is currently away from the station, and has assigned Trivedi to be investigating officer (IO) of the case, so they are now framing charges for criminal court.[1]

As we listen to Trivedi dictate the report, we hear him name two charges under the Indian Penal Code (IPC): one under section 378 for theft—a cognizable offense, meaning it does not require police to obtain a judge's warrant to investigate—and another under section 427, for "mischief causing damage to the amount of Rs. 50 [or more]," which is a non-cognizable or lesser order offense. This is procedurally correct. However, as Trivedi continues speaking, I notice that he is having Prithvi write into the report that the accused was picking pockets rather than damaging and stealing fence material. Confused, I ask, "Why don't you just report the actual crime?"

Trivedi explains that they are writing the report this way because they do not have the resources to gather the real evidence materials—large pieces of wood and steel and wire—and then lug them all the way down to the judicial magistrate's office in town for the arraignment. CRT generally does not have adequate staff at the station, nor a store of the proper tools, like saws and binding material, for gathering this kind of evidence. And because SO Yadav is "out of station" with the sole government-issued jeep, the remaining CRT staff officers do not have a big enough vehicle available to carry all of the evidence to town. They also lack authorization from the SO to compensate private laborers and drivers to help them—if there is even enough money in the *thana* kitty anyway—and say they cannot afford to pay out of their own pockets at the moment.

Besides lacking adequate resources, the CRT staff also lack adequate time to procure such resources. Because the man has already been detained, they are legally bound by what is colloquially known among police as the "twenty-four-hour rule," which under Criminal Procedural Code section 76 requires that a suspect in police custody be produced before a judicial magistrate within one day from the time of arrest and filing of the FIR (CrPC 2005 [1973], 48). Even though police who are caught illegally detaining someone may be punished for indiscipline, a common practice has developed of unofficially detaining suspects or their associates for several days in order to gather information. I witnessed such detention routinely at CRT. I also noted that while this practice clearly violates the detained persons' civil and human rights, police would claim that sometimes this unofficial practice ironically may be better for the detained because of another section of the law related to judicial custody. Specifically, if an accused person named in an FIR is produced in front of a judicial magistrate before police have managed to gather enough evidence to hold him or her under the twenty-four-hour rule, then under CrPC section 167, the magistrate may order that the suspect remain in judicial custody, which could potentially be even worse because the suspect could end up remaining in custody for a much longer period while waiting for guilt or innocence to be established. Thus, police "feel that the least amount of harm is done to the suspect in the event that he is innocent, and in the event that he is guilty he will get his 'just deserts'" (Kumar et al. 2008, 29).

But in this case, the CRT police are trying to follow the twenty-four-hour rule. With the deadline rapidly approaching, Trivedi and Prithvi say that the best thing to do is procure a small razor blade—the tool of choice for many local pick-pockets, so they can slice open a victim's clothing or bag to steal the booty—and present this to the court as evidence. If they present the evidence and report on time then, they claim, it is more likely that the judge will convict and they will be able to dispose of the case. And, they point out, the punishment meted out will be the same, whatever evidence is used, since pickpocketing and the crime actually committed both count under the IPC as theft.

An older constable named Aman, who is the CRT *diwan*, or secretary cum dispatch officer who keeps track of files and registers, stands by watching our interaction. I am reminded of Bassanio in Shakespeare's *Merchant of Venice*, who pleads "to do a great right, do a little wrong," when Aman says with a half-smile sometime later, "This the way it is . . . sometimes a little bit of dishonesty benefits everyone . . . the victims, the judges, the police . . . sometimes even the criminals. Therefore, it is not wrong."

As SI Trivedi and Constable Prithvi complete the false charge sheet and tell the accused man to sign it, another SI named Arun—who is fresh out of the academy, and now completing what is known as his "practical training" in the field—returns from his room in the CRT living quarters with a new set of twin straight razors, still encased in the cardboard covering in which they were bought. After writing up the charge sheet, Prithvi places one of the blades in a small cardboard box, wraps it in cotton cloth, and sews it up with string per regulations of securing evidence. As Prithvi stamps the box with the SO's seal and attaches it to the charge sheet, constable Aman plays with the other razor blade distractedly, carving away splinters from the rickety wooden table that serves as a desk.

This is clearly a commonplace thing to do, and the CRT police express no hesitation or embarrassment about it. Still, I inquire, "Would it not give you more peace of mind to produce the real evidence for the real crime? What if the accused says that he has been charged falsely, and that you are using fake evidence?" The apathetic and somewhat bewildered response by SI Trivedi is, "He [the accused] is signing the report. Besides, *every* criminal claims innocence and denies wrongdoing. This one will be no different. But the judges base their decisions on the evidence, not on what he says." Trivedi makes no mention of the possibility that other witnesses and evidence to the contrary of the fictitious story may be produced to the court; or of the IPC Chapter XI's "of false evidence and offenses against public injustice" (secs. 192–229). Finally, Constable Prithvi collects the charged man, the cloth-covered package, and the other relevant materials including the signed report and drives them all down to the magistrate's office on his personal motorcycle.

"Every dirty job that comes along"

During periodic fieldwork trips to northern India for more than a decade, I have witnessed police perform innumerable legally and morally questionable practices on a regular basis. Some, like the instance of false reporting and evidence fabrication just related, seem to be relatively benign if still highly dubious. Others are more extreme, discriminatory, and violent, such as an incident I witnessed of a young Muslim man and Hindu woman shopping together, who were hauled to a local police station, harshly interrogated, and detained without charge after someone reported a "kidnapping" (Jauregui 2013b).[2] The routinization of police practices that seem to be at best self-serving or lazy, at worst prejudicial or cruel, is accompanied by a banalization. Police rarely hide or express shame about such practices as part of some "intimate culture" of policing (Herzfeld 2005). Moreover, members of the public who witness or become involved in such interactions generally do not express surprise that police would act this way, and sometimes do not even express any moral indignation about it. The apparent ordinariness, prevalence, and repetition of such problematic engagements reveal a great deal about the legal, moral, and ethical frameworks within which police perform what they understand to be their professional duties. An analysis of the contours, conditions of possibility, and potential consequences of these frameworks constitutes my focus here.

This analysis develops a concept of an "orderly ethics" of everyday police practice as co-configured with provisional legal authority and *jugaadi* legitimation. Conceiving police practice this way helps to explain its integration with systemic corruption, cronyism, and coercive violence as shaped by broader forces and relations of sociocultural order. Provisional *legal* authority is a crucial element of this ethics since it involves procedural enactments and enforcements by police that provide a resource, service, or some other potential social "good" that is contingent on how the law as written code works in dialogue with other subjects, relationships, and circumstances considered relevant in a particular case. In the case of the CRT fence-cutter-turned-pickpocket, for example, the provisionality of legality itself is manifest in officers ironically following certain legal procedures and rules of evidence while also committing the illegal acts of writing a false report and submitting fake material evidence to the court, with an expressed understanding that this is the best way to get the job done.

When questioned about why they think such contradictory behavior is the best path forward, police display a form of what I call *jugaadi* legitimation. Building on the insights into the contronymic character of "doing *jugaad*" in chapter 2, I conceive *jugaadi* legitimation by police as a moral-cum-instrumental rationalization of using ad hoc or adaptive means to achieve a virtuous end, such as getting "the criminal" and "the evidence" to court in an efficient manner. *Jugaadi* legitimation by police of their enactments of provisional legal authority manifests what I call an "orderly ethics" of policing.

Like its conceptual cousin "provisional," the modifier "orderly" is polysemic. First, following from historical connotations of military institutional organization, it refers specifically to police operating in a social field in which "orders" are given and carried out by a group of specialized and authorized actors.[3] Importantly, police not only execute official orders given by senior officers in the chain of command, but also have a duty to meet the demands of a fractured public with its unofficial and unending "orders" for service. Working in a virtual minefield of conflicting demands on both of these vertical and horizontal axes, police are expected to somehow maintain a balance of legal, bureaucratic, and broader social orders—a tall "order" indeed.[4] This field of expectations and its concomitant pressures signal what is perhaps the most important connotation of "orderly" for this analysis: the unique subjectivity of police as disciplined institutional actors whose multiple roles in producing and preserving order are as amorphous, indeterminate, and provisional as their authority to do so.

A concept of orderly ethics does *not* imply that police simply act in ways that are consistent with a static role in a Durkheimian social order characterized by organic solidarity, as structural-functionalists might posit (cf. Dumont 1970). Rather it is somewhat closer to the Foucauldian concept of ethics entailing one's relationship with, and understanding of, possibilities and responsibilities for demonstrating moral agency under specific conditions as "truth" (Foucault 1998). Janet Roitman (2006) has followed this line in theorizing an "ethics of illegality" among moto-taxi men in the Chad Basin who engage in activities like cross-border smuggling and road banditry, and conceive this as rightful "work" in the face of depressed economic conditions. But unlike these moto-taxi men—one of whom Roitman even quotes as calling Cameroonian police "partners" in "exploit[ing] illegality" and exclaiming "long live the tolerant police! (ibid., 262)"—police in Uttar Pradesh (UP) and elsewhere are routinely expected to conduct their practice in direct dialogue with "the law." Thus, their orderly ethics does not hinge on exploiting illegality so much as it does on mobilizing and manipulating provisionality in all its senses, especially the provisionality of the law itself as a kind of subject with contextually shifting meanings, positions, and capabilities.

Police mobilization and manipulation of the law, and of other social goods and subjects, are not simply a unilateral expression of power as *Macht*. Rather, they express their provisional authority as a combination of moral and instrumental virtuosity in maintaining whatever "law and order" means in a particular time-space, and according to the continually changing expectations of, and new demands placed on them by, various others (Jauregui 2014b). In other words, and pace Louis Althusser (1971), *"the police" are themselves interpellated by various members of "the public" and various components of "the law"* as a peculiar type of authoritative orderly in the historic sense of becoming an institutional domestic servant, similar to a low-level soldier attending to the minute needs of high-level officers, or a hospital janitor responsible for cleaning and nonmedical care of patients, practitioners, and facilities.[5] Like these other types of orderlies—that is, subordinate subjects who are supposed to keep things tidy, well-managed, and running smoothly—police are expected to use their provisional authority in ways that will often involve their getting legally and morally "dirty" as a means to make society more "clean" and productive (cf. Jauregui 2015). Thus, police are variously, if not always in equal parts, commanders and servants (cf. chap. 4). Police recognize this social fact and incorporate it into their more or less conscious and contradictory expressions, especially in their rationalizations of the fraught relationship between means and ends in their work.

A theoretical concern with how public police relate means and ends in their everyday practices of order keeping has long been an object of inquiry in scholarly studies of policing, most notably in Carl Klockars's now classic essay on the "Dirty Harry Problem" (1980). In this analysis, Klockars examines the "ineluctable" and "insoluble" aspect of policing that renders what he calls the "genuine moral dilemma" of police officers and institutions constantly having to use bad means to achieve good ends, thereby figuring police as always already "tainted" actors (cf. Bittner 1970). Klockars analyzes a variegated class of Dirty Harry problems. But what he characterizes as the "core scene of *Dirty Harry*"—the 1971 Hollywood film starring Clint Eastwood and namesake for the problem—involves the fictional San Francisco Police inspector Harry Callahan standing on the bullet-wounded leg of known serial killer Scorpio in order "to torture a confession" out of him. The inspector does this ostensibly to learn the location of a fourteen-year-old girl that Scorpio has kidnapped in the hopes that she might still be alive and possibly saved. But he clearly suspects—and film viewers later have it confirmed—that she has already been raped and murdered, opening a space of ambiguity regarding whether his violence is more pragmatic, that is a means to gather information, or punitive, that is to wreak vengeful pain on the murder-rapist as a kind of "street justice" (see Van Maanen 1978).

Klockars's critical analysis of the Dirty Harry problem addresses vital questions about how illegal or immoral acts of police violence may be legitimated as "necessary" or "right" under specific circumstances (cf. Machiavelli 1966 [1513]). And I concur with his general line of inquiry to the extent that

there are undoubtedly myriad intractable dilemmas permeating everyday police work, especially in relation to the official authority of police to deploy coercion in the name of some "greater good." That said, by choosing a moment
of physical torture by an officer acting "outside the law" as the fundamental
scene of the *Dirty Harry* film—and thereby following a long-standing analytical assumption that the "core function" of policing is the potential or actual
use of "non-negotiably coercive force" (Bittner 1970, 46)—Klockars narrowly
focuses his inquiry on physical violence and extra-legality, at the expense of
recognizing and analyzing other types of dilemmas and transgressions configuring police work that do not necessarily involve bodily injury and may
also conform to specific elements of the law.

As explicated in chapter 1, a narrow focus on both physical violence and
extra-legality as being central to the role of public police has long configured
critical questions about state authority addressed by a variety of social theorists
(Bittner 1970; Muir 1977; Weber 1978 [1919]; Benjamin 1978 [1922]; Westmarland 2001; Derrida 2002). It has also formed the foundation of anthropological analyses of state security actors over the past several decades (Sluka 1999;
Robben 1995 and 1996; Das 2004; Pratten and Sen 2008). I would not claim that
these and other studies focusing on violence as a core component of policing
are wrong-footed. It is vital to continue to critically interrogate all forms of
police violence, especially those that manifest discriminatory or disproportionate ill treatment by police of others. Even I have employed this strategically essentializing focus on police violence in some of my own analyses of
policing in UP (Jauregui 2013b); and I will return later to the problem of police
violence, and elaborate on some of its perhaps less obvious conditions of possibility and unintended consequences.

For now, however, I want underscore the fact that the theoretical applications of analyses essentializing police as primarily violent actors are con-
stricted by their concentration on harm to human bodies and violations of
legality at the expense of other problematics. We must loosen and retract the
conceptual ligatures of the idea that police embody the originary violence of
law if we are to have a more nuanced and comprehensive understanding of
the conditions of possibility for all sorts of morally and legally questionable
police practices, from discriminatory acts of stop and search to deceitful interrogation. The public police raison d'être must not be reduced to en masse
deployment of excessive or extra-legal coercion, physical or otherwise, since
as most any ethnographer of police will agree, the vast majority of the time
police are not actively engaging in physically violent acts, or explicitly (or even
implicitly) threatening to engage in such acts. Moreover, even when police
are engaging in such acts, and especially when they are not, they are generally

acting in direct dialogue with legal procedures and strictures rather than dis-
missing them. Therefore, I here aim to retune the dialogue to consider ethical
dilemmas of police praxis that span a vast field of moral and legal boundary
transgressions associated with their multiplicity of roles, and the patterned
ways in which these dilemmas configure the discourses and practices through
which police relate means and ends in their everyday work.

Pace Klockars, I submit that the scene in the *Dirty Harry* film that best defines the moral, legal, and ethical dilemmas of policing is *not* Inspector Harry
Callahan's torturing a confession out of the serial killer, but rather a short in-
terlude in the story that actually has nothing to do with the main plot devoted
to the dramatic hunt for Scorpio. In this cutaway scene, the police officer is
called upon to prevent a man from jumping to his death from a tall building in
front of a crowd of gaping onlookers. Responding to the call, an exhausted and
exasperated Inspector Callahan arrives at the scene, rises several stories in a
mechanized cherry picker, and engages the suicidal man rather unsympatheti-
cally and sarcastically, saying that he is not going to try to save him from killing
himself, but is simply there to follow procedure and gather identification information, because the jumper is going to make "such a mess" when he falls to his
death that Callahan does not want to search through the bloody muck for his
wallet in order to fill out and file the necessary police report. The man becomes
so angry at Callahan's callousness that he lunges at the officer, which allows
Harry to grab him—a move the detective appears to have calculated all along—
and bring him down from the building, "saving the day" in an ironic way.

Immediately following this incident, Callahan says to his partner in his
typical wry tone, "Now you know why they call me Dirty Harry . . . every
dirty job that comes along."

Extrapolating from this scene—which is the only time in the film when
Harry Callahan articulates his own "dirtiness," an articulation that contrasts
starkly with those of other characters in the story[6]—I would revise Klockars's
thesis to argue that the Dirty Harry problem for police is not simply that they
are perpetually stuck having to use categorically "bad" (i.e., violent or illegal)
means to achieve categorically "good" ends (i.e., a just and peaceful order),
but rather that they are perpetually subject to—and subjects in—ongoing ne-
gotiations and contestations over precisely these categories of means and ends
and "goods" themselves. Police and their practices become "dirty" and "disor-
derly" not merely through the state authorized vice of routinely or excessively
deploying physical violence outside the law, but inter alia by virtue of their
being constituted by the publics that they are supposed to serve and represent
as a marginal "other." Police are outsiders on the inside charged with doing
various types of transgressive or "dirty" work—including but not limited to

coercive action—that most people would rather not do themselves, all while somehow remaining completely lawful and just.

In doing their work, police are compelled to traverse and sometimes even transmute the limits of legal, moral, and ethical practice (Jauregui 2011 and 2013b; cf. Das and Poole 2004, 14). Moreover, by breaching and bending the law's apparent limits, thereby revealing its inconsistencies, inadequacies, and contradictions—as well as its indeterminacy and provisionality—police compel *all of us* to rethink these limits, and question what is truly right, just, and necessary. This is key to why Dirty Harry is such a disturbing and even terrifying human icon. It is not simply the fact that he seems to wield his Magnum .44 gun with violent impunity ("Do ya feel lucky, punk?" he infamously asks while threateningly pointing the gun barrel in the face of a nabbed robber). Rather, it is that Dirty Harry has the ability and the will to both reveal and subject others to the vagaries of provisional legal authority. In so doing, he shows us that relationships and acts that appear to be "external to" or "in excess" of widely accepted moral, legal, and ethical codes are in fact coterminous with what may be considered justifiable or necessary.[7]

Taking all of this into consideration, it is less surprising that the vast majority of everyday police work in UP (and arguably elsewhere) seems to be conceived and enacted less as a rational-legal exercise in the discovery and collection of facts as "evidence" of a true crime, or as a discretionary intervention in conflict, and is instead constituted more as a praxis of purposeful adaptation and improvisation as a means to maintain order in a context where provisional authority is the main rule. This police praxis emerges in a field in which manipulable rules of evidence, personal relationships, gut feelings, long-standing systems of patronage, cultural conflict and local power plays must be navigated and managed on a minute-to-minute basis. Police serve various publics not merely as proceduralist bureaucrats or law-bound gatekeepers to the criminal justice system, but more importantly as "orderlies" working odd jobs at the coalface of the continual reproduction and transformation of legal, moral, and ethical boundaries. In what follows, we will see how the multiple roles demanded of police—especially those of first responder, crime investigator, and dispute arbitrator—and the concomitant orderly ethics that they practice may simultaneously ease and challenge peoples' access to the official criminal justice system.

Bodies of Evidence

On a hot morning in April, Constable Prithvi is responsible for swathing and sewing up yet another sharp object in white cloth to submit to court. This one is not a razor blade but a *baanka*, a long curved metal instrument that is generally used to chop wheat or bamboo. And this one is said to be the "real evidence" in a murder case. It has allegedly been used by a local villager to hack his grand-uncle to death in a violent turn to an ongoing land dispute, one of the most common and widespread forms of conflict leading to heinous crime in rural India, besides dowry. The police say this is most likely a case of *randwa pratha*, a sinister social institution prevalent in parts of northern India wherein people will sometimes kill off unmarried elderly male relatives in order to consolidate family land holdings.[8] I watch as Prithvi begins to wrap the dark stained weapon, while an SI named Pandey and another SI under training named Bahadur draft the FIR and industriously hand draw kinship diagrams and maps of property lines. They tell me that under some sort of "pressure" the alleged murderer decided to turn himself in directly to the court (instead of first going to the police), and is being remanded to police custody at CRT, since the murder occurred within the *thana* jurisdiction. The station chief, and several constables are now down at the courthouse picking up the suspect.

Pandey and Bahadur say that prior to leaving for court, the SO had ordered them and Prithvi to go to the murder scene and investigate. They claim that after arriving at the scene, they had discovered the bloody *baanka* and recovered the apparent murder weapon as a key piece of evidence. Now, they have returned to the station and are priming everything for when their boss comes with the suspect who has surrendered himself. Prithvi has already sewn up the weapon into the white cloth, and I think to myself that things seem almost "too ready." When SO Yadav and his entourage finally arrive with the suspect, he asks to see the *baanka*, meaning Prithvi must now undo his painstaking needlework. As Yadav fondles the blood-stained weapon with his bare hands and looks it over, he begins what seems an odd and stilted monological interrogation of the man in custody who stands before him.

"Tell me what you did!" the SO barks.

Without waiting for an answer, Yadav continues with a barrage of questions and commands: "Who did you kill? Did *you* kill him? Is *this* the weapon you used? Tell the truth! Where did you leave the weapon?" Eventually, the man in custody, who appears to be rather dazed and not especially clever mumbles a confession: "Yes, I killed my grandfather's brother. I bludgeoned his neck and head with this *baanka*. I left it in the sugarcane field and ran away."

"Sign here," the SO orders while pointing to the FIR. The suspect is assisted in attaching his thumbprint, the signature of the illiterate, to the report written up by SIs Pandey and Bahadur. Several constables and the SO himself then proceed to frisk him. Satisfied that he is unarmed and without some other kind of contraband, the police shove the man into the holding cell where he will await his trip to the government hospital for a requisite routine medical exam. The man says in a pleading voice that he has not eaten or drunk anything since the night before, and a constable is ordered to procure *samosas* from a nearby shop and some water from the station hand pump. When the constable returns, he pours water from a steel pitcher through the bars toward the accused, who cups his hands to funnel the water into his mouth.

Meanwhile, two or three other police in the room casually examine the *baanka* as they chatter about other matters, turning it over in their hands, eyeing it from various angles. They are not wearing any gloves or minding what they touch, even though they say that they intend to send the evidence for analysis to the Lucknow district forensics lab, one of only three in the entire state of UP. (I am later told by Pandey that the analysis will be of the blood, not fingerprints or other physical traces—he says the lab will determine, "whether the blood is of human or animal origin.") The weapon goes back to Prithvi for re-sewing up and then fastening with the SO's personal seal, imprinted in wax.

The SO explains to everyone how the charge sheet declares that the accused walked ahead of them through the fields where the murder took place, led them to the resting place of the incriminating weapon, and they then recovered it to bring forth as evidence. This clearly contradicts what Pandey and Bahadur related to me about finding the weapon themselves earlier that morning. I remain quiet until the other police are away from the SO, and then ask Yadav why he and the others are fabricating a story about being led to the weapon instead of reporting what actually happened: namely, that the police found the *baanka* of their own accord and acumen.

A man of few words, Yadav says, "We must follow the rules of evidence."

I request that he expound, and he relates that while this man just confessed to the crime in the presence of police, CrPC section 164, along with sections 24–26 of the still in-force Indian Evidence Act (IEA) of 1872, bar the content of confessions to police from being admissible as evidence in court.[9] However, IEA section 27 leaves a legal loophole for procuring and admitting evidence based upon utterances by the accused to the police. If the accused volunteers or "consensually" provides "factual" information to police while in their custody, then this information may be used by police to "discover" admissible evidence.[10] This means police must somehow "prove" in their reports that the accused willingly provided them with information that directly guided them to evidence, rather than offered them a confession of guilt.

This confounding twist in the rules of evidence commonly translates into practices like this case of falsifying the FIR to say that the suspect led police to the weapon rather than truthfully reporting that the police found it themselves. Legally, according to Yadav, if the police reveal that they found the murder weapon first and acquired a signed confession from the accused only afterward, then their evidence is more suspect in the eyes of the court and less likely to secure a conviction than if they perjure themselves and claim that the suspect led them to the evidence of his own free will. There are no rewards for good detective work here. And the provision of the right kind of evidence and its reported sourcing that maximizes the probability of conviction and case disposal matters more than truthfully reflecting how, when, or even by whom said evidence has been procured.

"This is our job," says Yadav. "This is what we have been trained to do. We apprehend the criminals and apply the legal codes and make sure that wrongdoing is punished. That is the will of the people. That is democracy. Justice is served."

These simultaneously grand and pithy statements, together with those made in relation to the fence-cutter-turned-pick-pocket, and the actions these statements rationalize, reveal an orderly ethics of practice in which the police must achieve a specific end—entering accused suspects into the official criminal justice system—by working with what they are given, both in the way of rules and regulations dictating their practice and in the way of available resources and capabilities, which are often quite restricted. This police work ethic, which I found to extend far beyond CRT, takes legal codes as an external given with which police practices of criminal investigation must be united or made to "fit" (*yug*) through adaptive and improvisational means using the resources at hand. In other words police must do *jugaad* to enforce the law (see chap. 2).

Rather than flagrantly flouting the law—as police are often accused of doing (and indeed, sometimes do)—and rather than metaphorically "making law" in the Benjaminian metaphorical sense of deploying discretionary violence with impunity (Das 2004), in practice, police generally take very seriously the law and its limits as enshrined in written codes. But police also seem to conceive of law as a kind of trickster subject that is both manipulative and manipulable. They understand as well as any judge or lawyer that legal codes are reinterpretable, mutable, and sometimes internally contradictory. Police therefore feel compelled to find means to try to trick the law into realizing a specific part of its potential, most often the potential to convict an accused criminal with hard and fast evidence. In so doing, police reveal the inherent indeterminacy of the law, and of legal evidence, as an unsettling social fact.

This may be read as police simply trying to maximize their clearance or case disposal rates (i.e., arresting and charging a suspect in a case). But it may also be read as a kind of service. Police understand that people look to the law for certainty, and for justice, and therefore demand that it work toward these ends. Such understanding leads many police in UP, and arguably elsewhere, to consider and manipulate case evidence not merely as a material artifact of an actual event, or as a scientific unit of analysis that somehow precedes or exists outside of and in service to legal proceduralism, but moreover as a product and producer of knowledge, decision making, and authority over others. They thereby reveal the limits of the law as a form of knowledge (cf., Valverde 2003). Police understand their duty to entail bending or breaking some rules in order to enforce the law in the fullest way possible, whether that means "getting the bad guy" in a criminal investigation or achieving some other end oriented toward "law and order." Thus, rather than analyzing their practice as simply acting illegally or immorally due to some sort of individual or institutional "corruption," and rather than their actions signifying an ineffable "force of law" originating in violence through abuse of authority (Derrida 2002), we may explain part of what police do as forcing the law itself to look in the mirror and face its own distortions, contradictions, and constrictions.

This is not to claim that all police officers and staff in UP are unanimous in their articulations and interpretations of legally and morally dubious practices, or that every one of them is always working sincerely in the interests of justice. It is fair to argue that out of sheer laziness or cynicism or some other questionable motive, particular police at particular times feel that it is simply easier or in their own best interest to fabricate or modify evidence, or to write a false report or even charge an incorrect suspect, in lieu of performing the difficult task of conducting a thorough and successful criminal investigation. And we must not ignore the often selective and self-interested character of some officers' investigative practices, nor deny the prejudices that may compel them to punish this "culprit" instead of that one. If a suspect is a member of some ill-favored social group, especially a rival caste or political party, then he is probably in a lot more danger of becoming a "real criminal" than, say, an official or unofficial affiliate or business partner of presently powerful or other favored entities, including the police themselves (see Jauregui 2014b). And there is also a ubiquitous practice of police fixing cases in response to bribes or some type of compellance, especially pressure from socially and politically powerful figures who have some direct interest in a case outcome (Jauregui forthcoming). Just as practices of *jugaad* and their various outcomes are not equitably possible for or distributed to everyone (chap. 2), one cannot substantively support an absolute claim that all police practices of evidence production are applied "fairly and equally" to all people, all of the time.[11]

But the fact that unfair and unjust practices regularly happen does not discount the fact that many police express that they *must* operate in ways similar to those described above in order to do their job right and well—that is, to act as ethical subjects. Police often claim—and my observations confirm (as do those of others—see HRW 2009, for example)—that they are too under-resourced, mistrusted, or pressurized to do everything that the law and their various constituents demand, including gathering evidence to convict a known culprit. Moreover, they have to contend with problems outside the ambit of their control like seemingly endless court backlogs, which mean that case evidence often must wait for a very long time to get through the door of the law, sometimes forever, like Kafka's country man (1925). As mentioned previously, much of the evidence awaiting trial simply rots away, or at best becomes fodder for a *thana* auction (see figs. 6 and 7).[12] For many police, this means that meticulous effort to find and keep evidence would be a waste of their time. By these lights, evidence is only as good as it is useful at a particular moment for a particular purpose, usually effective prosecution. Rather than letting it deteriorate because of factors far beyond their control, many police feel it makes more sense to do *jugaad* with evidence itself. Thus, a la finding a razor blade and substituting it for fence material to catch a thief, many police stuck sifting through the evidence room to find material to send to court will steal from Peter to pay Paul, using evidence from one case to submit to court for a different case. Summing up orderly ethics in relation to this type of practice, a sub-inspector leaves us with a lingering question: "If you are punishing the *asla apraadhi* (real criminal), then what does it matter where the evidence comes from?"

Judges in Khaki, Fixers of Criminality

The police process of investigating and deciding who may be a "real criminal" is configured not only by legal codes and official regulations, but also by a host of unofficial modes of sociality and power plays. Beyond manipulating evidence to fit with certain provisions of law, police in UP routinely act in ways that reflect (1) demands by government leaders to under-report crime and (2) decision making based largely on hunches and biases. These political and professional forces often work in tandem, especially when people complain to police about relatively petty crimes and civil disputes (Jauregui 2014b).

The largest portion of my fieldwork with the UPP took place during the run up to the Vidhan Sabha (State Legislative Assembly) elections, which are scheduled to occur every five years (see chap. 5). It was an intensely politically charged moment, with incessant and omnipresent candidate nominating and campaigning activity, and party-sponsored posters and "hoardings" (billboards) covering every free inch of space. In this context, I was told by several police of various ranks that there had been unofficial orders "from the top" (i.e., from the UP chief minister, or CM, via the director general of police) that amounted to what some called a "blanket ban" on official reporting of crime (see also Dhuru and Pandey 2007 and Kumar et al. 2008). In short, police alleged that they were commanded by their highest boss in the state government not necessarily to prevent and decrease the actual occurrence of crime, but rather to use whatever means necessary to ensure that reported numbers of crime took a downward turn (in some places in the US, this is known as "juking the stats" or suppressing crime figures; see also Simon 2004).

Many UPP officers claimed to have been told to register as few crimes as possible so that the ruling party could proclaim on the news and in campaign advertisements that official crime rates had dropped during the reign of the current CM. One of the more controversial outgrowths of this was when Bollywood megastar Amitabh Bachchan (whose wife, as mentioned in chap. 1, is a celebrity Member of Parliament for UP, affiliated with the then CM's party, the Samajwadi or Socialist Party) said in campaign ads, "*Uttar Pradesh mein hai dam, kyunki jurm yahan hain kam*" (There is greatness in Uttar Pradesh, because crime has decreased here).[13] Some police even told me that there were unofficial monthly maximum quotas for crime registration, which if exceeded would draw punishment, usually a transfer of the station chief out of a desirable post or into an undesirable post (see chap. 5).

In combination with this politicized pressure coming down on police from outside, a second factor leading to problematic police (non-)responses to crime involved officers simply thinking that they "knew better" than to believe every complainant who came their way with a problem, even though their job is officially to at least inquire (in non-cognizable cases) if not conduct a full-blown investigation (in cognizable cases). The SO and other staff at CRT would give various reasons for not taking cognizance of a case, including things like a personal belief based on "experience" that a complainant was lying or an observation that a complainant did not have their story straight. It seems there is no shortage of persons in UP trying to register false cases with police as a means to harass their rivals in disputes, the investigation and prosecution of which may end up being a huge waste of time and resources. Even so, police's ignoring of complainants amounts to illegal neglect of duty.

Another reason given by police for routinely ignoring complainants was that they do not consider some reported occurrences serious enough to warrant their assistance. One such case I acutely recall witnessing was that of an elderly woman coming to CRT and asking the police to use their heavy hand in stopping a group of village boys from bullying her grandson. "Put the fear of god into them," she pleaded. While officers would sometimes offer their assistance in such cases if it was convenient, or if they took a particular interest in doing so, they would more often appeal to IPC section 95 regarding an "act causing slight harm" which reads:

> Nothing is an offence by reason that it causes, or that it is intended to cause, or that it is known to be likely to cause, any harm, if that harm is so slight that no person of ordinary sense and temper would complain of such harm [*sic*].

Notably, however, according to this legal provision and depending on an officer's own "sense and temper" police could, and often did, reason that even an apparently more serious offense need not be considered cognizable. Along these lines, I witnessed countless persons turned away who appeared to need immediate attention, including people who had been physically assaulted and were visibly bleeding or maimed. There was also an especially disturbing trend at CRT of neglecting women who complained of domestic abuse. This happened in part because this particular form of violence against women, a routinized and ubiquitous problem in this region, is widely conceived by many people as a "private matter" and widely considered by many police to be a less serious offense not worthy of their attention, even in the face of the CrPC provision defining wife beating (or physical abuse of children or other women in the family) as a cognizable crime, and the 2005 Protection of Women from Domestic Violence Act emphasizing the point.[14] In opposition to these state laws designed to protect women and children, many people—both men and women—regularly invoke Hindu religious norms of *pati-bhakti* (devotion to husband) and *nari-dharma* (duties of a woman) to dismiss or even justify domestic violence as part of a woman's universal duty of self-sacrifice.[15]

With such strong cultural penchants toward ignoring or rationalizing domestic violence, it is not completely surprising, if still intensely distressing, that police will often claim that they are "too busy" with "real work" to help a woman alleging she is a victim of abuse or threat by members of her family. But crucially, in addition to these cultural tendencies, police also cite legal technicalities and supposedly experience-based "gut instincts" in support of such neglect. I witnessed a woman arrive at CRT around 11 p.m. one evening, accompanied by her brother—who served as her representative to as well as protector from the police (a common practice)—claiming to have walked some ten kilometers to file an application against her husband for continually beating her. The sub-inspector who received her complaint barely looked up from the paperwork he was doing and said, "It is too late, come back tomorrow."

I could not help protesting in disgust. "How can you say it's too late? She is in distress, why don't you help her? What is she supposed to do, go back home to be beaten some more?"

The SI shrugged it off saying, "The SO is not here . . . it is not my responsibility . . . besides, she is probably lying. I didn't see any bruises or broken bones."

Leaving aside for the moment the superficiality of his dismaying dismissal of the truth of her claim, I later learned that according to a particular legal provision, his callous statement that it was not his responsibility could be seen as technically correct, even if arguably immoral. This SI was not the CRT station chief, but a regular (and not particularly "take charge" type of) staff member assigned to the *thana*. The SO was away that evening, and the "second-in-charge" SI who served as acting chief in the SO's absence was also not present at that time for some reason, and had not specifically assigned anyone to take over as station officer-in-charge. Since, as per written law,[16] domestic violence is only "cognizable if information relating to the commission of the offence is given to an officer-in-charge of a police station" (CrPC 2005 [1973], 345–46), the dismissive sub-inspector was, for better or worse, in one sense following the rules.

This is one of the darker facets of a police orderly ethics founded upon provisional legal authority and *jugaadi* legitimation. On the one hand, police may break or bend some rules in order to adhere to others or realize a higher end of justice, as was arguably happening in the cases of the blade and the *baanka*. On the other hand, their praxis of sometimes arbitrary or ad hoc adaptive responses may also devolve into a type of hyper-proceduralism that allows officers like this CRT SI to absolve himself of responsibility for ignoring a complainant who happened to have bad timing. It also may result in instances like a moment I witnessed at CRT where a man bleeding from a severe head wound was ignored for more than an hour because the only officer present at the station had determined that stamping a stack of gun licenses and completing other paperwork that was overdue to be transported to district senior superintendent of police (SSP) headquarters took precedence over a person in acute need of medical assistance.

Similar dismissive responses would manifest in one of the other most common forms of police work at CRT: the unofficial arbitration of charges and mediation of disputes brought to police by local villagers. On Christmas Day, a typical but also relatively busy workday at CRT, I arrive in the morning to find dozens of people and less than ten police gathered in the main yard and under the tree outside the small station building. Local village headmen, or *pradhan*,[17] are reporting to the *thana* for an annual review, which is supposed to ensure that the police have the most up-to-date information on the happenings in the local villages under their jurisdiction for the past year: census information; births; deaths; criminal activity; disputes between neighbors; the names of people with gun licenses; the names of local leaders and business owners; the strength of political parties, etc. The information is kept in Register #8, also known as the Crime Register, which the CRT police tell me is "the most important of all the registers."

There is a lot of paper being filled in, and all the wooden tables and chairs from inside the station have been brought outside so that the police can work in the warming sun on this cooler winter day. Three sub-inspectors are doing most of the interviewing (the SO is still in his personal quarters on the *thana* grounds), and some constables are writing down information, while others are performing miscellaneous tasks like making sure the SIs have all the proper lists and registers, pens and paper, snacks and chai. After about half an hour of observing this flurry of activity, I see a group of four men approach, accompanying a woman in a red sari. They claim that her *pati* (husband), *jethani* (wife of husband's elder brother), and *nanad* (husband's sister) are all beating her in order to extract more dowry money. The woman's father speaks for her while she squats on the ground, and the SIs respond by informing him about the rule that only the SO can lodge an FIR in a case like this. The father tells the SIs present that he will wait to talk to SO Yadav. When Yadav eventually comes out, the woman's father and other male relatives offer the details of her complaint. They sometimes ask the woman to respond to a question or support a particular point, but she mostly remains submissive and quiet.

The SO calls the *pradhan* of their village on his mobile phone, and directs the *pradhan* to tell the people being accused of the crime to come to CRT for questioning. I am a bit mystified, since the usual process I have observed up to this point is for the SO to send another sub-inspector as investigating officer (IO) out to the village in order to inquire and personally bring people to the station; my guess is that for some reason, the SO feels this is not so serious a case yet. This is basically correct, because after calling the *pradhan*, the SO tells me privately that he thinks the woman is *badachlan* (of immoral or ill-mannered character) and lying.[18] Upon being asked how he knows this, the SO replies, "She says she got married three years ago; they would not be beating her for dowry after so long." I am left with a bad taste in my mouth, not least because the male relatives have been doing the talking and it is not clear how much of what they are voicing is the woman's or their own "character."

But I say nothing more for the moment, and note that Yadav seems to be basing his judgment on past experience, observation, and intuition. I also remember the remarks of many police and other people with whom I have spoken about these issues, who claim that some people will try to take advantage of special laws against dowry to file false charges against someone with whom they are having a dispute about some other matter, as a means to intimidate the other side. But then, as already mentioned, domestic violence and dowry death—when women are harassed by their husbands' family members, sometimes to the point of being maimed or violently killed, as a means to try to extract more dowry money or resources from her own family—are also not infrequent crimes committed in the countryside. The task of deciding which cases are "authentic" usually falls first to local police.

While the woman, her father, and their male relatives wait for the opposite party to arrive from their village, another group of men from a different nearby village approach the SO, in visible and audible distress. A couple of them have what appear to be blood stains on their clothes, and as they approach we note that there is a distinct smell of alcohol emanating from their general direction. They all begin talking at once in a mixture of Awadhi and Bhojpuri dialects of Hindi, which I have difficulty understanding. My research assistant says that there has been an altercation over the selling of pork, and the men are divided into two "teams" of two people each. For the sake of simplicity in relating the story, and since I did not record any names, I will identify them as follows:

Team A

(1)   An older man with a head wound bleeding through a ripped cloth
(2)   A young man with very muddy feet, perhaps a relative of the older man

Team B

(3)   A young man with a *beedi* (hand-rolled cigarette) tucked behind his ear
(4)   An older man with a swollen eye and reddish-brown spattered clothes

They make for quite a spectacle, and everyone present, including the various *pradhan* giving information about their villages for the local review, stops to stare and listen. Team A loudly proclaims that they were assaulted by Team B; and before Team B can get through much of their verbal protest, the SO tells one of the sub-inspectors present to go back to their village with them and conduct in inquiry. As they walk away, everyone returns to their respective activities.

About one hour after the inquiring SI and Teams A and B leave, the man accused of beating his wife for dowry comes, accompanied by at least a dozen kin. This mode of traveling to the police station in a pack to give testimony, or at least to offer protection and support, is quite common in my observation. The SO grabs a chair and places it in the shade of the tree. He then sits down, as if he is a presiding judge or a wise village elder, and signals that the two opposing parties must gather around and face him. They duly arrange themselves into teams of their own. As the SO proceeds to question the plaintiff wife and her father, the details of her story change several times; and as the inquest wears on, the SO indicates that he does not believe the charges. The father seems surprised and embarrassed, and asks the SO for ten days to try to better understand what has happened. The SO gives him five days to "get the story straight" and come back if he wishes. Then everyone leaves. Not one mark of ink has been spent on a police report.

This instance may be compared with a similar case in Chhattisgarh (another state in northeastern India) of a wife who complained to police that her husband was an alcoholic who would regularly beat her (see Kumar et al. 2008, 32). In this case, the wife did not want to file an official complaint, but just wanted the SO to talk to her husband, because, she said, the latter was scared of the police (cf. Hautzinger 2016). Ultimately, the SO did her bidding, for which she thanked him, and the SO explained to the observers that "doing things that [are] culturally accepted [is] sometimes more important than being guided purely by the law." Perhaps that is what the wife and her family wanted in this case at CRT, for whatever reason; but, if so, then what they got instead was embarrassment in front of the alleged assailant's whole family.

Not long after the adjournment of the participants in the alleged dowry beating case (who, to my knowledge, never returned to the station after that), the four men comprising Team A and Team B return, and Team B now seems more confident in giving its side of the story to the SO, who still sits in his chair under the tree like a judge wearing a khaki uniform. Man #4 claims that the two men on Team A opened a shop to sell pork without obtaining a license to do so, and were also selling meat from pigs that they did not own but had stolen from someone else (not him). He continues by saying that when he confronted them about it, they attacked him. Man #1 claims that this is not true, they had not stolen any pigs, and they were selling their own meat and have all their licenses in order. Man #2 is muttering inaudibly in support of his A-Team mate.

The SO gets up from his chair, walks over to Man #2, performatively sniffs the air (i.e., inhales the smell of alcohol still emanating from the man), and wrinkles his nose in an expression of disgust that makes the other people in the vicinity who are watching snicker with amusement. Then the SO sits back down, and continues to question both teams on the details of their story in a very casual manner. At certain points during the inquest the SO is typing text messages or even talking to someone on his mobile phone about other matters while the men are giving their testimony. At other times, he is cracking jokes and gossiping with some of the other nearby sub-inspectors and constables, literally talking over the four men as they volley accusations at one another. He is clearly not taking any of the complainants seriously. Eventually, he gets up without a word, and goes inside the *thana* building and into his office for a few minutes. When he returns, he makes a great show of carrying a stack of official-looking papers and readying himself with a pen. He tells the four men, "We are all going to come to a compromise [*samjhauta karna*] and put it in writing." Upon hearing this and seeing what look like official documents waiting to be filled in, the four men hesitate and each "team" begins to conduct a mostly inaudible conference. Eventually, they all appear to be uninterested in this solution of "coming to an understanding," and walk off, perhaps to their village, perhaps to the nearest liquor vendor. When I ask the SO why he thinks the men all left without following his lead to come to a compromise, he says that it is because they are just drunk and making a nuisance, and that he sees it all the time.

I then ask him to say a bit more about this process of compromise that he had suggested. He replies, "It is the traditional way of doing things, and a very common thing to do . . . and not everyone runs away from it like these men. In fact, both the police and the people usually find it a useful thing to do, much more efficient than going to court. It is not a legal process, but much of our work is done this way." His claim is partially supported by some historical ethnography. Bernard Cohn (1987 [1965], 581) has described the didactic element among village leaders in UP of *samjhana*—which literally means "to make understand, or explain" and figuratively means "to come to an agreement, or compromise, under wise leadership"—as a kind of alternative to official court procedures. More recently, Pratiksha Baxi (2010) has analyzed similar processes of *samadhan* in Gujarat to demonstrate how, for better or worse, a "culture of compromise" around many rape prosecutions may actually transform the behavior of both complainants and accused persons inside official court proceedings as well as in out-of-court settlements. Both of these analyses demonstrate, albeit in rather different contexts and more or less explicitly, how compromise brokering practices by police and other figures with provisional authority involve a complex interplay of coercion and consent as well as of official and unofficial channels of judgment by all parties involved.

I would add to these insights the suggestion that police engagement in these "traditional" practices also underscores the multiplicity of roles into which they may be interpellated by "orders" from various parties, including and especially the roles of ad hoc "judge" and "fixer" (cf. Berenschot 2014). The cases related here exemplify the ways in which Yadav would routinely be called upon in his capacity as station chief not only to conduct official police work—the forms of which, following from my reframing of the "Dirty Harry problem," seem to multiply infinitely—but also to unofficially, or quasi-officially, intervene in a host of matters, especially as case arbitrator or dispute mediator. The compounded pressures to respond to various exigencies, and the resultant shape of the responses themselves, are configured by multiple forces and relations of provisional authority, from the immediacy of people approaching him for help, to the pressures from other authority figures (and, of course, the routine offerings of bribes and other favors) to "fix" crime reports in a particular way, as well an expressed feeling of being able and duty-bound to help since "people usually find it a useful thing to do."

Multiplicity and Indeterminacy

The cases discussed here show how an orderly ethics of police practice founded in provisional legal authority and *jugaadi* legitimation may serve at cross purposes. It may offer a gateway to advancement through the official criminal justice system, as in the cases of the blade and the *baanka*, where police presumably arrested the correct criminal suspect, but felt compelled to fabricate evidence or falsify a report in order to follow procedures that would optimize chances of a conviction. On the other hand, this work ethic and its associated practices may prevent desired entry into the system and encourage neglect of people in need of help, with police appealing to experience over evidence or various types of external pressures discouraging thorough police work, such as demands from various "bosses" to minimize crime reporting. Moreover, the elbow room this ethic provides for laziness, abuse, incompetence, or self-interested behavior by police is vast.

That said, the leeway for extra-legal interventions, which may be preferable to moving through the official criminal justice system, also constructs police as useful and versatile resources. The practices related here—fabricating case evidence, manipulating official reports, unofficially disciplining and punishing alleged assailants, and mediating disputes—may be conceived as "corrupt" or "dirty," violating the spirit and letter of the law, and perhaps harming people. But they may also be "ordered" by public demand. While police routinely perform such acts of their own accord, and often in service to their own interests, they are also frequently called upon by others as jack-of-all-trades orderlies to do "every dirty job that comes along," even things like discipline village children bullies (cf. Perry 2009). And crucially, the work is never fully done—the dirty jobs keep coming in an exhausting and inexhaustible form of renewal of demand for police intervention. The resultant orderly subjectivity and its concomitant ethics evince both a multiplicity and an indeterminacy to police practice that reflects contradictions inherent to "the law" itself and has been noted more or less explicitly by various police studies scholars (Brodeur 2010; Marquis 1992; Bittner 1990 and 1970; Van Maanen and Manning 1978; Muir 1977).

Police the world over have developed in historically and culturally specific contexts to inhabit myriad and sometimes contradictory roles, like detective-investigator; guardian-protector; traffic director; crowd controller; dispute mediator; peacekeeper; law enforcer; interrogator, and first responder, among others, especially roles related to social work and public health. In all of these roles, police constitute public "servants" charged with trying to prevent or manage various kinds of social "messes" or, failing that, cleaning up after them. The social fact of this role multiplicity, its dialogue with law, and its co-production with social order—especially though not exclusively in contexts of extreme resource scarcity—compels us to confront the indeterminacy of legality and legitimacy inherent in police practices, and to develop theories and policies of policing that account for this multiplicity and indeterminacy: a tall order that this book's conceptual framework of provisional authority tries to answer. Next, we will consider these multiplicities and indeterminacies with regard to a specific police duty: the provision of violence as public service.

4

Expendable Servants

Ritual Remembrance and Reinscriptions

At about 8:30 on another bright October morning, I arrive at the district police lines, just a couple of kilometers up the road from Lucknow University.
Moving past hundreds of uniformed constables and sub-inspectors, I walk to
the sprawling parade ground along a dirt road lined with scores of makeshift
memorial structures each consisting of a steel Brodie helmet set atop a tripod
of bayonets stabbed into the ground. As I make my way to a tent-covered area
with long rows of folding chairs, in front of which sit large plush couches reserved for senior officials and invited guests, I notice a small area where a few
non-police women and even fewer children are sitting. But the vast majority of
persons present are either serving police officers in uniform or retired officers in plain clothes.

At 9:05 sharp, right on schedule according to the program, a marching
band starts playing a proud tune and more than one thousand police constables in full dress regalia move into position to begin a stiff stepping parade
followed by disciplined firearm formations (see fig. 14). Following the carefully rehearsed movements, a senior civil service officer walks to the podium
facing the colorful masses of constables, and makes an introductory speech
about the history of this ceremony celebrating national Police Commemoration Day, or as the Uttar Pradesh (UP) state government officially refers to
it, Police Smriti Diwas (Police Remembrance Day).[1] She reminds the audience that this annual event was inaugurated in 1960, the year after ten Central Reserve Police Force *jawan*s (soldiers[2]) were killed by the Chinese Army
in Hot Springs, Ladakh, near the India-Tibet border following the former's
mobilization to search for missing personnel who had not returned from a

Parts of this chapter were previously published in Jauregui 2015.

FIGURE 14. Uttar Pradesh Police constables in formal dress regalia line up in the background to begin the parade for national Police Commemoration Day. Lucknow police lines, October 21, 2006. Photo
by author.

reconnaissance mission launched the previous day. She reads the names of
the ten *jawan*s and then makes some general statements about the importance of continually remembering and honoring those who have sacrificed
themselves for the Indian nation.

Following this introduction to the event, the Lucknow district senior superintendent of police (SSP) gives a short set of remarks, during which he
states, "We are like the army, fighting against the enemy—but the army knows
its enemy, which is from the outside, while we do not always know our enemy, because it is from inside our own society." Then the UP director general
of police (DGP) arrives on the parade ground in a shiny white ambassador
car and marches up to the podium to exchange salutes with his subordinates.
Next, the UP chief minister (CM), Mulayam Singh Yadav, arrives in his own
ambassador car and struts toward the podium facing the calico corn rows of
constables standing tall under the sun. As commander-in-chief of the state
police, the CM exchanges salutes with them in concert with a parade song.[3]
He then stands silently and is handed a satin pillow on which rests a booklet
listing the names of all of the police officers in India killed in the line of duty
over the past year, a total of 669 police.

A glance at my own copy of the event program reveals that this past year (2005–2006) follows the pattern of previous years, in which the state of UP claims the largest absolute number in the country of police killed-in-action (KIA), scores more than the number of fatalities in national level paramilitary groups like the Border Security Force (BSF), and many more than in states with raging insurgencies or alleged international incursions, like Jammu and Kashmir.[4] The 136 Uttar Pradesh Police (UPP) KIAs—each of whom is listed in the program, about a dozen of whom have a photo next to a paragraph describing how they died—include one inspector, seventeen sub-inspectors, and thirteen head constables. The remaining 105 are all constables. As the DGP reads the "honor roll" in what seems like a monotonous rush—perhaps because the ceremony is supposed to be timed quite precisely and he cannot help but speed through the list—I note how the deceased individuals named belong to various caste and religious groups ("Constable 100 Rajesh Kumar Yadav . . . Constable 1217 Shakeel Ahmed Khan . . . Constable 20392 Dilip Tiwari").

After reading the entire list, the CM and DGP together somberly leave the podium and lay a large wreath at the foot of a statue of an anonymous uniformed figure that is already elaborately decorated with flowers, the pedestal of which reads *paavan smriti* or "sacred remembered" (see fig. 15). Then the UP governor and several other civilian dignitaries, including the state home secretary as well as several retired and serving Indian Police Service (IPS) officers, come up in pairs to lay additional wreaths at the foot of the statue. Following these processions, which move to a relatively upbeat tempo played by the marching band, the tone switches to one of mourning, and a tune reminiscent of the US military's "Taps" begins to play. Officers bow their heads, and a few appear to wipe away tears or sweat as the melody ends and a series of somber chimes ring out. Then there are two minutes of silence across the vast field, followed by the faint barking of a command and a force-wide salute in the direction of the *Paavan Smriti* statue (see fig. 16).

Following the solemn music, silence, and salute, the CM addresses the crowd, referring to the collective of dead police as "fearless heroes and soldiers, who lost their lives and took the path of sacrifice for the sake of society and country." He expresses pride in police "devotion and courage" and pledges to "boost morale . . . [by] making laws more stringent, . . . improving facilities, . . . increasing personnel head count, . . . ensuring the best and latest medicines will be made available as needed." As soon as he completes his speech—which combines mass-scale eulogizing with promissory notes echoing electoral campaign slogans—the CM returns to his vehicle to be escorted off the grounds in a convoy. Before the audience even disperses,

FIGURE 15. Paavan Smritii ("sacred remembered") statue standing (in) atop a pedestal for all police killed in action. The Hindi text on the plaque in the foreground reads in translation, "Memorial Column. The laying of the foundation stone for the memorial column honoring fallen police officers (literally, 'for those who have obtained the status of heroes'). Mr. Shripati Mishra. Chief Minister of Uttar Pradesh. Held on Thursday, October 21, 1982." Lucknow Police Lines. Police Commemoration Day, October 21, 2006. Photo by author.

hired laborers begin rapidly deconstructing the stage of the memorial, tearing down the white curtains and lugging away the chairs.[5] At the same time, the Lucknow district SSP calls logistical orders over the microphone from the stage, commanding the constable drivers of retired IPS officers to come immediately, since custom demands that these most senior status persons have the privilege of departing first. The driver of one retired IPS officer is tardy for some unknown reason, causing visible embarrassment, impatience, and irritation for serving officers who have to stand around waiting for his departure before they can leave themselves. In the interim, I listen to a small group of them discuss how well organized and executed today's annual ceremony was.

Finally, the retired officer's ride comes to whisk him away as I stand speaking with a few remaining senior officers, including the current Lucknow SSP. While we make small talk, three middle-aged women approach us. One of the women, calling herself Surajmukhi, claims to be the widow of a constable named Babu Ram who died in a police *chowki* (substation) in Moradabad in

1983. Surajmukhi alleges that although she received a lump sum compensation, other promises made by the state were never fulfilled, including that of her son being given a job with the UPP, a legal entitlement provided to all families of police KIAs. Another one of the women, claiming the name of Subhas Chandra Sharma, says that she lost her constable husband when he died on duty in 1985 in Badaun district. She says she was given Rs. 30,000 at the time, or about $2,400 in 1985 dollars, and still receives his pension payments.[6] However, she complains that the pension amount (paid at the now twenty-year-old rates) is not nearly enough to cover her rent and other basic expenses, and she also wants the UP state government to make good on a promised job for her son that has yet to materialize. As the women speak, several of the senior officers peel off from the group. In distracted and dismissive tones, those remaining refer the women to an administrative office at the police lines, and then make a quick exit. A couple of lingering journalists stand by scribbling on their notepads, and in the next day's *Times of India (Lucknow Edition)* a short article titled "Police Fail to Keep Their Promises to Cops' Widows" appears under the main headline story discussing the official ceremony.

FIGURE 16. Senior officers of the Uttar Pradesh Police salute their fallen brethren via the *Paavan Smritii* or "Sacred Remembered" statue (outside the bounds of this photo, to the right), which symbolizes the tomb of the unknown soldier (see fig. 15). Lucknow police lines. Police Commemoration Day, October 21, 2006. Photo by author.

Violence and Police Life

Since 1961, a reported 32,557 police personnel across India have died in the line of duty, one of the highest absolute numbers of such casualties in the world, if not the definitive highest, with most deaths occurring in contexts dissociated from conventional warfare (PIB 2014). Tens of thousands of other police in India have been badly injured or permanently disabled during the same period. In UP, at least 1,228 police officers have died in the line of duty just from 2003 to 2014, and are named on the rolls of police "martyrs" by the state government.[7] Reflective of its other dubious distinction superlatives, UP often claims the largest number of police KIAs in India, almost always well over one hundred persons annually, though the numbers vary year to year and from one report to the next.[8] Even taking into consideration that India has the second largest national population in the world—over one billion strong as of the 2011 census, with UP constituting about one-fifth of that number—these are staggering body counts. They far outpace many years of analogous statistics of police dead in other countries, and even supersede US and international coalition soldier deaths in war zones like Iraq and Afghanistan.[9] Yet there is little public ritual recognition of these police deaths save for an annual ceremony attended by almost no one other than a few official dignitaries and masses of police themselves (cf. Manning 1997 [1977]; Hornberger 2011); and virtually no public protest raised about them excepting occasional and short-lived complaints from family members, which usually end up having to do with the payment of ex gratia death compensation by the government. Why is this so? And what might it have to do with everyday police life and practice?

However it may be viewed (as "just a job"; as a vocation, or as a means of social mobility) and however it may end (in retirement; in honorable or dishonorable discharge, or even in physical death), being a police officer is a life course that may proceed in a variety of ways. We know this, and yet we rarely ask: What *is* this police life form, and what does it mean, for "the police" and also for "the policed"? How does police life acquire (or lose) moral virtue or instrumental value? How and why do the virtue and value of police life fluctuate so dramatically, running a gamut from inspiring hero worship and deification on the one hand, to inducing social ostracism and demonization on the other hand? And how does this moral and instrumental flux relate specifically to the unique provisional authority of police to deploy violence "as needed" against an alleged "enemy . . . from inside our own society," as the Lucknow SSP noted during his speech at the Police Commemoration Day ceremony?

Violent police interventions are often delegitimized as unjust and immoral

because they are interpreted as being either excessively brutal and discriminatory, or inadequate and inept. In large part because of this "damned if you
do, damned if you don't" quality of the state mandated authority to use violence "as needed," police the world over routinely conjure condemnation;
and importantly, this condemnation often leads to widespread feelings of in-
difference among the public regarding the dangers police may face in, or the
grievances they may have about, their work. At the same time, police are also
occasionally recognized as agents who may do great deeds that categorically
subject them to disproportionate risk of harm, physical or otherwise. I argue
that this paradoxical condemnation-cum-valorization relates to the specific
ways in which police may be figured as servants of violence.

Building upon chapter 3's framing of state police as "orderlies" interpellated by various sections of the public into multiple roles involving "dirty"
duties, I now analyze the figuration and social reproduction of state police
as "public servants" charged with the morally and physically dangerous duty
of maintaining social order through potential or actual use of violence. A
nuanced understanding of this figuration and social reproduction of police
life helps to explain why they are simultaneously honored, admired, feared,
distrusted and censured for their violence. To distill it for heuristic purposes,
police life itself takes on a polarized value that also polarizes public opinion,
with hyperbolic heroism on one end and trivializing scorn on the other. Analyzing this paradoxical figuration of police and its relation to their sworn duty
to "serve and protect" via "any means necessary" compels us to recognize a
broad public complicity in "ordering" (in both senses of structuring and demanding) police violence, as well as in ostracizing police as a perduring and
provisionally authoritative type of social "other."

My analysis focuses on how forces and relations of ordering and othering
police violence work in the context of UP specifically, and to some extent
in various other parts of India. Following a discussion of how both "the police" and "the policed" express ambivalence regarding the moral virtue and
instrumental necessity of various forms of police violence, we will explore
how avatars of police in public culture frame these state officials as sacrificial
soldiers and loyal servants providing violence as a service that is at once required and reviled.[10] This construction of violence as service figures the police
answering their "call of duty" as a peculiar kind of authoritative servant who
in doing his duty sacrifices not merely the physical body and common creature comforts but the metaphysical ideal of living and working as a morally
pure subject, what I call here "the good life." This sacrifice condemns police
to a life of expendability, a hard truth that is ironically reinscribed in some of

the very discourses and practices that purport to uphold police goodliness and godliness.

Ambivalent Orders of Police Violence

Before I even began my ethnographic research, I had seen many media reports and heard myriad tales from persons claiming to have experienced discrimination, intimidation, or unwarranted physical harm by police. As I proceeded with my fieldwork, I both personally witnessed and heard innumerable tales of everyday police violence, which manifested in a variety of forms including but not limited to ad hoc harassment and humiliation of people on the street or in the station; illegal detentions and beatings of suspects or their alleged associates; weaponized crowd control, usually a "*lathi* charge*" (police beating people with their batons) though sometimes it would escalate to police use of water cannons or even rubber bullets; and ongoing targeted harassment of individuals or groups, especially persons associated with social minorities or rivals of the ruling political parties. Police violence in UP is ubiquitous and woven into the fabric of everyday sociality. Like other morally and legally questionable practices as described in chapter 3, police violence was frequent and open, and I was struck time and again by the utter banality of it. It was not hidden or confined to some secret torture chamber, but generally quite diffuse and visible to the public eye (cf. Scarry 1987). Take this instance I witnessed at Chakkar Rasta Thana (CRT).

Upon returning from an overnight patrol around 2:00 a.m., my research assistant and I come upon a disturbing scene happening in the CRT front yard. By the dim light of the lone bulb strung atop the veranda, we see a shadowy group of four constables with shot guns strapped over their shoulders gathered around a man who is writhing on the ground. Two constables are pressing his torso down by stepping on him, and the other two are holding his legs up and forcibly spreading them apart, as if threatening to snap him like a wishbone. A sub-inspector that we do not recognize is standing nearby chewing tobacco *paan* and watching the scene looking nonchalant. We approach with some trepidation and explain who we are and that we have been conducting fieldwork here, dropping the name of the chief station officer (SO) and some other CRT staff to verify our connection, including Constable Aman, the CRT *diwan* or dispatch officer. Hoping I have done enough to establish our credentials, I ask the sub-inspector what is going on, and he tells us matter-of-factly that he is the chief officer at another nearby police station, and that he has ordered these constables to extract information from this man suspected of being involved in a violent robbery that has just been reported.

When the constables see us, they half let go of the man on the ground and stare at us, apparently curious and confused about our presence and status. But as soon as we speak to their boss and begin to walk back into the station, they return to their brutal "questioning" without hesitation. As we enter the station—by now barely flinching to the notes of slapping and grunting and crying still sounding outside—we proceed to Aman's tiny office in the back. He is slumped in his hard chair, looking tired and grumpy, and by way of greeting he shakes his head in what appears to be some combination of embarrassment and exhaustion, saying

> I hate when they do this. I hate watching the violence. But this is how it is. This is the condition we are in. . . . Everyone beats. . . . If we [police] do not beat [suspects and associates], then they do not tell us anything . . . but I hate it. I am getting too old for this job. It is too much. My eyes are getting bad, my health is deteriorating. I am almost sixty years old and I still have to stay up all night doing all of this paperwork; buying the paper with money out of my own pocket and never getting it back, watching while the other men beat people. It should not be this way. It is terrible.

Constable Aman's complaints express his own fatigue and professional grievances alongside a wan justification of the beating going on outside, which is laced with critical statements manifesting an embarrassed moral conscience. It seems to echo his previous statement rationalizing false reporting and fabrication of evidence: "This the way it is . . . sometimes a little bit of dishonesty benefits everyone . . . the victims, the judges, the police . . . sometimes even the criminals. Therefore, it is not wrong" (see chap. 3). But this time, his "this is how it is" aims to rationalize a specific moment of extralegal police violence as a function of a broader "condition." His claim that "everyone beats" is ambiguous: "everyone" could mean all police, and this is how I initially interpreted it (Jauregui 2013b); or it could also include persons outside the police institution since physical, structural, and cultural forms of violence seem to be omnipresent in UP, and arguably in many other parts of India, permeating many households, community living spaces, workplaces and public areas (again, see chap. 3 regarding domestic violence specifically). Interpreting Aman's statement in the broadest sense does not amount to an argument that police violence is simply an extension of other forms of social violence. Nor would I make the degenerative and essentializing claim that India is pervaded by an overarching (sub)culture of violence (cf. Wolfgang 1982). That said, it is vital to theorize not only continuities between apparently "ordinary" and "extraordinary" forms of violence (Das 2004 and 2006), but also the ways in which violence is "ordered", that is structured and demanded, by both the police and the broader public.

Police violence in UP, and arguably in much of India, is routinized and openly visible. It is also rationalized by police officers and various others as a means to prevent disorder and realize justice. Thus, police violence is a very "public" activity in both senses of being available for all to perceive and interpret, and being a potential resource or provision from which people may potentially benefit—or at least find something like relief. In my experience, many persons complaining of being victimized in some way would actively seek out police use of violence against their assailants or disputants. Even in instances where the police did not ultimately use violence—such as the cases I have discussed in chapter 3 of villagers going to the police to plead for intervention in their domestic situations and disputes—it is clear that police are often seen to have the authority to force a resolution, a provisional authority backed by the possibility of violence as consequence. Recall, for example, the elderly woman who asked that the CRT police go "put the fear of God into" some local village boys she claimed were bullying her grandson. In this and many other cases, it is clear that many people *value and call upon* the coercive power of police to achieve particular goals. Rather than presuming that police violence is categorically destructive, oppressive, or evil, people may see it as a resource, a positive provision, a public service geared toward realizing something like order or justice (even if some might call it vengeance or harassment) when other more or less "legal channels" seem to fall short.[11]

This unpalatable social fact is also evident in the ambivalent responses to a particular form of police violence in India that has captured the public imagination over the past couple of decades: encounter killings. Encounter killings, also known simply as "encounters," occur during ostensibly spontaneous confrontations between police and alleged criminals or terrorists, usually in the form of a reported self-defense shooting by law enforcement officials.[12] These homicides would seem at first glance to be a familiar mode of police violence analogous to the controversial police killings of unarmed persons from social minority groups in the US and many other countries. But encounters are different in at least one crucial respect: it has become public knowledge that these extrajudicial killings are in fact carefully planned and collectively executed operations that are explicitly intended to destroy targets, rather than the unfortunate results of systemic racialized or otherwise discriminatory confrontations following from a presumed intent by police to arrest and capture a criminal suspect. In short, encounter killings often may amount to state-sponsored assassinations.

A crucial fact to understand about encounters in India is that there is no clear consensus among either "the police" or "the policed" that these extrajudicial killings are patently illegitimate or unnecessary. In fact, there is often

expressed a substantial tacit or even active support for this type of premedi-
tated police violence among wide swaths of the public. News media outlets
routinely laud police "success" in encounters with "notorious criminals"; officers regularly receive gallantry medals and "out-of-turn" (faster-than-normal)
promotions for such successes, and several officers known as "encounter specialists" have become household names and veritable local or even national ce-
lebrities (Perry 2003; Peterkin 2008). Such figures are also widely represented
as heroes—or, perhaps more interestingly, as antiheroes—in popular films and
television serials. As one commentator remarked, when police are portrayed
in Hindi films, a good cop "is either a joke or, more likely, a vigilante who
flouts the law while claiming to uphold it. He has an extra-constitutional attitude and extraordinary powers to single-handedly solve crimes, punish the
wicked and protect family, society and the nation" (Ramnath 2014).

I have analyzed these developments in terms of a popular metaphysics providing moral and instrumental support to police vigilantism (Jauregui 2015),
which has developed and intensified across much of India since the 1980s for
reasons that remain debatable (Eckert 2005; Raj and Sharma 2007; Belur 2010;
Outlook India 2011; CHRI 2008). This metaphysics entails a deep ambivalence
among much of the public, which manifests in various ways, especially in the
coincidence of collective protests against violent police actions with widespread citizen support for it. Crucially, the protest and the support are not
neatly divisible along class, caste, ethno-religious, or other sociocultural lines,
and may occur simultaneously among the same groups. Moreover, the apparent support comes not simply from vocal "fringe" groups or social outliers,
but from many people of various social groups in various locales. One can
find numerous reports of crowds demanding that police officers kill persons
threatening them (Eckert 2005, 199) or rallying around officers accused of excessive violence (Jauregui 2011 and 2015). But the demand and the support are
not absolute. They are mitigated by moral ambivalence, which is apparent in
resigned comments like that from an editor of the prominent English news
daily the *Hindustan Times* quoted as saying, "We know the vast majority of
encounters are fake. . . . We do not think that this is a perfect situation, but
in common with the rest of the middle class we have come to the regrettable
conclusion that there is no real alternative" (Perry 2003).[13]

In an ethnographic study of encounters based in Bombay including interviews with both local denizens and police officers, Julia Eckert (2005, 183)
incisively describes the encounter killing as the avatar of the "double life of
the killing state: it is at once the vigilante, saving the nation from doom and
the outlaw who thrives on the destruction that threatens the nation . . . a
symptom of state crisis . . . [that is also] valorized as the last resort for an

embattled society . . . it is abhorred and it is demanded . . . promising order and signaling chaos." Eckert theorizes the public ambivalence inspired by this "double life" of extralegal police violence as a function of global trends in hyper-security, such as the conflating of crime and terrorism, and the dehumanizing of criminals and dehistoricizing of criminality. She also argues, correctly I think, that there is a growing sense among the *aam aadmi* (common people) in India that encounters may represent a necessary and last-resort "stand against the murky networks of politics and crime . . . the protector of society against [elite-led] 'politics'" (ibid., 195, 211). In this way, ironically, police violence may become not only legitimate, but increasingly the weapon of choice against systemic governmental corruption and other social ills.[14] This lends a postcolonial Indian twist to what was coined by Carl Klockars (1980), and remains widely known among scholars of policing, as the "Dirty Harry problem," or the intractable dilemma of police often having to use morally "dirty" means to realize "just" ends (see chap. 3). In short, there seems to be a broad-based popular demand for the provisional authority of police violence.

If this is so, then there is a perhaps surprising congruence between a police institutional ethos of coercion as a means to realizing a virtuous end—a police ethos which, crucially, is *itself fraught with ambivalence*—and what might be called a public culture of police vigilantism in India that may support or even *actively order* (i.e., structure and demand) certain types and instances of police violence as a means to realize popular justice (cf. Abrahams 1998 and 2008; Pratten and Sen 2008; Goldstein 2008; Hornberger 2013; Huggins 1991). This congruent police-public ordering of legitimated violence and its internal contradictions are reflected in statements like those of a retired Indian Police Service officer who in his memoir initially writes, "Every police department worth its salt needs its hit-men . . . [and being a hit man] requires guts . . . a willingness to be condemned for life" (Pereira 2008, 199). This officer expresses police ambivalence when he says of the increasing routinization of encounters "what I feel queasy about and object to is the attitudinal change over the years that has replaced the need to capture the criminal alive" (ibid., 201). Such ambivalence is even expressed by many celebrated—or notorious—encounter specialists themselves. Inspector Pradeep Sharma, who holds a record body count of well over one hundred encounter killings has been quoted as saying, "I don't enjoy killing. . . . But after we [police] shoot some mobster, his victims look at me like God. That's the best part of the job" (Perry 2003). In a far more assertive, even aggressive, moment that reflects less ambivalence and more a moral conviction about his role as a coercive orderly, a la his popular epithet as "Bombay's Dirty Harry," Sharma also says, "Criminals are filth . . . and I am the cleaner." Again, we see a manifestation of the police officer as both a moral and instrumental "orderly" purportedly "cleaning" society. Next, we will turn to how such conceptions of violence as a duty to keep things pure and tidy configure what I call "police *dharma*."

Children of a Lesser God

Similar to Inspector Sharma's boasts about one of the "dirtiest" parts of his job—namely, his being a "cleaner" of society as a vigilante killer—many police in India profess a substantive certainty about their murderous or otherwise violent actions. When they do, they often couch their justifications in religious or sacred terms, like Sharma's comment about being looked upon by others "like God." One of my interlocutors in UP—a senior officer reputed to have led and participated in many "successful" encounters, though he says he despises the term "encounter specialist"—said to me (in English) regarding his lethal exploits:

> Yes—I am "trigger happy." But I am completely confident in what I have done, and no one has ever questioned it. The line between good reasons and bad reasons is thin as a thread; but I am on the good side, because *I have a solid sense of ethics.* You know *even the Gods have killed people when it was necessary.* Our Gods have done it . . . your [he presumes] Christian God has done it with that Noah's Ark. *I am no God, but I pray every day for guidance. . . . I do not kill for personal gain, but for the greater good; when there is no other way out, [killing] must be done. And the people will praise you for it.* When my team finished off [a "notorious gangster"], the people in the towns and villages he had been terrorizing were so happy! They threw marigolds on me and put me on their shoulders and carried me around. They queued up by the thousands at the station to thank me for doing what the courts could not (emphasis and bracketed explanations added).

The police officer highlights public demand and support for his violence as "justice" for, or at least relief from, violence being visited upon "the people" by criminalized "others." His egotistical tone is punctuated by statements that he seeks guidance from his God, echoing both his subordinate colleague from Bombay, Inspector Sharma, and a host of similar statements by police officers and others who make explicit comparisons between police violence and that of anthropomorphized Hindu deities. In her study of police encounters, Jyoti Belur (2010, 146) quotes another Bombay-based officer talking about his involvement in these actions as saying, "There is a reason that my birth has taken place . . . why I must have come into the police service. So if great injustice is going on, I am not going to sit and think about means and ends." According to Belur, the officer makes this statement immediately after citing

a famous passage from the *Bhagavad Gita*, which will be familiar to Sanskrit-
ists and various other scholars and denizens of South Asia:

> *Yada Yada Hi Dharmasya Glanir Bhavathi Bhaaratha*
> *Abhyuthaanaam Adharmasya Tadatmaanam Srijaamyaham.*
> *Paritraanaaya saadhoonaam vinaashaaya cha dushkritaam,*
> *Dharma samsthaapanaarthaaya sambhavaami yuge yuge.*

In English, it translates roughly:

> Whenever there is a decay of righteousness, and a rise of unrighteousness
> O *Bhaaratha* [Mother India], then I [God] manifest Myself [as warrior]
> For the protection of the good and the destruction of the wicked
> For the reestablishment of *dharma* [natural law/universal order], I will
> come, in every age.[15]

This passage invokes the concept of *dharma* in multiple ways in relation to
universal structures of right, justice, and order. *Dharma* is as polysemic and
problematic to translate into English as terms like *jugaad* and *chalta hai*. In
this analysis, we may understand it generally to convey an idea of moral duty
in relation to social order, or laws of conduct appropriate to one's position
in the universe in a specific incarnation, at a specific moment, in relation to
specific others, for example, as wife (see chap. 3), or as warrior. The *Bhagavad Gita*—an oft-cited sacred text dating back to approximately 500–700 BCE
as part of the great epic myth of the *Mahabharata*—purports to recount the
Hindu deity Krishna[16] offering advice and solace to Arjuna, a soldier caught
in a moral dilemma at having to fight a war against a sibling clan, thus having
to rain down violence on some of his own people. Krishna counsels Arjuna
on the battlefield at Kurukshetra (a town in Haryana near the UP state border) regarding his duties as a consummate warrior to offer his people protection, provision, and the possibility of progress.

The above-cited passage also appears as an aural *shloka* (ritually chanted
couplet) at the end of a popular Bollywood police film, the title of which is a
direct allusion to this mythical battlefield, *Kurukshetra* (Manjrekar 2000). This
film relates the story of an assistant commissioner of police (ACP) in Bombay named Prithvi Raj Singh who, following repeated failed attempts to use
legal means of arrest and prosecution, finally resorts to "immediate justice" by
brutally killing three powerful men: the corrupt CM of Maharashtra state, the
CM's rapist-murderer son, and another politician from the opposition party
with whom the CM is secretly conspiring to consolidate power. After relating

his travails through an impotent legal system and his reasoning for committing the extrajudicial murder to a *janata ki adaulat* (court of the people) presided over by the editor of a popular national newspaper, *The Indian Express*, Singh is publicly though unofficially acquitted and vehemently supported by the citizens as a moral "innocent." But since he has been legally convicted of committing a heinous crime, the officer is taken away to jail in one of his own police cars as the above-cited *shloka* is sung in solemn tones at the film's end.

Officer Singh's fate signals a crucial aspect of the soldier-hero motif that is often applied to police: that of a sacrifice for, in the words of my own interlocutor, some "greater good" (and recall the UP CM's reference to police killed in the line of duty as "fearless heroes and soldiers, who lost their lives and took the path of sacrifice for the sake of society and country").[17] The epic figure who may best embody soldierly sacrifice, and has been referenced more or less directly in other filmic representations of police, is Arjuna's son, Abhimanyu. According to the *Mahabharata* story, at the age of sixteen Abhimanyu joins his father and others in their clan war and immediately proves himself as a courageous and able fighter. However, he becomes a martyr when he is lured into and eventually killed within the rival clan's *chakravyuha*, a labyrinthine military formation consisting of seven spiraling circles of soldiers, each line moving in opposite directions and using various magical weapons to trap and confuse the enemy in the center.

The *chakravyuha* form plays a key role in popular imagination in many parts of India, serving as a common metaphor for persons who feel ensnared by and unable to overcome or exit threatening and confounding systems that aim to defeat them. It also constitutes a central metaphor in another well-known Hindi language police film called *Ardh Satya* or Half Truth (Nihalani 1983), which features an antihero named Anant Velankar.[18] Sub-Inspector Velankar becomes inextricably caught between, on the one hand, trying to enforce the law and defeat what is colloquially known as "the nexus" of criminality and governmentality in Bombay; and, on the other hand, succumbing to the nexus in order to survive, to say nothing of thrive, as a police officer (see Jauregui 2015). Similar to ACP Singh in Kurukshetra, Sub-Inspector Velankar is repeatedly thwarted in his attempts to enforce the law. Besides receiving no official recognition for his "good work" leading a team in an encounter with a notorious bandit, his attempts to arrest local mafia dons and other criminals are routinely suppressed by corrupt or indifferent senior officers. Also like ACP Singh, in the end, Sub-Inspector Velankar feels he has no other option but to kill his main nemesis, a powerful and vile criminal-turned-politician. But unlike ACP Singh, who is represented as morally "pure" in the face of unquestionable evil, Velankar's character is constructed as morally ambiguous and out of control, if also pathetic. When Velankar turns to alcohol for solace and eventually beats to death a helpless (even if not fully "innocent") petty thief in his custody while drunk, the virtue of his penultimate act of killing his nemesis, and then turning himself in at his own place of work, is rendered questionable at best. But his violent eruptions are mitigated, or at least contextualized, by flashbacks of his interactions with an abusive father who was also a police officer, and by his ill-fated love affair with a left-wing academic-activist woman to whom he confesses his feelings of depression and impotence on the job.

I will leave to film and literary theorists the debates over the finer points of interpreting similarities and differences between the narratives and characterizations of ACP Singh and Sub-Inspector Velankar. What is important for this analysis is that they both are represented as empathetic antiheroes who sacrifice themselves in their battle with "the system" for some version of truth and justice in line with a greater cosmic order. As reflected in these and other invocations of specific tropes from Hindu mythology, the figure of the sacrificial warrior is a crucial component of the idealized *dharma* of police. In other words, the moral duty of police is structured by cosmic forces and relations to fight and use whatever means necessary to reinstate good order in the face of imminent (and immanent) evil. Perpetration of and subjection to violence is an inescapable part of this moral duty.

But the (potentially) sacrificial soldier is only one of the key avatars of police *dharma*. Another is manifest widely in routine appeals to a figure who appears in the other great Hindu epic myth, the *Ramayana*. In the film *Kurukshetra*, ACP Singh commits his triple homicide during the Hindu festival of Dussehra, an annual holiday celebrating the triumph of good over evil during which people burn effigies of Ravana, a ten-headed demon ultimately vanquished by the god Ram as related in the *Ramayana*. In fact, the murders occur in a spectacularly violent scene that splices the police officer's calculated beating and shooting of the villains inside the chief minister's house with fiery images of thousands of Dussehra celebrants frenetically drumming, dancing, and lighting fireworks at the public festival outside. The dramatic allusion to the *Ramayana*'s battle between good and evil explicitly links this particular police officer's actions—and more generally all police officers' *dharma*—with those of another Hindu deity: namely, Ram's loyal servant, Hanuman.

Hanuman, known and worshiped across India as the monkey god, is considered to be the unofficial patron god of police in UP, as evidenced by the fact that most state police stations have some sort of shrine to Hanuman on the grounds (see fig. 17). Hanuman is widely revered by many devout Hindus

FIGURE 17. Statue of Hanuman, unofficial patron god of police, on Uttar Pradesh Police station grounds. Hanuman idols and temples are present on the grounds of many police stations in UP. The shrine pictured here, and the offerings placed before it, are relatively humble, but those at other UPP *thana* may be quite grand and elaborate. Photo by author.

for his ability to fight evil forces with the gifts endowed to him by the greater universal gods, such as invincibility from war weapons, ability to shape-shift, and capability to fly over (or, depending on the version of the myth being told, to walk on) water. His primary role in the *Ramayana* involves rescuing Sita, the wife of Ram, after she is abducted and taken to the faraway island of Lanka (i.e., Sri Lanka) by the aforementioned demon Ravana, her (sexualized) honor thus threatened and thereby endangering the honor of her divine husband (cf. Jauregui 2013b and Baxi 2010). Thus, Hanuman is quintessentially defined as a hero by his acts of protection and rescue.

For all of his heroism, it is also crucial to understand that Hanuman may be seen as a kind of "lesser god," a servant to other gods insofar as he himself worships Ram and Sita (often referred to in tandem as "Sita-Ram") and professes that he would sacrifice himself for them without reservation. Hanuman's extraordinary and seemingly unconditional devotion to Sita-Ram is best exhibited in the part of the *Ramayana* following Ram's crowning as emperor in Ayodhya.[19] When Ram attempts to reward all of his servants for their loyalty, Hanuman refuses the gift offered to him for saving Sita from Ravana, saying

FIGURE 18. Hanuman showing Sita-Ram in his heart. Photo by Palagiri. Reproduced with permission.

he does not need or want it and only wishes to worship and protect Sita-Ram. When some of those present question or mock Hanuman's expressed reverence, Hanuman rips open his chest, exposing his heart in which everyone can see Sita-Ram, and nothing else, residing. This image of Hanuman—who is often represented as having an extraordinarily muscular and hyper-masculinized body—is ubiquitous in police stations and many other sites across India (see fig. 18).

Hanuman's service to Sita-Ram occasionally demands destructive force, as represented in the portions of the *Ramayana* recounting things like his burning the forests of Lanka with his long flaming tail as he seeks to rescue Sita from Ravana. But while he may deploy violence on occasion "as needed" to help destroy evil and preserve good order, unlike Arjuna or Abhimanyu, Hanuman is conceived less as a sacrificial warrior and more as a humble and devoted servant. Hanuman acts throughout his life in accordance with his own *dharma* as a daring and loyal protector, doing the needful for Sita-Ram as various new and threatening conditions arise, from an extraordinary demonic kidnapping to the ordinary vagaries of securing day-to-day living. It seems fitting then that for many people in India, and especially for police themselves, Hanuman's constitution as a courageous and able servant is an apt figure representing idealized police functions of order maintenance and protection. Thus, police are figured not merely as warriors and enforcers, but as servants of a peculiar kind: servants of violence, justified at least in part by widely influential religious ideologies.

Condemnation and Compensation

During my visit to the UPP training schools in Moradabad (see also chaps. 1 and 5), the senior officer acting as my guide requests that I speak about my research to a class of about two hundred cadets preparing to become sub-inspectors. Standing at the podium, I describe to the many young men (and a few women) my plans to observe the kind of "cutting-edge" police work that they will soon be doing, and express my interest in gaining a better understanding of police officers' worldviews. Following my brief lecture, I respond to their questions and comments, which include unrelated remarks like "where did you learn to speak Hindi?" and (from one of the women) "you wear *salwar kameez* very well." Afterward, one of the instructors introduces me to someone he characterizes as a "star student," a man in his early twenties named Aditya, who then volunteers to give me a tour of the school and allows me to accompany him for the rest of the day. As I shadow Aditya around campus and eat lunch with him and some fellow cadets, he tells stories about his father, grandfather, and several uncles who are or were UPP sub-inspectors, too, and how he has lived and traveled all over the state following his father from post to post, though he calls home a village near Gorakhpur in eastern UP. He speaks in a way that suggests he is already very proud, knowledgeable, and perhaps a bit resigned about the office into which he will soon be sworn.

In a more reflective moment, Aditya says to me in English, "Ever since your presentation about wanting to understand the world of police, one thing has been running through my mind . . . being in the police is not just a service, it is a sacrifice." I ask him to explain further what he means, especially the difference between service and sacrifice. In lieu of offering clear and distinct definitions of each term, he provides some illustrative examples that represent a very particular idea of sacrifice, one which seems decoupled from death in the line of duty—though that does come up later upon visiting a campus police memorial, a demonstration of how death in the line of duty is salient even during police training (see fig. 19). First, Aditya recounts some lessons from one of his academy instructors about how a person who becomes a police officer must make a very personal and difficult decision to place the job above all else and forego things like a stable family life, easy work, holidays,

FIGURE 19. Police Training Academy memorial for UP police who died in the line of duty. Moradabad, 2006. Photo by author.

comfortable living conditions, and convenient hours. He then describes some of the negative consequences of making such a decision, from the perspective of the oldest son and a young male relative of police officers whom he has watched suffer a variety of burdens like long separations from their families; rejection by some members of their communities; frequent transfers; low pay; and intense stress leading to poor health and concomitant exhaustion, depression, and anger. I later hear this perspective reiterated by the children of CRT SO Y. K. Yadav (see chap. 5).

Echoing the flashbacks of Sub-Inspector Anant Velankar's character in *Ardh Satya*, Aditya's remembering of his father's and uncles' misery then shifts into a commentary on how police are often unfairly blamed for problems that are not (solely) their fault, especially their use of force against suspects or crowds, and the part they play in the slow or unsatisfactory resolution of legal cases. As his fellow cadets nod and listen, occasionally adding their own comments, Aditya complains about systemic problems contributing to excessive police violence, problems like poor resources and low levels of manpower making police feel weak and fearful in the face of powerful organized crime rings, government corruption and "political interference" in policing. In light of such conditions, he avers that police are easy targets for becoming what is known colloquially as a *bali kaa bakra* (literally a sacrificial goat, most often one killed during the Muslim festival of Eid; the phrase is also used routinely to refer to a "scapegoat"). The *bali kaa bakra* is a familiar metaphor that I hear time and again during my fieldwork when police describe themselves or fellow officers as having been unduly denounced for apparent excesses, or for their *chalta hai* attitudes and actions (recall Sharma and Tiwari's complaints about people misreading police actions and motives in chap. 1). Aditya is adamant that people have the wrong idea about the intentions and lives of most police, and insists that his counterpoints and explanations be represented in my writing, "because police have such a bad reputation here for being violent, and people need to know that so much of it has to do with the terrible working conditions and a lot of misunderstandings."

Aditya's lament suggests that the police sacrifice lies not so much in the threat or actuality of physical death, but rather in a more metaphysical death of what might be called "the good life" in a dual sense. On the one hand, police forfeit a life marked by stability, autonomy, and creature comforts that might be collectively understood as welfare or well-being. On the other hand, and perhaps even worse, they may suffer disproportionate social condemnation and ostracism for what amounts to doing their job. This dualistic conception of sacrifice as separation from the good life is distinct from, but also related to, the dualistic figuration of police as sacrificial soldiers and devoted servants in association with Hindu deities like Arjuna, Abhimanyu, and Hanuman. These avatars signal the possibility of not just physical death through courting danger but also the metaphysical death of the good life in service to greater social "goods" or "others" that place undying demands on them. And among the many duties demanded of these provisionally authorized "orderlies" (chap. 3), the one that is perhaps the most problematic, the most fraught with moral ambivalence and ambiguous necessity, is the police duty to intervene with potential or actual violence in the everyday lives of the people living or moving within their jurisdiction.

The moral legitimacy of police violence is thrown into question by a variety of factors. In UP and various other parts of India, since police are often viewed as pawns of the current regime, shadows of the "real" authority figures, their violence is generally interpreted as serving special interests—especially the interests of VIPs and "elites" or persons from the "political classes" or otherwise influential status positions—rather than the public good or *janhit* (chap. 5). But even more generally, police are beleaguered by a doubly "impossible mandate":

not only are they supposed to deploy violence as a means to realize a perfectly "clean" social order in a context where the causes of crime are largely outside of their control (cf. Manning 1997 [1977]), they are also somehow supposed to work toward this ideal by deploying violence that is itself (only) ideally "controlled" in the dual sense of being directed and restrained by legalities and moralities that may be inherently in conflict (see chaps. 3 and 6).[20] Like other elements and manifestations of provisional authority, police violence *chalta hai* (chap. 1); the motivations for, and the interpretations, legitimations, and even content itself of violence shift according to the conditions and subjects in play. This means that police routinely and inevitably transgress and even transmogrify an imaginary line delimiting moral and legal right that is itself a moving target. They are thus always already both "inside" and "outside" the sphere of sovereign decision, as well as social acceptability and belonging, similar to the executioner (Foucault 1977). But the police role is far more ordinary, indeterminate, and dispersed than that of the executioner or even the soldier, even if they have structural similarities or relational links with both of these avatars.

The figuration of police in terms of moral-legal condemnation, sacrifice and simultaneous inclusion and exclusion may prompt comparisons with some recent reconceptualizations of *Homo sacer* (sacred man). Giorgio Agamben (1998 [1995]) revived this Roman legal term for a criminalized person condemned to death to theorize political subjectivity as a function of "biopower" or the sovereign power over life (Foucault 2003 [1976]).[21] The *Homo sacer* subjectivity proposed by Agamben is embodied in a life form that may be killed but not sacrificed insofar as it is included in the juridical order only by virtue of its exclusion from having the legal rights of common citizens. At first glance this might seem to apply to police as ostracized, criminalized, or even demonized agents. But the ways in which soldier and servant avatars construct multiple meanings out of police violence in UP (and some other parts of India), in combination with the types of "living sacrifice" grievances expressed by real (proto) police like the young Aditya and elderly Aman, outline a very different type of condemned man: specifically, one who is, as noted earlier by the retired senior officer regarding encounter specialists, "condemned for life" (Pereira 2008, 199). Police are not necessarily condemned to physical death—even if there may be a relatively high probability of their death vis-à-vis other persons, especially in UP—but they are certainly condemned to a life of violent service that can never be morally pure or good.

Concomitant with the service of violence being morally ambivalent, the figure of the police servant also faces problems of a pragmatic sort. The colorful idols and images of Hanuman leaping across oceans with his superhuman powers, unbleeding open heart and undying devotion to Sita-Ram fall far short of fully capturing the everyday realities of police life in India. In addition to being quite dreary and draining (cf. Fassin 2013), police work may also be considered dreadful and even dangerous, less for being filled with fantastical adventures and heroic battles, more for being fraught with the many systemic problems discussed throughout this ethnography, inter alia scarce resources, conflicting orders, internal contradictions of law, political interference, and fragmented knowledge. These and many other problems permeate and permutate a socio-cultural context rife with structural inequality and conflicts driven by class, caste, communal, and patronal power struggles. Amid all of this, police are officially (under)paid on a set scale, and have many of the same worldly worries and questionable loyalties as any other human subject, with the additional burden of embodying the state power to use violence. Extending Aditya's claim that being a police officer is a "sacrifice" in part for relinquishing enjoyment of worldly and material goods as well as moral ones, I would underscore the fact that police as orderlies or servants of violence categorically sacrifice the good life as *paid professionals*. And importantly, as previously shown, payments to police come not only through government salaries and pensions, but also via relationships of exchange that may involve black money earnings or reciprocation of favors and other types of provisions-as-compensation from all kinds of persons, be they *aam aadmi* (common people) or powerholders with uncommon *pahunch* (reach or influence).

Rather than *Homo sacer*, or even *bali ka bakra*, a more apt characterization of police in UP, and arguably beyond, would be an expendable servant, a figure that is *simultaneously condemned and compensated* by the very public that orders (i.e., structures and demands) his provisional authority to deploy violence. The simultaneity of condemnation and compensation signifies a peculiar economy of police life as one that is as devalued as it is demanded. Police life is expendable in both senses of being "normally consumed in use . . . allowed to be sacrificed" and also "employ[ed] for a specific purpose" (OED 2015). Understanding police expendability as a function of both condemnation and compensation sheds new light on, and reveals looming and disturbing shadows around, official discourses of police heroism and rituals like Police Remembrance Day, which, I would submit, ironically reinscribe and reinforce the devaluation of police life even as they perform a kind of hyper-valuation and valorization of it.

Serving Violence and Living Sacrifice

Each time I returned to my field notes and photographs of the 2006 Police Remembrance Day ritual on the Lucknow police lines, several aspects of the ceremony and its aftermath stood out: the general absence of persons other than police themselves at the commemoration; the many hundreds of constables, disciplined and decorated, standing and marching for hours in the blazing sun while scores of serving and retired senior officers sat as spectators on plush couches in the shade; the director general of police's rushed reading of the names of the 136 "sacred remembered" police, more than 86 percent (118) of whom died as constables or head constables; the chief minister's promissory notes of structural improvements to the police organization intended to "boost morale"; the rapid deconstruction of the stage set to honor the dead via the statue of an anonymous officer atop a garlanded pedestal; and the awkward moments of waiting for the retired senior officer's delayed constable driver, and watching the quick dismissal of the police widows following their complaints about inadequate "ex gratia" compensation from the UP state government.[22] All together, these occurrences strike a dissonant chord blaring a disquieting message: the extinguished police officers we were supposedly celebrating were in fact generally undistinguished (see also fig. 1). They had done what was expected of them, executed orders, and thereby been expended, executed in another sense.

Most police in UP (and elsewhere) are not blind to their generalized expendability in the social order that they work to produce and enforce; the ubiquity of complaints about their job reflected throughout this text suggests as much (see also Jauregui 2013a, 2014a, and 2014b). Still, it seems poignantly incongruous that the figuration of a police official as a condemned and compensated person, as an expendable servant, is strongly and publicly reinforced by police themselves, who make it a point to expend a great deal of time, energy, and other resources on actively and affectively participating in—or at least attending and going through the motions of—official state rituals like Police Remembrance Day. This incongruity may be explained on both moral and instrumental registers. On the moral side, like most other humans, police, too, wish to construct meaning out of their lived experiences, especially when confronted with the possibility of death, in the line of duty or otherwise. Collectively honoring the bodily sacrifices of fellow police each year serves as way for still living police to re-provision themselves with a sense of virtue, particularly in relation to their service of violence that inspires such ambivalence and dread. On a more pragmatic register—though one that also has a moral thrust—public rituals attended by other senior government authority figures provide an opportunity for recognition not merely of police virtue, but further of police claims to need a greater quantity and quality of provisions from the state, whether in the form of increased benefits and manpower or decreased demands and pressures.

But even the CM's promises for greater government expenditure on the police institution—often framed in terms of "modernization schemes"—work to reinscribe and reinforce police expendability. Several officers cynically remarked that they hear the same kinds of promises repeated every year, and not just during speeches at Police Remembrance Day ceremonies; but the hoped-for changes and improvements almost never seem to materialize. At best, such promises constitute a kind of didactic performance, where the CM as police commander-in-chief may transmit at will the claim that policing *should* change for the better, but does not need to act on it, or even really listen to police expressing what they think needs to change (and can make excuses later for why the status quo remains). Such frustrating performances work to reinforce not only police expendability but also their generalized subordination to more powerful forces and relations of political will, or the lack thereof.

As already indicated, most police in India who are expended through bodily death serve at the lowest rank of constable. Very few persons recruited and trained as senior police officers (IPS or PPS) die or suffer permanent injury on the job; and those seniors who do die in the line of duty are individually memorialized, their deaths often reported widely and sometimes generating spectacular controversy.[23] By contrast, as we have seen here, the death of "cutting-edge" or subordinate police is officially remembered in a ninety-minute once-per-year collective memorial service rather than in individualized funerals. Perhaps even more disquieting than this disproportionate expendability of the "rank and file" is the social fact that the vast majority of police who die each year do not even make it onto the honor rolls of the sacred remembered at all, because their deaths are categorized as unrelated to duty.

The annual reports of the National Crime Records Bureau (NCRB) tell a potentially more nuanced and disturbing story of police death and injury across India than do the speeches and roll calls of Police Remembrance Day ceremonies. It is a story worth reading and considering more closely in association with this analysis of the provisional authority of police to intervene in everyday life, sometimes in matters of life and death. The latest available figures show that out of approximately 2.2 million civil and armed police personnel across India (BPRD 2014), 3,714 died in one year (NCRB 2013, 157–60). While this aggregate of death comprises less than 1 percent of total police personnel, by any account it is still an outrageously large number of fatalities, and notably reflects a 10.3 percent increase in total police deaths over the previous year. Looking deeper into the NCRB report, we find that 2,739 or almost 74 percent of these police deaths were allegedly from "natural" causes; 740 or almost 20 percent reportedly occurred while police were "on duty"; and the rest, an alarming 235 or 6 percent, came about "by suicide." Crucially, of the

740 police recorded as being killed on duty, 598 or 80.8 percent were listed as due to "accidents."[24] And reinforcing the earlier point of an inverse variation between death rates and police rank, 682 or 92 percent of those who died while officially on duty were constables.[25] These and other figures paint a very different portrait of police service, sacrifice, and vulnerability than do their avatars in popular film or epic myth allegories.

Notably, in the same year the number of reported civilian deaths in "police custody" and "incidents of policing firing" were counted at 248 and 103, respectively (ibid., 151–56).[26] This means that in this one year, according to official government statistics, more than twice as many police were killed on duty (740) as the number of civilians killed by police (351), which seems shocking in comparison to other countries, especially those in "the West" where the number of people killed by police is usually much higher than the reverse. The Indian figures defy several common expectations. First, the greater than 2 : 1 ratio of police : civilian deaths nationally is an inversion of what we might assume to be the case if we attend primarily to repeated charges of police brutality as it is ubiquitously reported in the news media—namely, the assumption, apparently incorrect in this case, that many more civilians die in confrontations with police than the vice versa. Second, we might also believe that most police deaths on the job involve dangerous engagements, spectacular chases, or dramatic shoot-outs with aggressive criminal suspects, an assumption reinforced by the associations with the aforementioned avatars, and reflected in news and entertainment media relating to police violence, as well as in popular discourse more broadly.

But, in fact, as demonstrated in the aforementioned figures, most police deaths in India result from causes categorized as "natural" or "accidental," a social fact that requires deeper exploration and explanation if we are to better understand the complex character of police expendability in India. During my fieldwork, I learned that many of the so-called natural deaths among police of all ages, particularly those approaching the mandatory retirement age of sixty, were due to illness, especially cardiac problems, often ascribed to or amplified by extreme stress, un(der)treated chronic health conditions, and the inadequate access to medical resources and unhygienic living conditions generally associated with India's poorer populations, among whom the masses of police constables may be counted. Regarding the on-duty deaths attributed to accidents, the kind I would hear about most often from my interlocutors resulted from things like failing equipment (especially old and ill-maintained weapons and vehicles),[27] building collapses, and road collisions. While accidents do occasionally happen, it is crucial to note that many of the problems listed above result from systemic infrastructural deficiencies and are theoretically preventable. However, public outcry around such deficiencies is muted and there is rarely much concerted effort to improve broken or outdated police infrastructure, even with all of the government lip service to, and reported monetary allocations for, modernization schemes (HRW 2009). Many police of various ranks would tell me that most of the money for such schemes seems to find its way into the pockets of corrupt senior officials and their associates.

The systematic neglect threatening, and often resulting in, bodily harm to police manifests in other even more insidious ways. I visited numerous constable and sub-inspector barracks across UP that were in a barely habitable—what many officers explicitly called a "subhuman"—condition. UP constables and sub-inspectors would regularly complain to me about physical and mental exhaustion, both for lack of manpower and other resources and because there is no real concept of shift work, meaning they are essentially on call twenty-four hours per day, seven days per week. If they are fortunate enough to be assigned specific duties on station grounds, then they might get a cot in barracks that are, if enclosed at all, filthy and poorly ventilated; otherwise they must reside in places that expose them to the natural elements of extremely hot summers and cold winters.

As I learned while conducting participant observation in Allahabad in 2007 of UPP policing of the *ardh kumbh mela*,[28] if police are posted "out of station" for some kind of extended special duty, the most fortunate might get a semi-sheltered cot or straw mat for sleeping and a tent-covered cement hole for quasi-private defecation (see figs. 20 and 21); but many just have to catch-as-catch-can by sleeping in (or under) vehicles, trees or some other semi-sheltering structure. Many constables are malnourished and suffer extensive periods of what might otherwise be short-term illnesses for lack of necessary rest or available treatments. On one occasion, several UP constables even informed me that three of their colleagues had recently perished from hypothermia and illness incurred during harsh winter conditions. I could not find any official documents on these specific cases, but would guess that they and similar deaths were probably categorized and reflected in that year's NCRB report as the result of "natural causes" or "accidents."

My ethnographic observations of and interviews about police expendability manifest in everyday vulnerability in UP have been supported by a damning Human Rights Watch report. While primarily devoted to providing empirical evidence supporting protests of human rights violations committed *by* police in India, the report also critically details many of the above-mentioned problems chronically faced by cutting-edge police that may be considered human rights abuses *against* police. The report quotes constables making statements like, "We are being exploited. . . . My meals are unhealthy and below caloric

FIGURE 20. Shared sleeping quarters for UPP constables and Home Guard personnel assigned duty at the *ardh kumbh mela*, Allahabad, 2007. Photo by author.

FIGURE 21. Makeshift cement and mud toilet for use by UPP constables and home guard personnel posted at the *ardh kumbh mela*, Allahabad, 2007. Photo by author.

value. . . . It's just like I'm a prisoner. We are suffocating here . . . The funds allocated by the government to constables are taken away by the superiors. You don't understand the trauma of being here. . . . I took three days' medical leave and had 25 days' salary deducted" (HRW 2009, 36). One of my own interlocutors echoed the beginning of this quote when he made an unforgettable statement that haunts this ethnography perhaps more than any other:

> "*Is naukri ko shishtaachaar ke naam par shoshan hai.*"
> "This job is exploitation in the name of discipline."

These conditions and complaints paint an ominous picture of the contours of police expendability in India as being shaped not simply by extraordinary episodic violence manifest in spontaneous (or even planned) encounters with threatening criminal suspects, but arguably more so by the slow violence of public apathy and abandonment (cf. Biehl 2005). This is true not just in exceptional events like the *ardh kumbh mela* but more importantly in everyday life, including at sites like the residences of government VIPs. Every time I would pass by the UP chief minister's official residence on Kalidas Marg in Lucknow, I would see on the perimeter about a dozen khaki-colored tents matching the uniforms of the many dozens of constables who lived there while assigned the duty of guarding the state's top governing official (cf. ZMB 2013).[29] Similar if smaller open camps where police constables must eat, sleep, cook, wash, and eliminate human waste can be seen near the houses of other senior officials, including many IPS officers. Passersby hardly give them a second thought, probably for being jaded by the presence of all kinds of precarious domestic spaces around town, especially urban slums (cf. Anjaria 2011).

The banality and visibility of *both* police violence and police expendability ironically produce a public blindspot regarding the precarity of police life and the provisionality of their authority. The blind spot is worsened by the ways in which police may be figured as gods (albeit lesser gods) and self-sacrificing warriors, at best, and as domineering and corrupt enforcers, at worst, since both of these stereotypes figure them as hyper-empowered actors. It is also starkly reflected in a disjunct between continuing official state lip service claiming to be working to reform policing and governance on the one hand, and a clear routine of passing the buck and the blame for ongoing inattention and lack of improvement on the other. Putting these systemic problems into dialogue with things like Aditya's and Aman's personal commentaries on police stress, scarce resources, and generalized lack of well-being, it become clear that institutionalized police violence has deep roots in systemic sociocultural inequality and everyday structures of violence much more than in extraordinary threats posed by "criminal elements."

There are certainly many real threats to the people at large and to police specifically in UP and other parts of India deriving from things like the
widespread presence of firearms (licensed and illegal); communal conflicts
that may erupt in mass violence; countryside *dacoity* (banditry) and regional
insurgencies, including and especially in areas with a strong presence of Naxalite or separatist movements; occasional bombings or other forms of attack
by extremist groups, and a variety of booming organized crime syndicates
(cf. Skolnick 2011; Van Maanen 1974; Westley 1970).[30] Police responses to these
threats often demand violence that may appear inadequate, excessive, or perhaps manifesting the strength and virtue of avatars like Arjuna, Abhimanyu,
or Hanuman. But these apparitions mask the more mundane elements of the
"living sacrifice" of police as expendable servants who are simultaneously
condemned and compensated for their violence and other service provisions.
The expendability of police life wrought by the types of slow violence described here is paradoxically reproduced not only by oral traditions, films,
and other forms of unofficial public culture but also by official rituals that
devalue police even while ostensibly demanding they be valorized. Next, we
will witness a similarly paradoxical dynamic evident in the ways that the politics of bureaucratic transfer simultaneously politicize and depersonalize individual police officers as they try to fashion as positive and productive a life
as possible, even if they are ultimately separated from "the good life."

Bureaucratic Politics

Regime Change

It is April 2007, and the Central Election Commission (CEC) of India, based in the national capital of New Delhi, has come to Uttar Pradesh (UP) to monitor the upcoming state Vidhan Sabha (legislative assembly) elections. The CEC's responsibility is to enforce *aachar sanhita* (election code of conduct), especially the provisions regarding fair procedures for the nomination of candidates and the cessation of campaigning activities in the weeks immediately preceding polling. CEC responsibilities also include organizing the deployment of thousands of police from the central (federal-level) forces and from outside state police forces at polling stations, in order to prevent electoral irregularities and limit the potential for voter intimidation and "booth capturing" by the ruling party, known to be perennial problems in many regions of this country, touted as the world's largest democracy.[1]

In an effort to ensure that nonpartisan police officers occupy key posts during polling, soon after its arrival in Uttar Pradesh (UP) the CEC wields its power to order the transfer of several dozen senior officers out of key posts, including the UP director general of police (DGP) himself, whom I still had not met after more than a year of fieldwork (chap. 1). An Indian Police Service (IPS) officer named Chanakya, who was appointed to replace an Uttar Pradesh Police (UPP) district chief removed from his posting by order of the CEC, agrees to meet with me soon after entering his new office.[2] During our meeting, Chanakya opines on the greatness of Indian democracy. "Voting is the thing that makes India a true democracy," he says. "This is the only factor on which we are ahead of China," he continues, claiming that India is morally superior to China because "the people have a voice here" even if China is "ahead on development." He echoes arguments made by some economists that India's development may be slow like an "elephant" but that this is better over the long term than that of the faster Asian "tiger(s)" (Das 2002).

Chanakya makes it a point to highlight how ephemeral his current position is. "When the election is finished," he says, "I'll be kicked out and the new government will appoint a 'party man' to take my place. But now, I am here, and I will do my best to ensure that the democratic process goes well under my watch." When I ask him if he feels torn between answering to the UP state government and the Central Election Commission, he responds emphatically, "I answer only to the CEC, not to the CM [chief minister of UP]. . . . The CM can do nothing to me now. . . . I am not getting any calls from politicians trying to apply pressure on me. I am only hearing from other senior police officers." Chanakya speaks with a firm tone and a self-assured, bordering-on-smug expression about this moment of authority in which he is insulated from "political interference," a problem about which many of his colleagues continually complain. I am struck by how different he sounds from other officers I have met over the course of my fieldwork, most of whom report being harassed by this or that state cabinet minister, or Member of Legislative Assembly (MLA), or political party leader.

Before leaving Chanakya's office, I ask for his permission to take a photo of the two plaques listing the names and tenures of all the persons who have occupied his current post since India gained independence on August 15, 1947. He chuckles, "Yes, yes, please do . . . you know, you can gauge the political climate and stability by noting how long each person stayed in office." A cursory glance shows what he means. The older plaque contains a list of about three dozen persons who served as district chief over a cumulative period of almost fifty years, with some individuals enjoying a tenure of three to four years in office. The newer plaque contains a list of more than twenty persons, including Chanakya, distributed over a period of only thirteen years, with only one person lasting in office for just over two years, and everyone else having tenures of only a few months each. The shift to an ongoing pattern of shorter tenures in office clearly begins in the early 1990s, when the Samajwadi Party and Bahujan Samaj Party began to gain prominence in UP electoral politics (see chap. 1).

As we exit the office, my research assistant who has accompanied me for the entire meeting remarks on what he calls an "aberration": namely, the fact that this new district chief has not transferred any chief station officers (SOs) since entering his office. The arrival of a new district chief usually inaugurates a slew of transfers of station chiefs under his charge, which will be published in the local news dailies. The official line is that the transfers are part of a necessary "shake up" or "getting rid of the dead wood" that will provide the best possible police service under new leadership. Unofficially, people speculate that the personnel shuffle results from bribes and bidding wars, retribution against rivals, and systemic cronyism. "Transfers and postings are a very political business," my assistant observes.

Ironically, later that evening, I learn via phone text message that Y. K. Yadav has been transferred out of his own post as station chief of Chakkar Rasta Thana (CRT), my ethnographic base of operations. My immediate reaction, recorded verbatim in my field notes, is "Oh, shit, now I can't go to CRT anymore . . . my connection is gone." This turns out not to be true. Since I have by now become familiar with all of the other CRT police personnel who remain at the station even after Yadav leaves, they inform the new SO that I have been coming and going with Yadav's permission, and thus I am able to continue fieldwork with CRT police for several more months, with the new SO's somewhat befuddled blessing. That said, my reactionary fears make clear that as an anthropologist of police, I have become entrenched in the order of provisional authority in and with which they operate. Yadav's transfer and many other events and exchanges that I have observed during my fieldwork demonstrate the importance of cultivating particular types of relationships—namely, sustained alliances with elected or appointed officials and political party leaders—in order to gain and maintain access to state resources. In the same way that many citizens work to establish and preserve personal relationships with police and other government agents, anthropologists like myself and even police themselves have to strategically build and sustain a network of allies in order to advance personal and professional goals.

When I speak to Yadav by phone the next day and ask him what has happened, he begins his explanation by saying that an electoral candidate running for the office of MLA in one of the subdistricts under CRT jurisdiction had filed a complaint against him with the CEC. The candidate had charged him with being biased in favor of the ruling Samajwadi Party, claiming that he unlawfully seized this candidate's campaign vehicle and removed "hoardings" or campaign posters. Yadav says the posters were covering traffic signs, and that while he did not follow a legal technicality of first attaining written permission from the Lucknow district magistrate (DM) to seize the candidate's vehicle, his action was absolutely in keeping with *aachar sanhita* rules imposed by the CEC. He adds, "No one from any other political party is issuing complaints against me." In any case, following an inquiry, CEC authorities determined that there was a high probability that Yadav was guilty of the charge, and ordered that he be transferred out of the post.

Yadav says his order to report to the Lucknow police lines at 6:00 a.m., rather than to CRT, came through a "wireless transfer"—that is, over the police radio rather than through a written order sent to him directly.[3] But even before hearing it himself on the radio, Yadav first learned the news when another sub-inspector called him and asked, "Hey, what happened? Why have you been sent to the Lines?" Knowing from many months of observation that Yadav prides himself on acting according to legal regulations rather than bowing to political pressure, I wonder if such a removal from office makes him feel some shame. I ask if it was upsetting for him to find out about his transfer from others before receiving the order himself, and he says he is not upset about any of this; in fact, he claims, he is happy because now he will not have to cope with the stress of being a station chief during an election, which involves a lot of extra work and pressure. He plans to take "medical leave" and relax for a bit. "I was CRT station chief for more than one year, and this is longer than the usual time for holding such a post anyway. I had no time for my family, and now I can spend some time with them."[4] I am inclined to believe this, since I know his wife has been ill and recall his teenage children sharing with me their displeasure at how often he is absent and apparently under great stress (cf. Aditya's commentary in chap. 4).

Yadav repeatedly assures me that the charges against him are bogus and have been trumped up "for political reasons." When I ask him to expound on these reasons, he says matter-of-factly that he believes it is a "clear case of caste bias" because the candidate who complained against him disdains people from his own caste.[5] I then ask why he thinks he was found guilty of the charge, if this was such a clear case of caste bias only and the CEC is supposed to be a more neutral third party in evaluating such charges. He suggests that the CEC is hardly neutral and definitely working against the incumbent Samajwadi Party that is led by fellow members of his caste. He claims that since the CEC is based in New Delhi, where the Congress Party is currently in charge of the ruling coalition in Parliament, it is full of persons trying to advance the interests of that party, or its allies in other parties, in the UP state assembly elections. However valid this claim may be in practice, it resonates with the claims of hundreds of other officers with whom I have spoken over the course of my fieldwork, which may be summed up by my research assistant's declaration that "transfers are a very political business." But what does "political" mean here above and beyond practices related to elections? How personal is the political, and how political is the personal? How exactly do bureaucratic politics work on the ground, and exactly what kinds of "business" do transfers involve? And how is all of this integrated with a larger order of provisional authority? These are some of the questions I aim to answer.

Transfers and the Public Good

According to legal regulations, a transfer is a lateral reappointment of a ranking state official to a different department, division, or district. It is not officially equivalent to a promotion or demotion, though on occasion it may coincide with such a vertical change of rank in the chain of command. Even so, a lateral transfer is often unofficially interpreted as a vertical movement of some sort that expresses favor or disfavor toward the individual being shifted. Transfers happen much more often in an individual officer's career than do promotions. They are supposed to recur on a periodic basis, according to written rules, within bureaucracies of all types in India—the civil service, forestry service, police service, etc. They may be requested by individual officials and granted by superiors; but more often, they will be ordered by command of the appropriate arm of the state government, ostensibly as a matter of serving *janhit*, or the public good.

As indicated in chapter 1, there were a variety of theories about Y. K. Yadav's transfer out of the post of station officer, which were related to me by various mutual associates of ours as I continued to conduct participant-observation at CRT even after his removal from office. Some people believed that he did not pay the new district superintendent a large enough bribe to keep the post. Some claimed he upset one of the elected MLAs who had sway in the area, or did not "fix" a criminal case in a particular way for some other local "big man" with influence in the government. Constables Sharma and Tiwari argued that Yadav had questioned orders or in some other way offended his immediate superior in the local police hierarchy, a deputy superintendent of police (DySP)-ranked circle officer (CO) named Valmiki, and therefore had been recommended for removal. No one mentioned the CEC except Yadav himself, and while it is not clear whether or how their involvement became public knowledge, what is clear is that the incident provoked unbridled speculation. After debating various explanations, most people would shrug and say things like *"Bhagwaan hi jaantha hai"* (God only knows).

Only certain fragments of knowledge about a transfer like Yadav's may be known or knowable by the various parties involved, including and especially by the transferee himself. It is an enormous challenge, if not impossible, to pin down a clear decision maker, motive, or causal chain of events that would definitively explain why Yadav's transfer occurred when and as it did. And this is the case for most of the other transfers of hundreds of thousands of officers that have preceded and followed this particular event. Such widespread and long-standing collective uncertainty regarding the decision-making process that places someone into or out of office runs counter to the ideal typical Weberian bureaucracy characterized by the "'objective' discharge of business . . . according to *calculable rules* and 'without regard for persons' . . . [with] legal guarantees against [an individual bureaucrat's] arbitrary dismissal or transfer" (Weber 1958b [1918], 202, 215, original emphasis). A key component of Weber's ideal typical bureaucracy is a "spirit of formalistic impersonality . . . [wherein] dominant norms are concepts of straightforward duty *without regard to personal considerations*" (Weber 1978 [1919], 225, emphasis added). In practice, however, while certain laws in India make outright dismissal of government servants relatively difficult, police and other bureaucrats generally are not guaranteed any such protection against arbitrary transfer. Moreover, though it is often difficult to document or prove beyond doubt, decisions regarding postings are generally known to be intensely politicized and personalized.

In my early interviews with senior officers, most of whom were appointed to the IPS, the issue of transfers as a function of the larger problem of "political interference" in policing came up in almost every meeting as the *bête noir* of the bureaucracy.[6] Based on the ubiquity of their complaints, I initially thought that I would try to track the politicization of the bureaucracy by mapping rates and vectors of transfers. When I inquired about how I might find reliable statistics reflecting transfer rates, I was told by a senior officer that the UP government Gazette and district Gazetteer periodicals no longer list every single transfer, because there is simply "too much activity" to keep track of it all.[7] Another officer said that this may be true, but noted that there is a signed piece of paper floating around somewhere for everything that happens in the police bureaucracy (cf. Hull 2012); he then pointed me toward a room lined floor to ceiling with shelves full of scores of burlap sacks stuffed with quasi-cataloged paper.[8] I soon realized that trying to comprehensively map the movements of officers through offices would probably be an impossible dream, even if I limited my research to this task only.[9]

Later, when I ask a senior officer at the UP DGP headquarters in Lucknow about how one might try to chart and explain the rates and vectors of transfers, he says wryly, "Oh, you are treading on very dangerous ground." When I ask why, he echoes some of his colleagues by saying, "Transfers are the biggest problem of the police. The state government would never authorize sharing this kind of information." I find this statement ironic considering that both English and Hindi language news dailies regularly report on the transfers of police and civil service officials at all levels, naming names and sometimes even speculating on the reasons for the shifts. When I try to press the matter further, the officer clams up and changes the subject.

Why is a procedure ostensibly as banal and routine as personnel reappointments such a mysterious and sensitive subject for so many people? And what does this mass-level mystery and sensitivity reveal about the machinations, motivations, and meanings attached to a particular official position, to decisions about shifts in position, and to authoritative decision making more generally? My analysis demonstrates that the discourses and practices of personnel transfers in UP reveal another key facet of how provisional authority works through a continually shifting web of official and unofficial relationships that are concurrently moral and instrumental: namely, the social fact that the personhood of individual officers and the capacities of professional offices serve as sites of political contestation that subject state authority to localized strategic games of position. The police institution is not simply a rational impersonal public bureaucracy that is politically corruptible and cronyistic; it is a multi-dimensional sociocultural field through which the authority of the state itself becomes indeterminate and is continually reconstituted across time and space through valuations and exchanges of provision and coercion.

The point is brought home to me by an IPS officer that I meet at the UPP Headquarters (PHQ) in Allahabad. He sits behind a large desk in an air-conditioned office and, along with a colleague of his visiting from another division, begins talking with me about problems of police accountability. "I have only been in this post for six months . . . how am I supposed to be accountable?" he asks defensively. He then says that the only way to make police more accountable is to stop their frequent and arbitrary transfers by ensuring that officers stay in a post for a *minimum* of two years and that an independent board oversees decisions about postings. "At the moment" he says, "it is the DGP who ultimately decides on transfers, at least on paper," which indicates that other decision makers play a role not recorded on paper. When I ask how I might learn more about the decision-making process, he says with nervous laughter: "You see, when it comes to transfers, there is a formal process; and there is also an informal process, which cannot be discussed formally."

As I build local knowledge and deeper relationships with my interlocutors in the field, I end up learning a lot about the "informal," or the unofficial process, which most people consider to be the primary driver of transfer orders.[10] But first, we must clarify what exactly people mean by the "formal," or official, process of transfer of appointment. Regarding police transfers specifically, the DGP is appointed by the UP CM, and according to the UPP Rules and Regulations (Kabir 2005), the transfers of other gazetted officers in the PPS (Provincial Police Service) or IPS (as well as the DGP, in part) are made by the Governor in Council. I am told in interviews that, in practice, the official procedure for transferring gazetted officers usually involves a conference among the DGP, CM, and the Chief Secretary, Home, who is the top civil service bureaucrat in the state.[11] Subordinate or "cutting-edge" police at the rank of inspector or below are usually transferred by the district chief, but may be transferred by any number of IPS officers, including the district superintendent; the range (collection of districts) deputy inspector general, or DIG; the zone (collection of ranges) inspector general, or IG, or the DGP himself, depending on the circumstances.[12] Ideally, transfers are supposed to help individual officers gain experience and build new skill sets over the course of their careers, and to optimize the state government's deployment of its employees as human resources with specific expertise. On the darker side, transfers are supposed to prevent appointed officials from developing "vested interests" by remaining in a particular post or place for too long.[13] However, perhaps ironically, this procedure intensifies the entanglement of police with party machines and underground economies, even as it is rationalized as working to divorce them (cf. Fogelson 1977).

A transfer must be done in a lawful way, via an order by someone in a particular office. A transfer may also be disputed via legal means, either by a petition to a superior officer brought forward by the person shifted, or by their appealing to a judge to order a "stay" on the transfer. Anecdotally, some police officers claim that there is an increasing incidence of persons using these types of legal means to challenge transfer orders. But, as with transfer rates themselves, calculating and mapping challenged orders would be an incredibly painstaking if not insurmountable task. Suffice it to say that while such maneuvers may be increasing in frequency, they remain the exception to the rule. In a classic case of Weberian *Herrschaft*, the vast majority of transfer orders received by police and other civil servants are obeyed more or less willingly. And importantly, these orders are not necessarily related to—in fact, arguably they often work against—the so-called public good. We will analyze here how bureaucratic transfers are co-configured with electoral and identity politics, personal preferences, and professional trajectories to reveal how provisional authority shapes not only police-public interactions, but also the ways that police relate to one another as colleagues and conceive themselves as institutional subjects.

A Personal and Political Economy of Bureaucracy

Flipping through English- and vernacular-language newspapers in Lucknow, one will regularly come upon news of bureaucratic transfers. The reports are usually short and descriptive, listing names, old and new appointments and little else, though occasionally one may see an additive like "SSP [senior superintendent of police] says routine move," as if to say, "this is simply procedural." However, as suggested by most of the officers with whom I spoke, the vast majority of transfers are not routine by any practical definition. Instead, they tend to be configured by factors like an officer's connections with other authority figures and political parties; or his caste or religious identity; or attributions of his past performance under specific conditions like a communal riot or the investigation of a heinous crime.

Perhaps the most spectacular form of transfer is the removal of an officer from a post as a form of public punishment for some kind of negligence or dereliction of duty. It is almost a matter of course that a local station chief will be transferred out of his leadership position if a major crime, such as an egregiously violent murder or assault, or communal violence happens under his watch.[14] If there is a criminal charge against an officer (which is rare) or suspicion of his active involvement in some questionable incident, the officer may be temporarily suspended from duty (or *very* rarely, dismissed from service); but usually the officer is simply removed from his current post and placed into another one elsewhere. There is an observable pattern of "heads have to roll" associated with occasional public outcry against the government, such as happened when police in New Delhi, UP, and elsewhere were seen as being unresponsive or ineffective in combating sexual assault and other forms of violence against women, a long-standing social problem that became an acutely politicized national issue following a heinous incident of assault and fatal gang rape in New Delhi in 2012 that received international attention (cf. chap. 3). When people accuse the government of being lax on crime, and leaders want to appear to be "doing something" about the problem, transfers tend to come in waves.

As suggested by the case of Y. K. Yadav and the CEC, public transfers of UPP officers and other government officials also tend to happen around the time of elections. A change of the ruling political party will often bring with it en masse transfers reflecting the preferences of the new regime. Following the 2007 UP Vidhan Sabha elections, when the Samajwadi Party led by Mulayam Singh Yadav was superseded by the Bahujan Samaj Party (BSP) led by Mayawati—who then began her third nonconsecutive term as UP chief minister—I witnessed many of my theretofore interlocutors in various offices abide major positional shifts. More than three hundred transfers of both police and civil service officers were reported in the first week alone. One observer has remarked that Mayawati still holds the record for transfers of IAS (civil service) officers, ordering some 1,400 of them in the first year of her first term of office in 1996—and who knows how many IPS and other police officers were also transferred so that she could put her own allies in strategic positions (Luce 2006, 128). It is said that Mayawati, or "Behen ji" (Sister Madame) as she is known, who is a Dalit, would transfer some high-caste bureaucrats repeatedly, to marginalize or harass them (ibid.). After taking office in May 2007, she dismissed more than twenty thousand recently minted constables, citing irregularities and corruption in the recruitment process under the Mulayam Singh Yadav government between 2004 and 2006. After a long court battle, the constables were eventually reinstated (TNN 2012). But Behen ji is by no means unique in favoring people of her own caste, or in gaining notoriety for conducting what people call "vendetta politics," a category of punishing practices that also includes things like killing public programs started by persons affiliated with the opposition parties, or expediting prosecutions of political rivals accused of crimes. Persons from all political parties are accused of engaging in these types of practices on a routine basis.

All of that said, the personalization and politicization of bureaucratic transfers cannot be reduced only to punitive or caste-ist politics. Besides the aforementioned rolling heads and postelection "sweeps," there are other patterns revealing the workings of provisional authority through transfers, most of which revolve around qualities and possibilities attributed to particular types of postings. Postings that are considered to be nodes of potential *kaalaa daan* (black money) earnings or access to influence—"plum postings," as they are often called—generally have a lot of transfer activity around them. These include "kingpin" postings in a district, like district superintendent or station officer. As indicated by Y. K. Yadav and others, district and station chiefs may suffer an especially high-stress job, requiring extraordinary amounts of work and frequent engagement with members of the public. But these officers also stand to gain extraordinary things from being in a position to make decisions about case investigations, duty assignments, and the allocation of security, among other things. Because SSPs and SOs are in localized positions of official authority, many people will seek their help in unofficially fixing cases and ordering protection. They have a significant quality and quantity of what is known colloquially as *pahunch* or "reach" and influence. These postings thus provide individual officers with the opportunity to earn a lot of money and also to form relationships and interact regularly with various sorts of VIPs and other persons with *pahunch* who are hooked into the local networks and channels of *sarkar* (government) as well as private enterprise.[15]

Officers who wish to take advantage of such connections will seek out—and sometimes bid with enormous bribes for—kingpin postings. For example, several officers told me that because the *kaalaa daan* earning potential was so high in a few of the UP-borderland suburbs of New Delhi—which have seen exponential economic growth in recent decades, and thus provide a high probability for kickbacks for specific high-level bureaucrats—the "going rate" for gaining a post as district SSP in some of these locales was reportedly a bribe of approximately Rs. 25 lakh, Rs. 2.5 million or more than US$40,000 (cf. Gidwani 2015). I could not get a definitive answer on what the going rate for Lucknow district SSP may have been; but this kingpin post, too, exhibited many of the signs of a sought after or highly politicized posting, which is not surprising considering its location in the UP state legislative capital that is teeming with VIPs. Five different people occupied the post of Lucknow SSP during the longest continuous period of my fieldwork in 2006–2007, with an average of only three to four months in office per officer.

In stark contrast to this high rate of ordered turnover in certain postings, I also met many officers who had occupied the same post for two or three or, in a few cases, even five years. The distinction between these longer tenures in mostly administrative postings and the shorter tenures of many district-level "cutting-edge" postings relate directly to generalized attributions of authority and desirability. Non-district or purely administrative types of postings appear to be insignificant in the larger provisional authority system, often considered bad career moves or dumping grounds for *bekar aadmi* ("useless people"). Such non-field postings also usually have relatively little black money earning potential, so are not as interesting to persons wishing to maximize the economic opportunities of being a bigger player in what many call "the game" of government service. Some examples of these less attractive police jobs include postings at training academies, the Criminal Investigation Division (CID), or infrastructural departments like the police "food cell" or "housing office." That said, even posts in some of these latter divisions may offer the potential for earning kickbacks from contracts for building materials or other types of provisions. Conversely, even some apparently attractive kingpin postings like station officer are considered less desirable when they are located in remote rural areas with smaller, poorer populations or fewer local resources and opportunities than the bustling urban areas (U. Chatterjee 2006). Transfers to these types of less desirable jobs are unofficially called "punishment postings" (cf. Simon 2004).

While many people speak in terms of preferred and punishment postings, it should be clarified that there is not an immutable taxonomy of "best and worst" police positions to which everyone subscribes all the time. Although there are trends toward many police favoring postings with significant decision-making authority, alliance-building potential, and money-making ability, this does not mean that all officers uniformly like or dislike a certain kind of job. For personal reasons, plenty of police prefer postings reputed to be "undesirable" by many of their peers, perhaps because the job happens to be near family, or because a person wishes to remain on the fringes of "the game" and march to his own drummer, insofar as that is possible in this behemoth bureaucracy. Chanakya, the district chief appointed by the CEC whom I engaged in the opening to this chapter, seemed to embody this latter type of officer. He expressed visible pride in being generally "outside the system," but momentarily in a powerful position because a central government agency was temporarily in charge, expressing its own kind of provisional authority. Rumor had it that Chanakya had gained a reputation for being more "fair-minded" than many of his colleagues, not necessarily affiliated with a particular political party, or at least not with a locally influential one. This is a crucial and perhaps more "positive" way in which the personalization of the bureaucracy manifests provisional authority as a so-called public good. For better or worse, both particular people and particular postings are deemed to have virtues and capabilities that translate into commodities with both "use value" in a specific time-space and "exchange value" abstracted over time (Marx 1990 [1867]).

That said, the provisional authority produced by the personalized politics, and politicized personhood, of police and other civil service postings also comes at an enormous cost to both government institutions and individual bureaucrats, to say nothing of the public good. The social fact that transfers happen at a dizzying rate, both en masse and to individual officers, leads to a host of negative consequences. Criminal investigations and other types of legal cases are left hanging when the officer in charge of pursuing it is shunted off somewhere else; service-oriented and possibly progressive programs die in the middle of being implemented, or before they can even get off the ground; suspicion and competition abound among officers vying for posts and trying to strategize optimizing their careers at the expense of their peers'; and of course, various forms of corruption flourish in the "market for public office" (Wade 1985). For officials themselves, the unpredictability and indeterminacy of transfers and postings makes for an often painfully insecure professional life course. One retired IPS officer related to me a moment in his career when he was transferred five times in as many days, and did not even manage to arrive at several of his new offices before receiving another transfer order directing him somewhere else hundreds of miles across the state. Such absurdly frequent and arbitrary shifts can have tremendously oppressive and depressive effects on the morale and personal lives of many police officers, never mind the detrimental effects on institutional functionality and practice. And yet, something also fights against the potential fall into inert fatalism: namely, the forces and relations of provisional authority founded in *jugaadi* agency and legitimation I have previously discussed. Now, I turn to the affective economy of police transfers, and the co-configuration of this economy with personalized modes of system navigation and operation that subjectivize police in various ways.

Structures of Feeling, Strategies of Movement

It is the end of February 2009, and I am having a second meeting with Manu Anand, a recently promoted DIG. Just one week earlier, he was transferred from one administrative division to another, following some field postings that had him in relatively more frequent contact with cutting-edge police. Our first meeting was in his office in one of the main hubs of state bureaucratic activity in Lucknow city, a site located between the district SSP's camp office and the UPP DGP Headquarters. But on this sunny Saturday he is technically off duty and out of uniform, so he asks me to meet him at the bustling Café Coffee Day in the heart of Hazrat Ganj, Lucknow's central commercial district. Officer Anand, a "general caste" man in his early forties—though his drooping eyes and greying mustache make him seem quite a bit older—says that he still feels quite "unsettled" in his new post. After apologizing for having to take several phone calls between our ordering sandwiches and soft drinks, he relates that he is under quite a bit of stress, because in addition to having to learn the ropes of his new posting, he also has been assigned to do the work of a second administrative position in another office where there is a temporary vacancy.[16] He says that he must do this double duty because "the state government keeps creating new posts and this means there is a shortage of senior officers to fill vacancies."

We begin talking about some of the problems associated with the continuous shuffles of senior officers like himself, and he says the following (in English):

> When you're in a post for just a few months, you have no time to do anything. You may start some project, try to make things better wherever you find yourself . . . but as soon as you begin to make some headway, or even before you really make a dent, you are shunted off again. For example, in one posting I held, I began a program to return stolen vehicles to their owners, which the police are notorious for neglecting. More than eight hundred vehicles had been confiscated in the area I was overseeing, and they were just sitting at the various *thanas*.[17] So, I began to compile a database of which vehicles were at which stations, then contacted the car companies and license and registration offices to match the vehicles with owners, and tried to get in touch with the owners to

return their vehicles. But by the time we had returned fifteen to sixteen out of
the eight hundred, I was transferred to another post, and that was it. Now the
program is no more, and the newspapers continue to run stories about how no
one can trust the police to return their property . . . but the real problem is that
things are just too fluid . . . we feel too uncertain to be comfortable starting any
new projects. It is not just that they will not reach completion, it is also hard
even to get a team of people together interested in doing the project, because
they all feel the same way, too uncertain—or they are just not interested because they think it is pointless even to try.

Here, Anand describes one type of negative impact that frequent transfers of
officers may have: namely, hampering what UPP officers would colloquially
refer to (in English) as "good work," clearing cases by making arrests and submitting charges to the judicial system or, depending on the reported crime,
making amends that would increase the probability of victims expressing satisfaction with the outcome (cf. Sherman and Strang 2007; Braithwaite 2002;
Strang and Braithwaite 2001).

As mentioned above, another type of negative impact from transfers relates to the interruption of ongoing criminal investigations, especially since
the post of station chief or SO (who often leads investigations) tends to be so
coveted and contentious, resulting in a high rate of turnover, and SOs make
the decisions about whether and how cases under their jurisdiction will proceed. After Y. K. Yadav was removed from his post as CRT station chief, I
witnessed a number of in-progress cases flounder under the new SO, not necessarily because he was incompetent or new to this type of job (though he
did say that this was his first post as station chief), but mainly because he was
subject to the steep learning curve of having to figure out what was going on
both in the station under his charge and its jurisdiction—who was who, what
was what, where was where, etc. This meant that the new SO would sometimes
"drop the ball" on hot cases; or do investigative work that was redundant with
work already done by his predecessor; or make "rookie" type mistakes because
of his lack of familiarity with the locale and the entailments of the job.

Now, imagine this kind of thing happening continually on a mass scale
across the state, and it begins to become clearer why police may express the
ineptitude, shoddy case work, corruption, and cronyism of which they are routinely accused. It is not just a matter of resource scarcity or bad training or
even the fraught "orderly ethics" that undergirds the routinization of things like
falsifying reports and fabricating evidence, as discussed in chapter 3. It is also a
function of the provisionality of their authority resulting from the extreme and
extensive temporal, resource allocational, and legal-moral flux of personnel
transfers. The sociocultural fabric of the police institution is being continually

shredded and rewoven by wayward weavers working a machine with too many moving parts, and producing a messy patchwork of mismatched and knotted materials, gaping holes, and fraying threads. Preventing "vested interests" can cut both ways. While transferring officers out may prevent the influence of unofficial relationships that promote "corruption" howsoever it may be defined, it may also prevent officers from becoming familiar and forming productive relationships with the people they are supposed to serve, which many of those in favor of "community policing" in other places would argue is necessary and favorable for best police practices (cf. Skolnick and Bayley 1988; Mastrofski et al. 1998; Skogan 2003).

Concomitant with deleterious effects on police work and institutional functioning, frequent transfers also tend to sap individual and group morale (cf. Diphoorn 2015). The overarching feeling expressed among police officers about transfers tends toward cynicism (cf. Van Maanen 1978 and Chan 1997). This cynicism manifests in various ways, and is often couched in jokes or nervous laughter similar to that of the IPS officer quoted above who alluded to the "informal process, which cannot be discussed formally." Nayanika Mathur has also noted a tendency toward joking and "ironical attitudes" among other types of bureaucrats in India (2012, 203). Following anthropological work with government officials in Turkey by Yael Navaro-Yashin (2002), Mathur analyzes cynicism among government officials as a practice of discursively critiquing an ideological or political system, and yet acting in the world as if deluded by the very system that they verbally disparage.

My fieldwork reveals a similar phenomenon being common among police in UP. However, it further demonstrates that in addition to Kafka-esque expressions of irony and absurdity, many officers express a rather more serious and dejected pathos—among them Manu Anand, whom I begin to find rather pathetic as our dialogue at the Café Coffee Day wears on. His expressions fluctuate along a dark and depressing spectrum of exhaustion, deflation, and disdain. As we begin to discuss how politicized transfers can be, and he rifles through some old papers, he suddenly says with visible and audible dismay, "Here, take a look at this piece of trash," and throws a folded piece of paper with crumpled corners onto the table. I unfold it to find an old facsimile of a message typed in Hindi on letterhead topped by the official UP government seal, with the inclusion of some hand-written scrawl in English (see fig. 22). Anand explains that this letter was sent to him some time ago from a senior officer in the "Establishment" division of the DGP headquarters, which is responsible for personnel transfers, along with a written note to be forwarded to the SSP of Gorakhpur district in eastern UP. The letter requests the transfer of a senior sub-inspector (SSI) out of his current post.

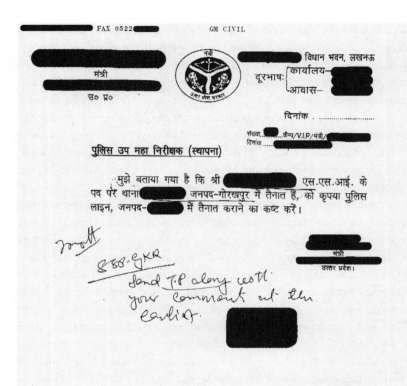

FIGURE 22. Facsimile letter from a UP state minister to a senior police officer in the UPP division responsible for posting personnel. Names, dates, telephone numbers, and other identifying information have been redacted to maintain the confidentiality of my interlocutor. The typed Hindi text below the underlined address to the recipient reads: "I have been told that Mr. _____ has been posted as SSI at _____ *thana* in Gorakhpur district, please take the trouble to have him sent to the police lines in [a different] _____ district instead." The handwritten scrawl below the typed text directs the Gorakhpur district chief to "send T. P. [transfer particulars] along with your comment at the earliest." Source: "Manu Anand," DIG, Uttar Pradesh Police. Reproduced with permission.

It comes from a UP state minister heading a department related to commerce whose official job has absolutely nothing to do with policing or decisions about personnel appointments.[18]

Anand indicates that this is not a unique document, but rather the type of thing that passes over the desks of senior officers like himself every day, in relation to transfers and various other forms of governmental business. According to a nongovernmental organization (NGO) campaigning for greater transparency and accountability in Indian governance, such "undue political interference in policing is now an axiom" (Kumar et al. 2008, 30; see also Verma 2005). And this letter is only one example of what people mean by political interference. Such interference may work in someone's favor, if they can mobilize their connections and other resources as *jugaadu* to realize a desirable outcome. But there are no guarantees. And as an unofficial rule, police from the top to the bottom of the organizational hierarchy know that if they do not act in line with the wishes of more powerful authority figures—especially, though not exclusively, persons affiliated the currently ruling party or coalition—then they could be courting disfavor that may lead to a variety of undesirable outcomes for them, not least a transfer out of a more desirable post into a less desirable post. While senior officers like Manu Anand are occasionally in the authoritative position of being on the "transferer" side of the process, *all* police are subject to being a "transferee."

Police subjectivization by the immanent *and* imminent threat, to wit, the high probability of being transferred at any time produces a complex of competitive mistrust, collective anxiety, and a generalized sense of being simultaneously scrutinized, manipulated, and devalued by other officials, by the public at large, and by the law itself. It also generates a sense of being pressed between a pervasive process of depersonalization on the one hand, and hyper-personalization-cum-politicization on the other. The term "depersonalization" as I apply it here should not be confused with Weber's aforementioned ideal typical "impersonal" bureaucrat who only follows legal and calculable rules and is awarded "merit" for producing good results, often in the form of the bureaucrat following a predictable path of movement and promotion through "the system." Rather, depersonalization works more as a kind of deindividuation and, again, commodification of both the person and the post as items of exchange and consumption with fluctuating value. In this order of things, professional merit is, if not wholly absent or chimerical, then largely an arbitrary and contingent recognition of an officer or an office as a "good" based not on "calculable rules" but on the strategic calculations of the current rulers and those subject to their provisional authority.

Police and their posts are depersonalized insofar as each individual becomes both expendable (chap. 4) and exchangeable. But the flip side of this depersonalization is the fact that sociocultural attributes like one's caste or religious affiliation, professional reputation, or access to various resources leads to a kind of hyper-personalization that provides each officer with political value for their occupancy of particular posts in particular contexts. This hyper-personalization manifests especially, though not exclusively, in appeasing the needs and desires of electoral constituencies. For example, on New Year's Day 2014, a senior officer named Rizwan Ahmad was appointed as the UP DGP—the third and not the last DGP appointed in a period of less than one year (Gidwani 2015)—even though he was only two months away from retirement and would have to depart almost as soon as he settled into the post. Why? As usual, it is difficult to tell with any certainty, though there were undoubtedly plenty of other equally suitable candidates for the job. Many pundits claimed that Ahmed's appointment—the first time a Muslim had ever been appointed DGP in the history of the state—constituted a move by the UP state government (at that time again led by the Samajwadi Party) to appeal to Muslim voters in the face of upcoming parliamentary elections. I also met several serving and retired senior officers who related stories of being posted in leadership roles in specific districts at times of high alert for communal tension, because they had past experience and a reputation for "success" in riot control, whatever that means.[19] Individual police officers gain reputations for things like being "tough on crime" or "the dog of political party X" or "feeble," or "a *crorepati*" (i.e., someone who knows how to work the system well enough to gain black money earnings that make his net worth exceed Rs. 10 million). In short, while transfers generally work to depersonalize officers and offices, they simultaneously hyper-personalize and politicize them, since posting a specific individual in a specific position in a specific time-space sends various political messages from the government to the people. Such actions also send various messages to the police themselves, among them: "Follow the orders—legal or otherwise—of the ruling party and its affiliates, or else you may well be sorry" (cf. Jauregui 2013a).

It is probably fair to say that "the politicization of policing is an undisputed fact in every country . . . and there is no police organization anywhere in the world where politicians do not interfere in management decisions" (Verma 2005, 165). But because of the historically and culturally peculiar ways in which identity politics intersect with electoral politics in postcolonial India—including but not limited to the development of modes of governance based on very unstable party coalitions—some have argued that "every small time politician exerts *disproportionate influence* . . . [and considers above all else] personal benefits, status and power of office" (ibid., 166–67). This is one of the many ironies of a "vernacular democracy" (Michelutti 2009) in which the power of "the party" claims itself as the great vehicle for the power of "the people." But I would add to this that even relatively "small-time" bureaucrats like cutting-edge police may exert disproportionate influence over their superiors in the hierarchy. Witness the aforementioned sub-inspector, someone relatively low-ranking in the police organization, who managed to convince a state minister to write a letter on his behalf requesting a transfer to a more desirable posting. It is not clear how the officer achieved this; but one thing we know for certain (though you will have to take my word for it since I redacted peoples' names in fig. 22) is that the minister who wrote the letter and the sub-inspector whom he is trying to help are both of the same caste.

Back at Café Coffee Day, in a statement reflecting the type of blatant and detrimental caste-ism of which CRT SO Yadav complained following his own transfer, Manu Anand goes so far as to claim that the leaders of the Samajwadi Party and Bahujan Samaj Party in UP have a kind of "personal vendetta" against the police as an institution. He expresses a belief that since people from "lower castes" came to power, they want to keep as weak as possible the police and civil service bureaucracies—which have historically been populated by officers who, like him, are affiliated with "general castes"—and to punish them for decades of oppression. Such statements seem self-pitying and problematically conspiratorial. And ethnographic work in other parts of India suggests that coercive practices by persons of castes that have only recently been able to populate elected and appointed government offices may be less a matter of revenge, and more a matter of adopting tactics long existing among formerly dominant general caste political leaders (Witsoe 2011). That said, Anand is certainly not alone, nor is he necessarily incorrect, in claiming that elected officials of the state government and their fellow party or coalition members—in short, "politicians"—want to keep the police and civil services under their thumb in order to serve their own purposes, which often have to do more with short-term gains for themselves and their constituents than with realizing long term visions of cultivating "the public good" for all.

Another senior police officer serving in the Vigilance Department who, like both Anand and Chanakya, explicitly seems to pride himself on staying "above the fray" or "outside the game" (and who therefore usually seems to occupy unpopular administrative "punishment postings" like this one), sums it up in the following way (in English) while complaining about what he calls the "transfer industry":

For the dishonest and the weak, the system forces you to succumb, if not in the first decade, then definitely in the second. For the good officers, it is demoralizing and demotivating because you know that if you remain honest then you will probably be punished for it by the majority, who do not remain so. You try to fight the temptation, but after so many transfers, your will is broken. You meet resistance wherever you go, you get a reputation, your family is miserable and starts to pressurize you. So you get some help.

The meaning of "get some help" is the crux of the matter. Getting some help means forming and mobilizing strategic alliances and exchanging provisions of various sorts with other persons in positions of authority who can try to influence where you are posted. Such persons are usually elected officials, party leaders, or local "big men" known to have strong ties to a political party or "*party bandi*."[20] Sometimes such persons may also include specific fellow police officers known for being savvy system operators. This is where *jugaadi* agency and legitimation come into play, not just in the sphere of executing everyday police work but also in the realm of conducting and navigating bureaucratic politics. Similar to common citizens who form relationships with police and other government agents to increase chances of achieving goals (cf. Hornberger 2013), police feel compelled to do the same thing with other persons displaying provisional authority.

Recall the IPS officer mentioned in chapter 1 who, after being called upon to do so by the MP relative of my acquaintance, was immensely helpful in providing me with access to various campuses of the UPP training academies in Moradabad (see also chap. 4). Though I did not know it at the time of my police academy visits, about a year later, my acquaintance informed me that the main reason the officer was so obliging in helping me was that he was trying to obtain a transfer into a police division near New Delhi that is known for being a very lucrative black money earning post because of its links with smuggling activity. The police officer had previously approached the politician to form a relationship—a meeting which likely involved monetary exchange in the form of a campaign-related "gift" of some sort—and the latter promised to try to help the officer gain his desired posting. This lesson regarding my unwitting "strategic complicity" (Jauregui 2013b) and ethnographic entanglements with bureaucratic politics forced me to recognize how my provisional all-access-pass to the police training academies and various other wings of the organization was itself made possible and configured by this web of relationships and exchanges.

I was also later compelled to reckon with the fact that my anthropological access to the world of cutting-edge police opened channels of hoped-for reciprocity for which I was unprepared and ill-equipped. I was not surprised to learn that, like the sub-inspector who received help from the minister in the form of the letter Manu Anand shared (see fig. 22), Y. K. Yadav obtained his post as CRT station chief by beseeching a prominent member of the Samajwadi Party (he claimed that the value of their shared caste affiliation was enough and that he did not have to pay a bribe). "This is just how it works," he said matter-of-factly. But thinking myself relatively divorced from such relations and machinations, I was caught off guard when, sometime after he was removed from the office of CRT SO and reassigned, Yadav called and asked if *I* could help him get transferred out of his current posting in another district, which separated him from his family still living in Lucknow. He said he thought that I might be able to put in a good word on his behalf with the newest Lucknow district chief. I fumblingly replied that I could not help him because I did not know the new chief very well and did not have any *pahunch*. I sincerely felt that this was true and that Yadav had misrecognized the quantity and quality of my own connections and capabilities. But I also felt so uncomfortable with the request and what it would demand of me that I did not even try. Yadav was clearly disappointed, and I suddenly felt the burden of my complicity with provisional authority in a new and intensely disheartening way.

It was a most poignant moment, reminiscent of an incident recounted by Clifford Geertz (1968) in which he bungled his relationship with a longstanding collaborator by suddenly discontinuing allowing the man to borrow his typewriter, which he had been doing for quite some time. Geertz wrote of this encounter as an exposure of the tenuousness of their relationship, the disjunct in their understandings and expectations of each other, and the fiction that their two cultural worlds could be regarded as one. Over and above these three things, Yadav's request of me, and my awkward refusal to grant it, together exposed some very inconvenient truths about the provisionality of our own forms of personhood and their co-configurations with authority. As an anthropologist of police observing their work "in the field," I was forced to confront the possibility that by building knowledge about this life world—indeed by authoring this very book—I could reproduce and reinscribe the questionable morality and legality, and the social inequality and violence, that so often inhered in their everyday practice. As a police officer inviting me to learn about his life world, Yadav ultimately reminded himself that his authority is contingent and precarious, his personhood is expendable and transferable, his capabilities are rescindable at any moment.[21] A la Praveen's rookie wisdom (chap. 2), if Yadav wished to trade his current position for a more desirable one, then he would have to keep "looking for the right connection" since I turned out to be a disappointment; he would have to continue engaging in the eternal game of speculation, betting on who would be the best help. And

I would have to continue reckoning with what Holly High (2010) has called the ongoing "spectral return" of the ambiguities, incongruities, tensions, and disappointments wrought by exchanges made between anthropologists and their interlocutors during fieldwork encounters. Our respective quests, and questionable requests—which had converged in one moment only to diverge in another—would continue into the unknown.

Speculations and Navigations

Police officers discussing what the above-quoted Vigilance Department officer called "the transfer industry" would often describe their experience by using the analogy of chess, sometimes invoking the term *shatranj*. Those police inclined toward citing ancient history would note with some pride how chess was invented in India more than a thousand years earlier and spread across the world via the Persian Empire.[22] Then, often in concert with some expression of the cynicism mentioned previously, they would usually compare themselves to pawns being moved about by other greater "masters" and often sacrificed as part of some grand strategy that they, the most ignoble and least mobile game pieces, could not fully understand except in a very general and vague sense of elites gaining and maintaining "power" (cf. the discussion of police service and sacrifice in chap. 4). One deputy superintendent of police once said to me explicitly, "We are tools. If a powerful person wants us to do something, we do it."

The chess analogy makes a certain kind of sense considering the structure of feeling described above, characterized by experiences of being depersonalized-cum-politicized. But from the anthropologist's point of view, this field of transfer activity is not merely an "industry" economically churning out commodities with volatile use, exchange, or even moral "values"; nor is it simply an interminable zero sum power play wherein wooden pieces are wholly manipulated by players of singular consciousness and purpose to "win."[23] The game of bureaucratic politics involves a much more complex interplay of transmographying actors, motivations, and productions of meaning around collective control of provision.

Returning to Sherry Ortner's delineation of a serious game involving "shiftingly interrelated subject positions . . . [wherein] actors play with skill, intention, wit, knowledge, intelligence" (1996, 12), I would argue instead that the multidimensional field of relationships and exchanges of which transfers are but one part reflect an ongoing game of state governance that is less about kingly conquest and more about resourceful authority. This game, configured by forces and relations of doing *jugaad*, orderly ethics, and the production of expendable and exchangeable servants subjects governance in India to the whims of provisional authority. In this game, police are often pawns being moved about and sacrificed by other players. But these pawns may also become other types of players with greater powers and the reach of *pahunch*, and some may even become little kings of a sort for a time. For all the limits on their authority, police obviously are not completely powerless whether doing their duty or advancing their career goals. Even as pawns, they can find ways to compel the multiple parties that constitute the imaginary figure of the "chess master" to move them into and out of particular positions, especially since the parties that combine to transfer a bureaucrat are themselves only contingently authoritative. They, too, can be shifted or shunted out in some other way; the ruling coalition may be reconfigured or the ruling party changed; some other more powerful "big man" or social force may soon rise to replace them (Jauregui 2014a).

Everyone's authoritative position in government is contingent on their access to resources, as well as on their luck and decisions about how to maneuver through the system. And "working the system" or "playing the game" of provisional authority involves an ongoing mass-scale trade in resources of various sorts. It also entails a significant amount of risk that one may choose the "wrong" ally or path. Somewhat similar to Yadav wrongly choosing me as one possible avenue of career advancement, Praveen, the Home Guard from chapter 2, also told a story of a young man he knew who failed in his attempt to bribe his way onto the constable recruitment roles. The young man went to the trouble of gathering "insider knowledge" about the correct amount of money (more than Rs. 200,000), collected the enormous sum from a variety of sources, and found a broker who would deliver the bribe to the DIG who was the head of the recruitment board only to be foiled by outdated or incorrect information. He gave his money directly to the DIG appointed as head of the recruitment board; but as it turned out, he should have given it to the relative of a prominent minister in the ruling party, whose list of preferred candidates ultimately trumped that of the DIG. For what it is worth, he reportedly recouped most of his money, though not all of it. He was lucky. Many are left empty-handed.

Playing the game of state authority is a never-ending gamble. It demands continual strategization involving risky gambits of various types, which may be advantageous or disadvantageous in the short term or the long run. But you don't stop playing. Indeed, the indeterminacy and mystery of the game have an ironic social effect: the very order that produces intense cynicism and demoralization also produces a vibrant field of exchange in which virtuosity, and sometimes even something like "merit" may be enacted and rewarded. Rather than causing everyone to throw up their hands and concede to their fate as determined by other "masters," the game frames police practice and professional postings as an exercise in speculation. Many people become determined to express both authority and agency by finding just the right mix of mobilizing "the right connections," maintaining access to provisions they could offer to others, building strategic knowledge, and thereby skillfully maneuvering in the game. They try to control their luck by making offerings to deities as well as to living humans in positions of authority. In this way, there is as much aspirational as cynical energy in the provisional authority order.

Tara Schwegler (2012) describes a similar phenomenon in an ethnography of the Mexican development bureaucracy. She explains how government actors would spend considerable time and effort trying to "read" and make sense of the political field, form alliances for later mobilization, and "discover viable pathways through which to advance their agendas" so that they could get *both* official and unofficial work done. I witnessed a similar hermeneutics of personnel turnover among my interlocutors in the UPP, who would spend an inordinate amount of time discussing their own and others' transfers, as if able to divine the "real" motivations, machinations, and meanings of specific personnel shifts (including those that had not yet happened), similar to reading tea leaves or horoscopes.

Police and other bureaucrats, especially in the more senior ranks, seemed to spend at least as much time attending to their past, present, and future positions in and movements through the web of bureaucratic politics as they would spend performing official police work. Almost daily, I would hear police making jokes about someone's "midnight marching orders," or questioning official reports of recent transfers by adding to the mix something they had heard through unofficial gossip. And though I was rarely able to witness actual attempts by individual officers to mobilize their networks and resources to direct their own transfer, they would regularly tell me things like, "I'm working on getting out of here" or "I've got someone helping me to obtain a post closer to home" in an offhanded way.

It is vital to understand that many officials speculating in and navigating the system strategize over the long term. For example, the aforementioned IPS officer who provided me with access to the UP training academies by request of the politician from whom he sought help with his own transfer made it a point to tell me that he was trying to time a posting in or near New Delhi to coincide with helping his children find places at good schools in the national capital (not surprisingly, he made no mention of any desire to be posted with a division that might provide increased black money earning potential, which was reported by my acquaintance as mentioned in the previous section). I also observed a multitude of repeated "casual visits" between district police officers and other persons with influence and authority in a locale, indicating that mobilization of social connections and resources is integrated with everyday interactions over an extended period of time (see Jauregui 2014b).

While it may seem ironic that a nominally rational-legal system of personnel shuffling has the effect of intensifying "vested interests," it is less surprising when one considers that in the cultural-historical context of postcolonial India, legitimate authority is associated not only with state law (which, as demonstrated throughout this text, is not so much flouted or dismissed as it is strategically harnessed and manipulated for its power) but also with forms of social status embodied in long-standing modes of dynastic rule by prominent families, and with relationships structured by donor-servant sensibilities (Jauregui 2014a and Piliavsky 2014, generally). More than an official chain of command, whom you know, who (and what) you are known to be, and what you and those you know have to offer one another at any given time are paramount factors in configuring both agency as the relational power to advance projects, and authority as the probability that a command will be obeyed.

These social facts mean that while there are distinct classes of "elite" and "subaltern" police that span official and unofficial relational fields, the latter may subvert the legal authority of the former. For example, soon after I began my fieldwork in 2006, I read in the newspapers about a local station chief who was transferred out of his post on direct orders from the DGP himself, only to be transferred back in twenty-four hours later by the district chief, apparently on orders from elected officials in the state government, which was a major embarrassment to the DGP. People speculated that this SO must have had connections very high up in the ruling Samajwadi Party. The SSI calling on the UP state minister, who wrote the letter requesting transfer shown in fig. 22, was working within the same system of provisional authority that so irked the deputy inspector general (DIG), Manu Anand.

Toward the end of our chat at Café Coffee Day, I relate to Anand some statements made by my constable interlocutors about feeling downtrodden under pressure from senior officers and not being allowed to take leave (see chap. 6). Anand claims that because district SSPs used to receive more resources from the state government, they used to be able to do a better job of "solving the problems of rank and file men . . . so the constables would look up to us." He continues, "But now, the constables go to the courts if they are dissatisfied with a transfer or are being punished for something. Or they go to local politicians or clans for help. They do not come to us senior officers for help, because our power has been so reduced and weakened."

He completes his thought by saying, "Your authority comes from your resources."

States of Insecurity

The Remains of the Day

The sun is setting and the almost week-long Lucknow *nagar nigam* (municipal council) elections are coming to a close. Now that the voting has wound down, and the counting has begun, there are fewer pressures on police guarding the voting booths. At this polling station just beyond the Chakkar Rasta Thana (CRT) jurisdiction, scores of cutting-edge police of various ranks, many of them bussed in from other state districts, are milling around waiting for orders, most of them tired-looking and probably hoping to go home. I begin chatting with a couple of Uttar Pradesh Police (UPP) constables from the eastern region of the state who are leaning on their *lathi*s, and once they learn that I have been observing everyday police practice in the area for some time, they start to vent their job dissatisfaction. One of them says, "I'll tell you the real story." He says it is almost impossible to get leave from work since the state government always demands police presence for special duty like this. He then complains about senior officers not communicating well, giving conflicting orders for duty and then blaming constables who are confused and sending them to the orderly room to be disciplined.[1] As the minutes pass, about a dozen other constables gather around, and the venting cascades:

> I missed my son's birth, and could only see him for one day before returning to work for several months. If you have a sick family member in the hospital or a wife going into labor, too bad, you cannot get leave in this job. . . .

> We don't get our salaries or uniform parts and allowances when we're supposed to. The senior officers do uniform checks and say, "Where are your shoes? Why do your pants have holes? Why is your shirt dirty?" But they don't ask, "Have you eaten or slept or bathed?" Then they write in their reports that

government money has been distributed and properly spent, when it's really gone into their pockets, or into those of the clerks at the pay office. . . .

The government doesn't help pay for our children's schooling as promised. They take Rs. 17 out of our monthly check for buses and services then do not provide them . . . and we still have to spend most of our salary on tuition. . . .

They're also supposed to reimburse part of our medical expenses, but it takes many months and we never get the full amount promised . . . and by the time the doctor takes his fee, and the medical file clerk and pharmacist and others take their [unofficial] payouts for quicker service, we are broke. . . .

If a senior officer has duty out of station like this, he gets a nice guest room, runs the air conditioner or the heater, eats good food, watches television, or has fun with visitors. We [subordinates] have to stand outside the whole night, in extreme heat or cold. Sometimes, if there is some space, we can sleep in the jeep; but usually we just get a chair or the ground. For the whole night, only tea keeps us company. . . .

When we die in the line of duty, there is no big ceremony. But when a senior officer dies, he gets much fanfare, the politicians come and mourn him. Nobody remembers us, and the family of the deceased does not get support, does not always get the pay or the pension or the job they are promised . . . they don't even get money to travel to the memorial ceremony.

I look around at the group of khaki-clad men as they speak, noting some of the differences in their uniforms: oversized summer shirts, frayed winter sweaters, some with starched and ironed pants, some with sandals and sneakers instead of regulation brown shoes. I think to myself how they resemble a motley "sackful of potatoes" (Marx 1978 [1852], 608), then ask, "What do you do to change these things?" One constable snaps at me, "What *can* we do? Who do we complain to? The people who are supposed to help us are the ones stealing from us." I recall that Uttar Pradesh (UP) constables and sub-inspectors are legally banned from joining or forming unions, while senior officers may have professional associations for "social purposes" only. Another remarks, "You should ask why constables are 'going crazy' and beating up or even killing senior officers," referring to a case of such a homicide in another state that had made the news recently. Another reminds me that police suicide rates are also quite high, and says, "You should also ask, 'Why do the police smoke so many cigarettes and take so much chai and *paan* (beetle nut chewing tobacco) and even alcohol? Why do they need to get high and drunk?' Investigate *that*."

These entreaties echo things I have been seeing and hearing from my interlocutors at CRT and elsewhere, always out of the sights and away from the ears of the officers who supervise and discipline them. So it is not surprising when, as three sub-inspectors walk over to see what the huddle gathered around a foreign woman is all about, the constables abruptly stand up straight, don stony faces, and cease their grumbling. The sub-inspectors stare at me amid the sudden silence with an admixture of suspicious, bemused, and amused expressions, which compel me to introduce myself as a researcher studying the "*roz ki zindagi*" ("daily life") of police in UP. When one of them asks for more detail about what I am studying and what I have learned, I say simply, "*Lagtha hai ki bahut pareshani hain*" ("It seems like there are a lot of problems"). In response, he says curtly in English, "I am part of a disciplined force, so I cannot tell you much. But yes, there are many problems." This concludes the exchange.

After the sub-inspectors wander off, there is an almost audible collective sigh of relief. Eventually, a few of the constables ease into some casual conversations, but the air remains heavy and awkward. I stand by quietly and begin to tune in to the voice of someone I learn is a newly minted constable. He is eighteen years old and has recently completed training. The older men in the group tease him in avuncular and fraternal tones about his inexperience, one of them joking, "How can he do police work? He doesn't even have a moustache yet!"—causing the others to chortle and question his manhood in other more vulgar ways. The smooth-faced rookie says defensively, "*Arre! Siikh reha huun*" (Hey! I'm still learning). I take the opportunity to ask him, "What is the most important thing that you have learned about police work so far?" and he responds with a serious countenance: "Do whatever you can to keep your job; because there is always someone coming up behind you ready to take it."

Conditions and Contentions of Police Authority in India

As an ongoing engagement with interlocutors and an analysis intended to inspire further conversation, an ethnography is never really complete. Still, we must find some way to conclude this story of the UPP life world and discuss what it may mean for understanding policing and the state in postcolonial India and beyond. The narrative began in the field with Sharma and Tiwari, a couple of constables going about their everyday work in a rural area of Lucknow district, which involved routine tasks of intelligence gathering, sensitive site vigilance, and spontaneous dispute resolution. The interactions described also included the constables' thwarted attempt to extract a bribe from someone, framed by their claims that police are misunderstood and misrepresented, even mistreated and misused, by some members of the public as well as by their own superior officers—hardly the hallmarks of excessive empowerment and entitlement with which police are generally associated. Their contentions resonate with those of the constables just related here, many of which have more to do with what they experience as a misallocation of resources rendering them deprived and devalued. All together, these expressions reflect a social world in which police life and work are confusing and demoralizing, despite—and also because of—their presumed power and promised benefits as employees of the state.

Police in UP, especially those comprising what is colloquially known as the "cutting edge," live and work under intensely precarious and pressurizing conditions. The complaints of the constables recounted above reflect those of many other police who express feeling misled about government provisions for their welfare, overwhelmed by physical and mental stresses and unable to take any action that might realize substantive redressal for work-related grievances (cf. Baxi 1982; Chande 1993; Ghosh 1982; Subramaniam 1988). Their expressed troubles reflect a sensibility shared by many people across India regarding the state violation of expectations that it will provide for public welfare (cf. Tillin, Kailash, and Deshpande 2015). Indeed, the state in postcolonial India is widely perceived as having the responsibility to care for its subjects, and this "care" manifests not only through provision of material resources like farmer subsidies and food rations, or of public services like legislating and policing, but also through provision of compensated "official" and authoritative employment—including but not limited to police jobs—that may engender social mobility. This is why appointments with the government bureaucracy have been so coveted and competitive, particularly among people from disenfranchised social groups whose abilities to grow private wealth or occupy elected office historically have been limited to nil (Arora and Radin 2000; cf. Witsoe 2011).

In postcolonial India the state constitutes the locus of provisional authority. While this authority manifests in many avatars—elected politicians, party leaders, civil servants, military soldiers, and others—the civil police represent the most publicly visible and omnipresent figures. Police authority therefore has foundations not just in "non-negotiably coercive force" (Bittner 1970), but inter alia in moral-instrumental valuations and performances of collective beneficence, resourceful adaptation, and even cosmological forces and relations that both bestow rights on and demand duties from persons occupying contingent and contested social positions. Crucially, "collective beneficence" here does not imply altruistic or selfless motives, nor is it synonymous with an ideal typical liberal democratic sensibility of "the public good" as something benefitting everyone equally (see chap. 2 and chap. 5). The so-called public is always already divided along various fault lines (cf. Habermas 1991 [1962]; P. Chatterjee 2006; Warner 2002). And the idea of the collective here refers instead to multiple parties that are connected through shifting exchange networks—or, in the words of constable Tiwari in chapter 1, through ongoing arrangements making people more or less directly "known to" one another—that may allow or compel provision of some good to all parties involved, if unevenly so.

In addition to relying on biological or affinal kin for help, people form tenuous relationships of trust with various others over time with the hope and expectation that they may call on one another for assistance. Everyone knows that if you have the means to provide something for your associates—be they family, neighbors, co-workers, caste or religious affiliates—then you do so in as much abundance as possible, knowing that favors may be returned in the fullness of time with divine blessings. If you fail to do so, then you are considered at best weak and incapable, at worst vile and corrupt. A shared understanding of corruption as misallocation of resources is demonstrated in chapter 2, where we witness the intertwined forms of agency and authority allowing-cum-compelling certain actors to provide greater things than others at certain times. These actors include but are not limited to police—who themselves often have to call on civilians for help to do their job—and through the provisional agency and authority manifest in giving things to others, they acquire social virtue. This virtue itself is provisional and manifests in forms of particularistic accountability (cf. Martin 2013) that are grounded partly in official institutions and legalistic command and control, and partly, arguably more so, in personalized performances of making offerings and responding to demand, in a continual moral-instrumental recalibration of "what is the good" and "who is going to provide it" (Jauregui 2014b and Piliavsky 2014).

As we saw in chapter 3, these ongoing moral-instrumental recalibrations dialogue directly with the law as official codification of right, and with unofficial demands of political pressure, personal entreaty, and experiential knowledge to configure an "orderly ethics" of police practice. This ethical sensibility is founded on negotiable terms of who is most in need of receiving, and who is best positioned to allocate, particular resources in a specific time-space, which in turn shape claims about what is the most reasonable course of action in the face of fluctuating constraints and capabilities (cf. Roitman 2006). Acting in accord with such ethics may involve police writing a false report or submitting fake evidence to prosecute a "real" criminal; or making an arbitrary judgment as to who is a real criminal or real victim of a crime based on hunches or biases; or resolving a dispute through brokerage of an unofficial compromise rather than filing an official legal report categorizing people as "criminal" or "victim" at all. These are only a few of the ways in which police may be called upon to "enforce order," (cf. Fassin 2013) and interpellated into the amorphous role of being state orderlies cleaning up society's "messes," a job that is "dirty," multifaceted, and never complete (cf. Marquis 1992).

The multiplicity and indeterminacy that configure public demands on police are further complicated by the unique role that police perform as servants of coercion by violence. As explicated in chapter 4, "the police" as the muscle of governance are simultaneously vilified and valorized by "the policed." More pointedly, police are condemned and compensated by a public that both fears and demands their violence. Since it is impossible for police to reach a perfect pitch of potential or actual violence—that is, a quantity and quality of coercion agreed upon by all to be just right (or "just" and "right")—their service becomes concurrently excessive and inadequate (cf. Ben-Porat 2008). Concomitant with this paradoxical figuration, police vulnerabilities and grievances are often summarily dismissed—especially, and ironically, in ritual public performances meant to honor them, like the Police Commemoration Day ceremony described earlier. Such critical evaluations and wholesale dismissals subjectivize police as statist "others" external to "society"[2] and separate them from the possibility of living "the good life" in both moral and material senses, even as they must continually meet the unending and wildly varying demands for their services. The value of police life and work is thus as provisional as their authority, figuring them as jack-of-all-trades orderlies who also happen to provide violence on demand while being equal parts expendable and fungible.

The social forces and relations figuring police expendability and fungibility play out in their engagements with various sections of the public they serve and also, as analyzed in chapter 5, in the politicization and personalization of official postings in the police bureaucracy. Thousands of transfers of police and other bureaucrats at all levels are occurring across India every day, usually individually, sometimes en masse and especially in the run up to or aftermath of local, state, or national elections. While transfers are officially billed as routine procedures performed in the interest of *janhit*, or the public good, the provisionality of any police officer being placed in a particular posting with variable qualities and quantities of official authority is configured by a host of unofficial influences and interests, from reward and punishment, to offerings of bribes and bidding wars, to government leaders demonstrably favoring personal or political party affiliates. The indeterminacy inhering in this burgeoning field of ordered (i.e., demanded and structured) movement has multiple negative consequences on police work and morale, forcing many people to "succumb" to the system by "playing the game" as noted by more than one officer. This "serious game" (Ortner 1996) galvanizes players to find ways to gain a sense of agency by mobilizing personal and professional networks in an effort to make the best life and do the best work possible for oneself and one's associates. Let us now consider how understanding these sociocultural dynamics in terms of provisional authority may help us to rethink some of the most commonly critiqued problems of police practice in India and beyond.

Reframing the Usual Suspects: Global Police Problems

The ethnographic data and derivative analytical frames discussed throughout this text may be considered contextually unique, particular to certain Hindi-speaking regions of northern India in the early twenty-first century. This analysis recognizes the cultural and historical specificity of social dynamics related to things like *chalta hai*, *dharma*, *janhit*, and *jugaad*. Even so, when presenting analysis of these dynamics to various audiences, I have been repeatedly struck by suggestions of their potential comparative value made by persons familiar with policing and related South Asian socio-legal practices, and also by those knowledgeable about police in places as far flung as Detroit, Johannesburg, Lagos, Moscow, Paris, Sao Paolo, and Taipei. This raises the possibility that a conceptual framework for understanding police authority in postcolonial India as provisional may inform research on police more generally.

Police have recently been analyzed by anthropologists as a "global form" that has "a distinctive capacity for decontextualization and recontextualization, abstractability and movement, across diverse social and cultural situations and spheres of life" (Ong and Collier 2005, 11, quoted in Garriott 2013, 2). Rather than referring to an interlinked architecture of knowledge and practice in a transnational state system (Bowling and Sheptycki 2012) or to a universal condition or structure of law enforcement as originary violence (cf. Benjamin 1978 [1922]; Derrida 2002), conceptualizing the police as a global form indexes a set of institutional ideals and interactive practices of governance and order that have emerged and transformed across space and time, not least through centuries of colonial expansion. The global form of police is co-configured with sociocultural, legal, and political developments at local, regional, national, and transnational levels (cf. Loader et al. 2016). Since there now exist what some have called "glocal" discourses around police institutions, it seems fair to say that some of their inadequacies, inequities, and iniquities also constitute global forms. I will here address four such problems as conceptual fields, what we might call "the usual suspects" that oppose or violate "the good" and lead to "crimes" of which police and their authority often may be "convicted": violence, bureaucracy, discrimination, and corruption. These issues seem to spur the most heated claims and debates about police and their possible reform. How might the conceptual framework of provisional authority elaborated in this ethnography help to reframe our thinking about these vast and variegated categories of concern and critique?

Police engage in all kinds of "dirty" work that most of us would rather not do ourselves, or perhaps even have done by others, even if conditions seem to demand it. But their deployment of potential or actual violence "as needed," which is often questionably legal and legitimate, seems to be the most intractable problem associated with their authority to intervene in everyday life. If, as argued here (see esp. chaps. 1, 3, and 4), police coercive authority is founded less on their embodying an idealized and externalized state monopoly on violence, and more on conditional and conflicting demands for provisions of state—including and especially for violence as a "service"—then we "the people" must contend with a host of uncomfortable and often unarticulated questions about our own complicity in reproducing police violence, even as we may work to question, curb, or eradicate it. How does the thrill and sensuality of violence often reflected in public culture figure police authority generally as coercive authority specifically? What types of police violence come into the spotlight as objects of critique or demand in specific moments and locales, and what other types may be eclipsed or dismissed in the process? Precisely when, against whom, and to what extent do we need or want police violence to come into force? These unsavory questions spur further questions, like, What effects may the public demands for police violence have on police officials themselves, and on their family members, associates, and communities (cf. Mangold 1997)?

These are perennial problems that we have not adequately addressed in theory or in practice.[3] Conceiving police coercive authority as not only political but also provisional—that is, as a contextual and contingently available moral-instrumental resource or "good" in much demand—may compel us to shift the terms of debate regarding "excessive" or allegedly "militarizing" police force (Balko 2014). How have the legal, moral, and ethical limits of demands for police violence historically been defined, and how *should* they be defined? Assuming we are not calling for the annihilation of public police institutions altogether, we are compelled to ask not simply how their violence might be limited, but further how it might be harnessed or guided in accord with shared ideals of truth, right, and social justice? Even Mahatma

Gandhi—the revered icon of Indian national *swadeshi* (self-rule) who pro-
pounded nonviolent resistance to oppression in his program of satyagraha
("truth force")—said, "I do believe that where there is only a choice between
cowardice and violence I would advise violence. . . . I would rather have India
resort to arms in order to defend her honour than that she should in a cow-
ardly manner become or remain a helpless witness to her own dishonour"
(Gandhi 1951, 132).[4]

The social reproduction of police violence occurs not simply through a
sensualized or vicarious horror fascination associated with a "wound culture"
(Seltzer 1998; cf. Sontag 2004), nor even through a logic of "necessity" (Hussain 2003) or "exigency" (Bittner 1970), but inter alia through a more or less
conscious and unconsolidated set of social desires to control police violence—
that is, to mobilize and direct it as a means to realize various ends. Put another
way, police embody the ideal of disciplined violence, an ideal that is arguably
as impossible to realize as a legal and legitimate monopoly on violence.[5] The
modifier "disciplined" refers to relational forces of institutional normalization
and subjectivization (Foucault 1977 and 1990 [1976]). But rather than a structuring social force working in service to "power" as a key driver of "governmentality" in toto (Foucault 1991), discipline is here conceived as a historical
form of bureaucratization working in service to "order" not only as sovereign
command but also as an arranged response to demand in everyday life.

As demonstrated throughout this book, especially in chapter 5, the police
bureaucracy is co-configured with ongoing sociocultural transformations and
reproductions of moral-instrumental good operationalized by both official
and unofficial agents who occupy shifty status positions with fluctuating capabilities. The authority of any individual officer and, crucially, of any particular state office itself is chronotopic, resource-oriented and conditional.
This is starkly reflected in the moment that the sub-inspector quoted at the
beginning of this chapter said, "I am part of a disciplined force, so I cannot
tell you much. But yes, there are many problems [in the everyday life of po-
lice]." It is a moment in which he has the authority to shape, and also to shut
down, conversation among a social group with a specific composition, namely
constables whom he outranks. But it indexes other moments and possibilities
of his (and others like him) being outranked by others—for example, earlier
that day, I had watched as a station chief, also a sub-inspector, dashed around
his own office serving tea and snacks to the Lucknow district magistrate and
district police chief sitting at his desk, his position momentarily analogous to
a domestic servant deferring to VIP guests.

The utterance "I am part of a disciplined force . . ." and its immediately
observable predicate of the (military) subaltern comportment demonstrated

by the constables would seem to figure the police officer, and moreover "the police" institution, as an exemplary Foucauldian subject that internalizes normative rules of conduct and manifests disciplinary power in ways that reproduce patterns of knowing, relating to and limiting the self and others, which could potentially inspire resistance (Foucault 1990 [1976] and 1977). But this assumes "the police" to be a unitary subject. Recalling and building on one of the most incisive and invaluable critiques of an apparently different kind of subject, the (sociocultural) subaltern, I would argue that police, too, are "irretrievably heterogeneous" (Spivak 1988, 284) while also bureaucratically disciplined in a way that depoliticizes them, for better or worse, quite often for worse. As demonstrated throughout this text, especially in chapter 4, police are, if not "subaltern" in the sense explicated by Gramsci (1971) and later the Subaltern Studies collective to describe oppressed and colonized "others" (Guha 1982), then uniquely condemned and compensated in ways that restrict or even destroy a critical political voice. And this unique form of subjectivity and its associated practices work to restrict or destroy the voices of others, including and especially those others that may be subjugated to a greater degree or in a qualitatively different way from subjects affiliated with historically powerful social groups and norms of "the good."

In the specific case of the UPP, and among most other police organizations across India, making critical-cum-political statements publicly—especially in a way that accuses the state government they represent and serve of not looking after their welfare, as these constables were doing in the vignette opening this chapter—is officially considered an act of "indiscipline." Such acts constitute a serious violation of legally binding regulations, including state and national codes of conduct and the Police Forces (Restriction of Rights) Act that was enacted by the parliament in New Delhi in 1966,[6] as a postcolonial rearticulation of a 1922 act passed by the British colonial administration banning "Incitement to Disaffection" following several violent uprisings associated with the nationalist movement. Evaluations of such activity as "violations" occur among police bureaucracies in many contexts, though there is wide variation in laws and regulations regarding these types of things. In any and all cases, however, it is vital to recognize how the sociolegal demand for a police force disciplined through bureaucratization may eclipse the sociocultural demand that police both provide security for the public and have it provided for themselves (cf. Foucault 2003 [1976] and 2009 [1977]).

Recognizing the disciplining force of bureaucracy as a potential source of insecurity, disempowerment, and depoliticization for police allows us to see how holding state office may reproduce various problems associated with provisional authority, especially in relation to generalized aspirations and demands for social mobility. The constable quoted in chapter 4 as saying, "This job is exploitation in the name of discipline," signals the possible development of a collective (subaltern?) consciousness among police around broken promises, alleged abuse, and unmet demands. Whether this development actually comes to pass and how it plays out politically will, of course, vary by context (Marks and Sklansky 2011; DeLord et al. 2008). It is worth noting that since India gained independence from Great Britain in 1947, scholars and popular media have recorded at least seventeen major uprisings of subordinate police personnel across the country, several of which have involved deaths and violent confrontations with para/military organizations, none of which have resulted in structural reform that substantively improves the abject living and working conditions of many police.[7] And it is clear that in many time-spaces, many people's aspirations for building their social and economic capital via employment with public police have been revealed as, if not wholly misplaced, then certainly a much taller "order" or unrealistic expectation than they may have previously believed. This is so not simply because bureaucratic realities invariably stray from the ideal typical forms of impersonal and calculable motives and actions into the realm of political contestations, but also because the authority of these state police is continually subject to question, negotiation, and demolition. As related in chapter 1, police authority *chalta hai*; it moves, sometimes changing so fast that police may hardly notice how violently or irrevocably the ground beneath their feet has shifted until they find themselves in a confusing, dismaying, and often humiliating condition, like when constable Sharma was beaten by the family of wealthy media moguls and then taunted by his boss.

Bureaucracy is a social institution commonly critiqued in terms of its hyperrational proceduralism and concomitant "red tape" leading to inaction, stagnation, and systemic prevention of needed access and assistance that perpetuates structural violence (Gupta 2012). While there is no denying these problems are rampant, we must acknowledge that bureaucracy is also a field of hyper-mobility and volatile fluidity shaped by various, often conflicting demands and collective ideas of the good that filter through agents moving into and out of its multiple nodes at a maddening pace and a vast scale. What new problematics may present themselves if we foreground the social fact that bureaucratic structures, motives, means, and ends are not always decelerating and impersonalizing, but as or more often characterized by accelerated movement and transformative possibility that includes for many—including and especially bureaucratic agents themselves—the potential for personal, professional, and political "progress" howsoever defined? This question is particularly important in time-spaces of apparently extreme or increasing social inequality and competition for resources. Clearly, employment with the police is not the great "equalizer" or even power generator that many presume, and this has significant and still undertheorized effects on police interactions with various sections of the public.

The complex imbrication of police authority with social inequality forms the bedrock of the third usual suspect of police: discrimination, more specifically the prejudicial treatment of social minority groups. In postcolonial India women, Muslims, many persons of traditionally "lower" Hindu castes, and Dalits or other "out of caste" persons (from Adivasis or "tribals" to various religious minorities like Sikhs, Buddhists, Christians, Jains, Jews, and Parsis, to name just a few) have historically been unduly and simultaneously harassed and neglected by police and others.[8] Put another way, social minorities across India suffer routinized "overpolicing" and "underpolicing" (Ben-Porat 2008), notwithstanding myriad special laws developed to protect them from such excesses and inadequacies. Discriminatory actions by UPP officers against some groups have been described throughout this ethnography, with special attention to the ways in which electoral-cum-identity politics, local influence, and socioeconomic exchange may shape officers' decision making and interactions with the public. None of this is surprising, nor is it unique to UP or to India. The exercise of police authority—to say nothing of the demographic composition of the police institution itself—in most times and places entails differential treatment of various groups along lines of context-specific social categories like race and ethnicity, gender and class, which reflects and reproduces historical inequalities (Fassin 2013).

Police discrimination is often critiqued in terms of how it affects the legitimacy and accountability of the institution. Police legitimacy has been analyzed synchronically as a function of perceived fair and equal treatment, or "procedural justice" among various sections of "the public" (Sunshine and Tyler 2003; Tyler and Huo 2002). It has also been analyzed diachronically as symptomatic of larger historical processes and events that directly engage police and affect their image, like decolonization or deindustrialization (Reiner 2010). In this latter vein, and as suggested throughout this book, most explicitly in chapter 2, the conceptual framework of provisional authority highlights how legitimation (and delegitimation, and relegitimation) is an ongoing, partial and uneven social process rather than a condition that is either wholly present or absent (Jauregui 2013a). A similar dynamic is at work when it comes to police accountability. Since provisional authority is neither distributed nor obeyed equitably across a homogenized political subject in the form of "the people," it disavows the democratic promise that every citizen subject is at all times free and fair before the law. This social fact is, again, neither new nor unique to India, and its myriad manifestations have been interpreted in various ways in various contexts, from liberal democratic racism in North America (Henry and Tator 2005, Murakawa 2014), to the criminalization of the postcolonial state in sub-Saharan Africa (Bayart et al. 1999), to mass-level self-serving instrumentalism in postcolonial India that is completely opposed to any ideal of democratic accountability (Brass 1997). But in many parts of India, and perhaps in other places as well, the discriminatory and unequal ways in which state authority is expressed may also work to produce a kind of contingent and particularistic "accountability" that ebbs and flows with changing demands, and gets recharged and rechanneled through a web of ordinary exchanges and relationships conceived as both moral and instrumental, involving both official and nonofficial actors, again for better or worse (Jauregui 2014b; Martin 2013; Witsoe 2011).

If we reconsider police discrimination as particularistic accountability in dialogue with provisional authority, in this or other contexts, then we may also shift our questioning and nuance our understanding of police knowledge and ethical frameworks as reflecting pluralistic and context-specific public demands for state resources. In other words, rather than presuming that all police channel an always already reigning logic of "power" that reduces social difference to a zero sum game of dominance through sovereign decision, we may instead work to analyze how dramatic shifts in particular concepts and practices of social difference reconfigure amities, enmities, access to, and benefits from state provisions. For example, we must further investigate how the aforementioned rise of political parties led by "lower" (and out of) caste persons, and the concomitant system of reservations (affirmative action quotas) in public institutions—which have produced claims of "reverse discrimination" by some persons from historically dominant groups—have reconfigured concepts and practices of police authority. Many claim that these conditions and developments have had profound, and not necessarily positive, effects not only on the demographics of police organizations but also on the patterns of police discrimination, specifically the patterned rise of police officers of particular caste or religious groups simply "taking care of their own" while passively neglecting or actively harassing various others (see chaps. 1 and 2). And these patterns seem to shift frequently with the winds and waves of electoral and bureaucratic politics (see chap. 5).

Whatever else they may be, police are "knowledge workers" (cf. Valverde 2003; Stalcup 2013). As part and parcel of their routinized practices of categorizing people into various "types"—officially in station registers and unofficially in practices of profiling and arbitrating disputes (see chap. 3)—police serve as both repositories and reproducers of cultural transformations in collective knowledge about social difference that shape ordinary interactions. And, importantly, these shifting knowledge forms may be mobilized *both* by police themselves *and* by others toward various positive and negative ends, from prevention of victimization and alleviation of fear, to exacerbation of oppression and intimidation of rivals. Like police violence, police discrimination as knowledge of social difference may be seen as a contextual and contingent social resource variously demanded, drawn upon, and deployed to help realize (often competing or conflicting) human needs and desires. In this sense, for better or worse—and very often for worse—there are public demands for police discrimination, if not as a conscious and purposeful collective call for prejudicial mistreatment of "others" (though sometimes they may be so bold and bald) then as an appeal for authoritative recognition and support of specific interests, even as calls for equality and liberty for all may resound in the halls of government buildings and spaces of public protest. Repeated demands for police protection of certain religious events and processions that may incite mass violence (especially against certain minority groups) constitute just one example of such an appeal.

Police discrimination between "criminals" and "victims" ideally answers general social demands to identify and control sources of insecurity. However, social groups who already have more influence and access to resources will have a higher probability of being able to actively mobilize or passively benefit from police discrimination, while those who historically have had less reach and capability will suffer the most. Therefore, here again we "the people" must acknowledge the parts we may play in reinforcing and reinscribing police discrimination in light of the specificities of our own social positioning vis-à-vis various others. We must ask: How do our direct or indirect engagements with police, or with others about police, rely upon and reproduce a host of stereotypes and fears of various social "others"—including of the police themselves as condemned and compensated servants of violence (chap. 4)—even as we work to promote equity and fairness? How do the public demands for accumulation and mobilization of police knowledge subjectivize police themselves in problematic ways, including and especially police officials who are members of social minority groups that have been historically disenfranchised or abused? When and how might framing charges of systemic police discrimination polarize discourses of reform in ways that constrict the terms and forms of debate, perpetuating "us versus them" dichotomies in lieu of cultivating collaborative possibilities? And how can, and how should, we conceptualize the legal, moral, and ethical limits of the demands for and use of police knowledge and discriminatory capabilities under various conditions, especially conditions of intensive precarity, when there is so much elbow room for their misuse?

This brings us around to the fourth "usual suspect" of police authority in the contemporary world: corruption. As suggested throughout this text, police practices across India are routinely synonymized with corruption, so much so that this word (in English or in Hindi as *bhrashtaachaar*) is almost invariably one of the first used by people in UP and across India to describe police and explain many other elements of official governance. As mentioned in chapter 2, an entire political party named for the *aam aadmi* (common people) emerged from an anti-corruption social movement in India that peaked around 2011. Popular charges of corruption as the rotten core of the state extend well beyond India, especially though not exclusively in postcolonies (Comaroff and Comaroff 2006) and countries often referred to as "developing" economically or "transitioning" to democracy. Following from this social fact, scholarly research and policy programs regarding corruption as an out of control "informal economy" have burgeoned over the past few decades, and some analysts have argued that corruption may even promote development or be an inevitable evolutionary stage on the way to a society realizing a full transition to an ideal typical liberal democracy (again, see chap. 2). But the frames of reference for what corruption means or implies across different contexts remain unclear—even as lawmakers, envoys, and activists continue to call for government transparency and accountability at local, national, and transnational levels, and to trade strategies and "toolkits" for mitigating or, ideally, eradicating this amorphous global plague.

This analysis of police authority in India does not propose a new or universally applicable theory of corruption, to say nothing of offering specific policy directives for its mitigation, eradication, or prosecution. Rather, it aims to inspire further critical questioning of a widely shared assumption that corruption among the police specifically or the state more generally is more prevalent or severe in the world's less economically wealthy or more politically unstable nation-states (see also Loader et al. 2016). My focus on the categorical shiftiness of moral virtue and instrumental virtuosity, and on the centrality of collective beneficence to everyday exchange in a place that, for all of its problems, is still considered a global power and the world's largest democracy, reveals the folly of considering corruption, howsoever it may be defined, as simply a symptom of an "incomplete" transition to liberal democratic governance. I submit instead that perceptions and practices of corruption may serve as an index of how the liberal democratic state reproduces itself as a site of insecurity for its own subjects, not merely through a volatile politics of the electorate but more commonly through exercising its provisional authority to govern and produce

order. Some have conceived this ongoing reproduction of insecurity as a function of subjective precarization under contemporary conditions of biopoliti-
cal and neoliberal global governance (Lorey 2015 [2012]). There may be some
strong empirical support for this argument. But we may also want to add to
the theoretical debate questions of how provisionality as a foundation of governance and order is also vital to shaping states of insecurity among various
subjects, and to configuring the authority of "the state" *as insecurity itself* (cf.
Weldes et al. 1999).

As explicated in chapter 1, the state is here conceived as a set of institutional ideals and interactive practices around governance and order embodied in authoritative office. If the sources and capabilities of state authority
are provisional in all the senses described and explained here, and thereby
associated with fluctuating conceptions of virtue and value, and fluctuating
capabilities to allocate resources, then it is less surprising that the state as a
figure of everyday life, and the police as figures of the state, are always already
corruptible. I will develop this point further by considering how everyday
experiences of and interactions with police configure the simultaneous opening up of possibilities and closing down of imagination regarding what state
authority is, may be, or ought to be.

Police and Insecurity

Every time I return to my notes of the conversation with the UPP constables
at the close of the Lucknow *nagar nigam* elections, I am struck by the lesson imparted by the fresh-faced "rookie cop" that a police officer should "do
whatever you can to keep your job; because there is always someone coming up behind you ready to take it." After spending more than twenty-four
months doing fieldwork with the UPP, I believe that most of his colleagues—
including those sharing the litany of laments that preceded his claim—would
agree with him, if begrudgingly. This statement throws into relief a widely
shared sensibility that, for all of the substantive disadvantages and even dangers associated with police employment in contemporary India, it still entails
immediate benefits and positive possibilities that, for many, seem to outweigh
the costs and discontents. This social fact is brought home by an interaction I
had with another recently minted UPP constable named Vikram, which I will
relate now in one last "return to the field."

It is Christmas Day and my research assistant and I are accompanying
Vikram on what is known as "picket duty." He has been assigned to guard
a local bank on the main road connecting CRT to the outskirts of Lucknow
district, since highway robbery is a particularly vexing problem along this

path. The constable is in his early twenties and has about six months of on-the-job training under his belt. CRT is his first district police posting. Like Praveen (chap. 2) and Aditya (chap. 4), Vikram comes from a "police family" with three uncles, two cousins, and a brother already being members of the force (cf. Sinha 1981). When I ask Vikram how he likes his job, I note that unlike many of his more seasoned colleagues he still carries a somewhat hopeful tone, although he indicates that he is becoming more disillusioned day-by-day. He says that he used to have dreams of being a police "hero," but has already seen that hope dashed by the common experience of doing good work—specifically, catching a thief—and then not being recognized for it because someone who outranked him took credit for the operation. He has also realized the folly of thinking that he would always be honest "like the police in the movies."

"Now, I have to be practical," he sighs. Vikram tells us that his wife is "in poor health" and has already lost two babies. The young couple lives far away from their families, a common scenario since police are legally barred from being posted near their home in order to prevent problems associated with "vested interests" (see chap. 5). They have not managed to secure subsidized police housing, which is in high demand but very limited supply—I recall CRT chief station officer (SO), Y. K. Yadav, saying it took more than ten years of service and a fair bit of "doing *jugaad*" for his family to finally be allotted a modest Type III flat on the grounds of another district station. Vikram and his wife are having trouble keeping up with rent payments. "Now," he says, "I want to learn one thing only: how to make [black] money. People will exploit you, and you have to survive." He goes on to express unhappiness that for today's assignment, he is partnered up with a Home Guard (see appendix and chap. 2). He finds this discouraging, "because nobody respects or fears them, so nobody gives them money." He goes on to claim that his partner for the day "doesn't know the business [of attaining sizeable bribes]. . . . I want to work with an experienced constable, someone who knows what they're doing, so I can learn how to make more money."

When I ask what he has learned about "the business" so far, he says that common people will often initiate a bribe to police. Echoing his more seasoned colleague, constable Sharma (see chap. 1) Vikram opines, "He who is doing something wrong or wants some favor always gives money. We don't even need to ask." As if the gods hear his claim and want to provide supporting evidence—or perhaps one in particular wants to inspire a Christmas holiday "gift"—a few minutes later an ox-drawn cart with an obviously, and illegally, oversized load approaches on the main road, moving in the direction of the market a few miles away. As the cart comes near, a skinny middle-aged farmer sitting next to the younger driver leaps off the makeshift seat, runs directly to Vikram, and proceeds surreptitiously to shove a faded red Rs. 20 note into the constable's hand while muttering, "*Le lijiye, saheb, le lijiye* (please, sir, take this)." Vikram leaps up, apparently embarrassed and trying to block this from our view. He performatively refuses the bribe, pushing the man away and not looking into his eyes. But the man is insistent, and eventually Vikram takes the crumpled note and sits back down next to us. I hear the *chai walla* (tea seller) who is standing nearby chuckle knowingly, and after a few seconds even Vikram himself is giggling abashedly. As the rickety cart slowly trundles by, he asks, "Why not take it? He is giving it." He then remarks, "This is how it is . . . it's part of 'the system,'" echoing many of his senior officers who have said to me that "corruption is built into the system" since the masses of cutting-edge police are paid "peanuts." Vikram's claim also echoes that of his colleague, constable Aman, who said to me, "This the way it is . . . sometimes a little bit of dishonesty benefits everyone . . . the victims, the judges, the police . . . sometimes even the criminals. Therefore, it is not wrong" (chap. 3).

The provisionality of police authority, in all of its senses, clearly carries with it a positive valence. Even if most police in India must endure low pay and great hardships, their social position marked by occupying state office clearly represents something desirable. Every time there is a recruitment drive, tens of thousands of people go to great lengths to try to obtain this type of employment, many of them industriously gathering outrageously large sums of bribe money and going into sometimes insurmountable debt in the hopes of gaining a spot on the training enrollment lists (see chap. 2 and fig. 13). Such mass-level "corruption" of the police recruitment process, in dialogue with everyday interactions like Vikram's spontaneous exchange with the farmers on the road, shows how both police officials and the people passing through their spheres of jurisdiction may conceptualize, and mobilize, the authority of the state and its official agents as conduits of various types of "goods" (cf. Smith 2007). The police officer potentially has greater access to, and an enhanced ability to deploy, multiple types of social and material resources *as state authority*. In addition to being a "force to reckon with," this authority itself may become a resource for others to mobilize or exchange, making police potentially virtuous and highly valued members of their communal networks. All of this signals how the provisionality of state authority may open up possibilities for mobility and transformation that otherwise seem beyond the reach of most "common people."

The provisionality of police authority also, of course, has an intensely dark side with many negative facets, burdening each officer, each office, and the institution at large with an uncommon culpability. Besides acknowledging the high probability that police authority may be applied in abusive ways, we must also recognize that it is *subject to misuse by others*. Its interdependence with social and material resource allocation and valuation renders it inherently unstable as both a commodity of exchange and a relational force. Moreover, many police, especially those with "cutting-edge" posts, are disappointed to learn that their avenues of access to resources, and concomitant social mobility, are in fact far more restricted than they may have imagined, stymied by glass ceilings, partial entries, and various obstacles of other sorts. These constraints lead to a generalized structure of feeling characterized by disillusionment, depression, anxiety, anger, and resentment. In the midst of this, police experiences of expendability and fungibility reproduce practices that may be counterproductive or even harmful to others, from foot dragging to ignoring or even harassing vulnerable people, perhaps as a means to feel less vulnerable themselves (cf. Scott 1987). Thus, for all the possibilities it may open up for social mobility and perhaps even the critique of social problems, police authority is severely constrained by insecurity in ways that limit the imagination. Such limits are blatant in the hyper-conservatism of the rookie's didactic "Do whatever you can to keep your job."

Like everyone else, police have to wake up each day and try to find or make meaning in their lives. And like everyone else, they struggle along a winding path toward some understanding and realization of "the good life." Unlike everyone else, their sworn duty as state officials and its authoritative force mean they must contend with the incessant dirty work entailed in conflicting demands and duties of order keeping. In so doing, police both struggle with and signify the state as a site and source of insecurity, as its beating and bleeding heart.

As I have explicated throughout this text, for all of its promised benefits and the supposed security of government employment, police life and work are also characterized by extreme insecurity, not just from the occasional danger of interacting with criminal(ized) elements, but more pointedly from the signs of the provisionality of their state authority, particularly the slow violence of their own welfare being ignored by the very state they represent and serve, producing vicious cycles of inability, instability, inequity, and iniquity. The masses of police in India, and arguably elsewhere, exist and operate under the same precarious conditions as the general populous, with some added benefits and protections to be sure, but also with some added burdens and vulnerabilities, not least being both first responders and the last resort in moments of emergency and exigency. Police proceed in their practice only a few steps removed from the "subalterns" they have historically neglected, harassed, and worked to oppress; and the revelation of the tenuousness of their authority is a disquieting reminder that the state authority to provide security is at best ephemeral, at worst illusory. This the real hard lesson of the quoted rookie cops, who are just beginning to tread the path of provisional authority and—unless and until some sociocultural and legal sea changes come to pass—will keep it going for years to come.

Coda: States and Stakes

Police represent an idealized state monopoly on the authority to intervene in situational and structural exigencies with, and as, the legal and legitimate means of provision and coercion. But the grounded realities of this authority reveal how its various ambivalences, ambiguities, and contingencies render a "damned if you do, damned if you don't" police subjectivity and practice that is saturated with excess, inadequacy, and insecurity. Various expressions of police authority, from physical violence and economic extraction to dispute mediation and traffic direction, routinely transgress moral, legal, and other social boundaries. Police powers of discretion may mutate into discrimination that reproduces or exacerbates social inequality and allows them to neglect the needful or hide behind hyper-proceduralism. Their appeals to investigative demands and order keeping work against calls for transparency, accessibility, and accountability. At the same time, police face the impossibility of deploying their authority in a way that is morally and pragmatically right for all people in all time-spaces. They are subject to conflicting public demands and contradictions inherent to law that render much of their work dubious and despicable. The value and virtue of police life and work fluctuate in relation to a generalized lack of control over various contextual factors, from political economic conditions and communal conflicts to local relations of patronage and situational power plays. All of this calls into question the sources and capabilities of the state authority to produce order and provide security.

As I discussed explicitly in chapter 1, "the state" in general is often theorized as a peculiar kind of subject, its forces and relations somehow working externally from "society" and its authority emanating from the will or power of "the sovereign" or "sovereignty" howsoever conceived. The concept of sovereignty has its own strange subjectivity and history, having been variously understood as the Leviathan commanding with the consent of the governed (Hobbes 1968 [1651]), as a totalizing structure of capillary biopower (Foucault 2009 [1977] and 2003 [1976]), as something originating in violence that may be "never present for itself . . . unlocatable" (Derrida 2002, 276), as a "formless . . . nowhere tangible, all-pervasive, ghostly presence" (Benjamin 1978 [1922], 287) or, as more recently proposed by some anthropologists, as a pluralistic "tentative and always emergent form . . . that is performed and designed to generate loyalty, fear, and legitimacy from the neighborhood to the summit of the state" (Hansen and Stepputat 2006, 297), to list just a few reigning conceptions. But if we follow the logic of Manu Anand's statement at the end of chapter 5 that "your authority comes from your resources," and add to it the argument presented here that authority is always already provisional—that is, chronotopic, contingent, and configured by changing and conflicting sociocultural demands rather than sovereign command—then a rather different foundation of state emerges: one in which authority is insecurity writ large.

Expressions and recognitions of authority as insecurity may often serve to close down the imagination of possibilities for productive transformation. People may "work the system" to protect or promote themselves at the expense of others; to kill programs or even other people that do not seem to fall in line with their own politics or interests; to instigate or augment divisiveness, exclusion, and inequality; to gather with persons of their "own kind" in offensive or defensive acts toward their "others"; and to condemn, harm, dismiss, or discriminate against various others who may be vulnerable. Such violent and exclusionary practices signal mistrust and fragmentation that constrain collaboration geared toward good governance and the realization of civil or human rights. At the same time, and as demonstrated throughout this ethnography, the provisionality of authority as expressed inter alia by state police in UP, may also work to open up space for aspiration, agency, and action. Police and their more or less distant associates may work the system to obtain gainful employment with the state and support their families and communities; to proceed with investigations and prevent or prosecute crime; to protect potential victims or compensate designated ones; to mediate or arbitrate disputes and reach some kind of resolution; and perhaps even to realize some version of "justice" in the world. Whatever their intended or unintended consequences, these practices signal aspirations for change, and may be motivated by the hope for positive transformation for some social collective, even if not necessarily working in the interest of the "public good" in toto. The tension wrought between these aspirational and mistrustful relations, where a politics of hope meets a politics of cynicism, configures and reproduces state authority as insecurity incarnate. And the police constitute the primary figure of this state of insecurity.

Appendix

Uttar Pradesh Police Organization

Rank/Pay Scale*	Recruitment Level	Proportion
Class I/A* Indian Police Service (IPS), Gazetted Officers, recruited and trained at the national level		
1. Director General of Police		
2. Additional Director General		
3. Inspector General		
4. Deputy Inspector General		
5. Senior Superintendent		
6. Superintendent		
7. Assistant Superintendent	←Level 1	<1% of police
Class II/B Provincial Police Service (PPS), Gazetted Officers, recruited and trained at the state level		
8. Deputy Superintendent	←Level 2	<1% of police
Inspector, Non-Gazetted Officers, recruited and trained at the state level		
9. Inspector		
10. Senior Sub-Inspector		
11. Sub-Inspector		
12. Assistant Sub-Inspector	←Level 3	<5% of police

(*continued*)

Uttar Pradesh Police Organization (*continued*)

Rank/Pay Scale*	Recruitment Level	Proportion
Class III/C		
Rank and file personnel, recruited and trained at the state level		
13. Head Constable		
14. Senior Constable		
15. Constable	←Level 4	>90% of police
Auxiliary support, not sworn-in police		
Home Guard***		

*Class I/A–IV/D are rank-based pay scale groupings for government employees. They are not congruent with the four lateral levels of recruitment to the UP police, which are indicated above preceded by ← and distinguished from the next level down by ——.

**The minimum education requirements for each level are as follows: (1) Constables: 10th standard; (2) Sub-Inspectors: 12th standard; (3) PPS and IPS: bachelor's degree.

***Home Guard (HG) are not regular police personnel, and are often referred to as "volunteer police." HG are irregularly assigned duties for which they are paid daily wages rather than monthly salaries, and do not receive pensions or other government benefits.

Notes

Chapter One

1. Except in cases of referencing persons whose names have been published elsewhere, I have changed the names of individual persons and local places to protect the identities of interlocutors. I preserve characteristics like regional caste identifiers (e.g., Bihari Brahmin) and religious affiliation (e.g., Muslim), since these are crucial factors in the constitution of personal, professional, and political relationships and interactions in India.

2. In May 2015 the Parliament of India passed the Black Money (Undisclosed Foreign Income and Assets) and Imposition of Tax Act. At the time of writing, just over six hundred official declarations had been made under this act, by or of people having black money deposits amounting to more than Rs. 3,700 crores (Rs. 37 trillion or approximately US$565 million). Critics claimed that amount was only a small fraction of the lot in circulation.

3. Interlocutors generally spoke with me in a mixture of Hindi and English, depending on their facility with the languages. Many senior officials with the Indian Police Service (IPS) spoke fluent English, while most officials in the subordinate ranks of Provincial Police Service (PPS), sub-inspectors and constables (see appendix), spoke little to no English. For readability, I have generally translated any utterances made in Hindi into English without writing out the statement in the original Hindi. Occasionally, if I feel the original Hindi (or Urdu) word or phrase has a particular linguistic or lyrical value, I transliterate it into Roman script and follow with English translation. With the exception of several semi-structured interviews, mostly with retired IPS officers, none of the observations or interactions discussed herein were recorded as audio or video files, but instead were reconstructed in field notes hand written and typed by myself. I systematically wrote notes in both Hindi and English immediately during, or as soon as possible following, an observation or interaction, sometimes in consultation with my research assistant if he was present, in order to record as much detail and analysis as possible, and to recall terminology and phrasing as precisely as possible. Even so, I acknowledge the intractable problem, especially in long block quotations, that an utterance represented as manifesting an interlocutor's "voice" is always inflected by my own.

4. If the regular payments are made on a weekly instead of monthly basis, they are referred to as *hafta*, the Hindi word for "week."

5. For an in-depth account and analysis of this story, see Jauregui 2013a.

6. It is relatively easy to guess the identities of some police personnel, especially senior officers, by triangulating their rank with their posting at a particular time, especially since this information may be publicly available. Therefore, I will generally engage in some "strategic imprecision" when describing people and their positions. For example, when I believe that it is important to specify the division or department in which an officer serves at a particular time, I may refrain from specifying his or her rank or title and instead use generic terms like "senior officer."

7. I was less surprised when in April 2007 another riot broke out between police and lawyers in Allahabad, Lucknow, and Varanasi (PTI 2007).

8. See Spencer 2007 for an incisive critique of the assumption of state externality in the South Asia context specifically.

9. I purposely use the analytical terms "official" and "unofficial" to index the subject positions, expressed motivations, and potential capabilities of state office holders, rather than the less precise terms "formal" and "informal" unless quoting or referring to someone else's usage of the latter terms.

10. Weber has been translated as writing both "legal coercion by violence" (1978 [1919], 314) and "legitimate coercion by violence" (1958a [1918], 78). Obviously, the difference matters, and this analysis aims in part to explicate the relationship, and the distinction, between legality as codified rules and legitimation as plural social processes of rendering moral support and justification. See also chapter 3.

11. Cf. John Comaroff 2013. For discussion of this point in the South Asia context see Kolff 1990, and a critical response in Alavi 1995. See also Das and Poole 2004.

12. Egon Bittner (1990) refers to policing in all three of these senses, in terms of police officials' (temporal and allocational) empowerment to "coerce a provisional solution upon emergent problems without having to brook or defer to opposition of any kind" when called upon by "citizen demand" (234, 252), and in relation to the history of the public police having a direct relationship with the expansion of "the provisions of criminal law" (236). Bittner focuses more on considering the various sources and consequences of what he calls the core police function of deploying "non-negotiably coercive force" (1970, 46), rather than on theorizing questions of police authority and its legitimacy per se, though he does make it a point to discuss the stigma attached to police work (ibid., 44–45).

13. *Herrschaft* is sometimes translated as "legitimate domination," qualifying coercion as subject to the will of "the coerced" to some degree.

14. Cf. Austin 1995 [1832] on law as a species of command handed down by the sovereign.

15. The rule is listed under Point 1, List 2, Seventh Schedule (Article 246) of the Constitution of India.

16. Unless directly quoting or referring to another source, on the few occasions in this text when mention is made of certain major metropoli in India like Bangalore, Bombay, Calcutta, or Madras, I generally will use what many consider to be the older "colonial" names for the cities, rather than the names Bengaluru, Mumbai, Kolkata, or Chennai, respectively, established as "official" by regionalist or nationalist parties. I do this purposely to keep the ongoing and problematic influences of the colonial past at the forefront of consideration of various social and political problems of policing (especially the imbrication of police rank hierarchy with class conflict), and also to signal my preferred distance from the chauvinistic ideological leanings of some of the parties who have called for some of these name changes. For example, the demand to refer to Bombay as Mumbai has strong links with the often virulent identity politics of Marathi dominance and right-wing Hindu nationalism in the region, spurred on by collectives like the Shiv Sena (Hansen 2001).

17. For further reading on crowd violence and ethnoreligious communalism in India, see Guha 1983, Freitag 1989, van der Veer 1994, Kakar 1996, Brass 1997 and 2008, Rai 1998, Hansen 2001, Srivastava and Chauhan 2002, Khalidi 2003, Engineer and Narang 2006, Nussbaum 2009.

18. Part of the reason for this shift had to do with the Mandal Commission, which was established in 1979 to analyze the needs of historically disenfranchised castes in postcolonial India. The Commission submitted recommendations in 1980 to implement a system of what are known as "reservations" or affirmative action quotas in public postings—from school students to government servants—for persons of castes and tribes designated as historically oppressed or underserved social minorities. This system includes reserved voting constituencies wherein only persons from certain designated minority groups could contest seats. The recommendations began to be implemented in many states in the early 1990s, inciting protests from persons associated with "general castes" or historically elite groups. To date, there continue to be enormous backlogs of reserved entitlements to government postings (in the police and other departments) and ongoing litigation around such issues in many states, including and especially in UP.

19. Note also that the incongruous social categories of caste and class themselves are not statically hierarchical (cf. Dumont 1970). There are wealthy or otherwise influential "lower caste" people, and there are "higher caste" or "general caste" persons who are poor or relatively lacking in social influence (Jauregui 2014a; Price 1999).

20. The 2011 national census reports the population of Lucknow city at just over 2.8 million, and the population of Lucknow district, including its surrounding rural areas, at just over 4.5 million (http://www.censusindia.gov.in/).

21. For an incisive critique of theories positing a clear, static, and memetic Royal Irish Constabulary "model," see Hawkins 1991.

22. Police lines also serve as sites of abeyance or refuge for subordinate officers who are between postings, and thus categorized as *line haazir* (literally, merely "present" or "existing" on the Lines) or attached to the police lines without a specific post for the moment. Y. K. Yadav was assigned this status for a while upon being removed from his post as SO of CRT, as discussed in chapter 5.

23. A *chowkidar* usually inherits his position from his forebears. At CRT, one or two *chowkidars* from a local village would be assigned to come to the station each night to perform minor duties like mechanical maintenance or throwing water on the ground to minimize dust storms during dry hot months, for which they would receive a nominal income: it was reportedly Rs. 500 (USD $10) per month in 2006, and Rs. 1500 at the time of writing. Beyond being asked to do manual labor, a *chowkidar* would be expected to share information with the police about what was going on in his village—who was arguing with whom, what sorts of strangers had happened by, what sorts of unusual events had occurred, etc. For more on this and other precolonial policing institutions, see Cohn 1971, 1987 [1965], 1996 [1989]; Gupta, 1974; Kolff 1990.

24. There exists a quota system demanding that at least one out of three IPS officers be promoted from the PPS rather than directly recruited to the IPS. And apparently, on very rare occasions, an individual may jump two levels up. I heard an unconfirmed rumor about a man recruited as a constable eventually rising to the rank of PPS-level deputy superintendent of police, or DySP, because he was particularly "well-connected." Such mobility may be possible for a few individuals, but it is improbable for the masses of police.

25. There is surprisingly little scholarly analysis of police union movements and labor politics in postcolonial India, including and especially police strikes and uprisings, of which there

have been many since 1947 even though they are legally banned (see chap. 6, notes 6 and 7). There was a particularly violent uprising of police constables across Uttar Pradesh in May 1973, which has been mentioned in passing by a few historians and political economists (see, for example, Roy 1974; Baxi 1982; Frankel 2005; Brass 2010). The event has also received brief and mostly descriptive treatment in several historical or sociological analyses of problems of policing in India written from the perspective of retired senior police officers or civil servants (Arun 1995 and 2010; Chande 1997; Ghosh 1981; Dhillon 2005; Subramanian 1988; Maheswari 1978). But the dominance of senior officers' perspectives is problematic, especially considering many constables involved in union movements and uprisings have viewed senior officers as their primary nemesis. There remains much research to be done on these issues.

26. For further examples and discussion of this idiomatic use of "cutting edge" in India, see Chande 1997, 213; Subramanian 2007; Erayil and Vadackumchery 1984; Mehra and Levy 2011, 4, 47, 276; Banerjea 2005, 54–55, 71, 74; Ghosh 2007.

27. For more on how politicized and common it is to appoint specific officers as DGPs toward the end of their careers, see ENS 2015a.

28. The same was true for my attempts to visit the national-level Sardar Vallabhai Patel National Police Academy in Hyderabad, where the IPS officers train before being deputed to the states. I did not manage to visit the NPA until 2010, as part of a teaching team based at the University of Cambridge contracted by the Government of India to conduct mid-career training courses for senior officers.

29. Because the capital city of UP changed several times under British colonial rule, the "center" of policing in UP historically has been divided. Today there remains a dual headquarters structure. The DGP Headquarters, which functions as a kind of center of executive operations, is located in Lucknow, while the official UPP Headquarters (PHQ), which constitutes more of a center of administration (the home of budget, personnel, and various other types of files), is located in Allahabad, about 4–5 hours from Lucknow by train. The UP High Court is similarly divided, with a center in the earlier capital of Allahabad and a "Lucknow Bench."

30. While smaller districts usually have chiefs at the rank of superintendent of police, several larger districts have a senior superintendent, or SSP, and at certain times some large cities like Lucknow have even had a chief with the rank of deputy inspector general (DIG) (see appendix for UPP rank organization). As with just about everything in UP, the required minimum rank of district chiefs and even the administrative structure itself are "provisional" and subject to change, since various regimes and executive leaders may have different preferences for how best to govern. Some may prefer a more "direct" control from the center, while others may prefer a more delegated form of governance. Over the many years that I have been doing research with the UPP, I have witnessed, among other changes: the number of state districts change from seventy-one to seventy-five, the dissolution and reinstatement of zones of jurisdiction, and multiple shifts in the ranks of officers selected for particular leadership positions. See also Sharma 2014 for a discussion of how the recruitment structures for government teachers may shift depending on the regime and then get "stuck in litigation," a problem that plagues most government service sectors (see also chap. 1 note 18).

31. I would occasionally read articles about myself printed in both Hindi and English news sources reporting various fictions—for example, claims that I was in Lucknow studying the voting habits of women—or showing a tabloid type photo of me on "Page 3" as a kind of celebrity moving about town or attending some local event. Like many anthropologists in the field, I stuck out like a sore thumb.

32. I am well aware of critiques of Geertz's conception and valuation of anthropological "rapport" between ethnographers and interlocutors, especially in the postcolonial context (see Clifford 1988; Rosaldo 1993; Marcus 1997; and Gupta and Ferguson 1997). And I do not mean to suggest that my access to CRT or to any other part of the UPP "world" was unlimited (see chap. 1, note 34), nor to imply that my subject position as a visibly foreign woman and an American scholar had no discernible impact on my police interlocutors' willingness to engage with me, and on their interactions with and around me (see chap 5, note 21). But the unusual and unprecedented access to the world of "cutting-edge" police that I did manage to attain—however partial, problematic, or even performative it may have been—also may not be reduced simply to my enjoying the fruits of (neo)colonial global power structures. A variety of factors came into play, not least my Hindi and Urdu language training, gender, age, and personal biography (Jauregui forthcoming).

33. This is not to say that other social science methods—including archival research, case studies, sociological surveys and experiments, or political economic, legal and policy analyses—fail to provide much needed knowledge and insights about many crucial elements of policing. But these methods of knowledge production do not routinely attend to the fundamental roles of ordinary interactions, relationships of exchange and cultural modes of meaning-making that are vital components of how policing is co-configured with social order and security.

34. See chap. 1 note 32. My access was something that had to be continually negotiated and repeatedly "reclaimed." And notably, there were several instances, especially early on in my ethnographic relationship with CRT personnel, when the SO did require me to obtain more "official" permission from a senior officer in the chain of command to conduct observations in the field. For example, on the first day of the 2006 Lucknow municipal elections—some of the goings on of which are discussed in chapters 2 and 6—Y. K. Yadav said that I could only accompany him and other CRT police on "election duty", which involved visiting and surveilling activities around polling booths, after receiving permission from "a higher authority." I called the district SSP, with whom I had already met several times, and he said it was fine with him and that he would make sure the appropriate subdivision officers were aware that I had his permission to observe.

35. In 2014 the UPP claimed that they would finally replace .303 rifles with hand guns, but that the process would take a long time (PTI 2014a).

36. For more on the village community atmosphere at CRT, see Jauregui forthcoming.

37. This may be compared with a larger *thana* in Lucknow city that I visited early on. The officially sanctioned number of personnel at this urban police station was more than one hundred sworn officers including the station chief; but, according to the register, the actual allocation of officers working on the day I visited, either in the station or out in the field, amounted to about half that number. So, it was functioning at about 50 percent capacity. I was told this is common.

38. In Jauregui 2013a, I discuss at some length what police often refer to as the "VIP problem" in India. See also ZMB 2013.

39. See esp. Kabir 2005, Criminal Procedural Code Chapter 12, "Information to the Police and Their Powers to Investigate," esp. secs. 154–59 and 166–68.

40. By calling this authority "unique" I do not mean to suggest that police in India—or anywhere else—do in fact constitute the Weberian ideal of a state monopoly on legal and legitimate violence. Any number of other actors besides police may be seen as legitimately or even legally deploying violence, especially in self-defense; and of course, police may be seen as illegitimately or extralegally deploying violence.

Chapter Two

1. CRT police and others also used the word "jack" for *jugaad*. I could not determine the origin of this synonym, which seems to be an English, or what some jokingly call "Hinglish," derivative. One of the crudely gendered and sexualized "humorous" maxims in circulation was that in order to get any "unofficial" work done, one needed to express or apply (in English), "money, jack, and back." The last of the three terms refers to the more or less willing submission of one's "back side" to the powers that be.

2. To view clips of these portions of the film, see YouTube.com 2010a, 2010b.

3. It is worth considering this statement by the filmmaker in light of a popular Bollywood comedy film titled *Jugaad* (Kumar 2009). The Bollywood film portrays a wealthy entrepreneur on the brink of financial ruin after his office is shut down during an infamous real-life "sealing drive" in New Delhi in 2006 resulting from changes in zoning laws disallowing businesses to be located in designated residential areas. The protagonist of the story must apply *jugaad* to reopen his multimillion-dollar advertising firm and reclaim his life in the face of obstacles constructed by corrupt government officials abusing their powers to regulate. Significantly, the film signals that *jugaad* is the necessary tool of the "everyman" but also represents it as an ability that is vital to upper or aspiring middle-class persons realizing neoliberal ideals of capitalist progress and individual enterprise.

4. *Hamraah* translates to "traveling companion." When referring to *a hamraahi* relationship between constables and their boss, the chief station officer, it signifies the SO's "favorites," near and dear subordinates whom he likes to keep with him for assistance with "special" duties. Sometimes a caste or other communal bias shapes *hamraahi* police relationships. The relationship reflects a mixture of favor based partly on personal factors—such as a constable being obsequious or enjoyable company or being well liked by the SO's children—and partly on work-related pragmatic factors, such as a subordinate being especially adept at negotiating compromises among disputants or, indeed, bribes for service on behalf of a superior officer. In any case, *hamraahi* police are rarely assigned by their seniors to do less desirable duties and in some cases may be able to earn more black money than their peers because they have a close relationship with an officer who has more decision-making power and, thus, higher unofficial earning potential. At CRT, Constable Prithvi emerged as SO Yadav's key *hamraah*. For more on how police cultivate personal as well as professional relationships with colleagues as a means to get things done, see chapter 5 and Jauregui forthcoming.

5. See chapter 1, note 24.

6. See Ruud 2000 for a discussion of similar expressions among persons trying to obtain positions as government school teachers and Class 4 employees at public hospitals in West Bengal.

7. Including piecemeal allowances for cost-of-living increases, monthly pay for constables at the time of writing can reach Rs. 10,000–12,000 (US$150–180 at the exchange rate of Rs. 60/US$1). But when I was doing fieldwork in 2006–2007, and prior to a UP state government approval of recommendations by the Sixth Central Pay Commission in 2008, the starting salary for constables was Rs. 3,050 per month, about US$76 at the then exchange rate of about Rs. 40/US$1. This amount hovers on the poverty line, and was often cited by senior police as the reason why corruption was "built into the system" (see chap. 6), meaning constables *had* to supplement their meager official incomes just to make ends meet. While in the field, I heard numbers ranging from Rs. 5,000 to Rs. 15,000 quoted as the "average" *kaalaa daan* (black money) earnings a constable could make in a month. And note that constables were also paying bribes, not just

taking them. Crucially, constables complain that they rarely receive the full amount of pay and allowances they are owed because of "hidden fees" and deductions and more or less explicit demands for bribes by the clerks issuing their checks and by bosses for a cut of their earnings in return for giving them desirable duties (again, see chap. 6). Regarding similar situations among police in Ghana and Nigeria, see Beek 2013 and Rotimi 2013, respectively.

8. These problems are very gendered. I have not worked closely with any women constables, but I know that there are other types of domestic pressures placed on women in addition to or instead of being economic "providers."

9. Ergo the previous notes, another important relative who is often intimately involved in fixing deals for police family members are spouses, especially (since the vast majority of police are still men) wives. Police wives often become actively involved in making "arrangements" for their husbands, not only because this deflects any possible blame away from the actual officers if things go awry, but also because the officers themselves are so busy with other aspects of their jobs that they do not always have time to take care of such "menial" business themselves. Occasionally, wives may also have better social connections than their husbands.

10. For an analysis that compares this socioeconomic form with practiced concepts in other cultural contexts, especially *guanxi* in China, see Jauregui 2014a.

11. Few bother to problematize the cultural essentialism inherent to increased global lauding of *jugaad* and its pride of place in books with titles like *The India Way* (Cappelli et al. 2010; for an exception, see Philip et al. 2010).

12. Cf. discussion of police *dharma* and violence as service in chapter 4.

13. The idea of corruption as service and its implications may also be directly related to the idea and implications of violence as service, discussed in chapter 4. Further exploration of this relationship, in India and elsewhere, could open a vast and fruitful field of inquiry.

14. I write "Mumbai" rather than "Bombay" here to reflect Anjaria's use of the term. See chap.1, note 16.

15. See Juggadinnovation.com 2011, associated with the book *Juggad Innovation* (Radjou et al. 2012).

Chapter Three

1. I note during my fieldwork that the terms "suspect" or "accused" are rarely used by police to describe persons listed in reports, arrested and charged. In the Crime Register at CRT and most UP *thanas* where I have conducted observations, there is a column reading *apraadhi ka naam, pita ka nam va puura pata* (criminal's name, father's name and full address). Another column lists the *tafsiir karne wale kaa naam* (name of the person giving the detailed account), which is often translated into English as "opposite party." When I am shown individual station statistics for "solving crimes" (i.e., framing charges and sending an accused to court, the usual proportion of which hovers around 60 percent), I see that most of the cases in which the "opposite party" is not named remain unsolved. This, combined with the routine "unofficial" resolution of cases I observe proceed with little to no evidence except for "witness testimony," indicates that verbal reporting is a more common form of "evidence" than material forensics, and that framing a crime as a dispute between aggressor-cum-criminal and complainant-cum-victim is also common (cf. Valverde 2003 regarding law's "flexible collage of knowledges").

2. Complaints of "kidnapping" are routinely brought to police when young couples elope and their families or community members disapprove. These reported "crimes" usually have more to

do with the ways in which *izzat* (social honor) works through gendered control of bodies than they do with signifying actual abduction or coercion. For more on this with specific attention to a "culture of compromise" around rape prosecutions, see Baxi 2010.

3. Beyond the military, the idea of "orders" in association with rank in a hierarchy actually comes from the Christian church in association with clergy members who are consecrated in a particular community by receiving "holy orders" (OED 2015).

4. Cf. Fassin 2013 regarding "enforcing" a social order of othering that exists beyond the police institution.

5. The military orderly is a subaltern officer who "carries out orders and performs minor tasks for a superior officer" (OED 2015). The "orderly room" or "a room in barracks in which the business of a company is carried on" (ibid.) is an ongoing institution on the police lines in Uttar Pradesh, which includes "the business" of senior officers disciplining cutting-edge police for minor infractions.

6. Early in the film, Harry's new partner, Chico Gonzales, asks him, "Why do they call you 'Dirty Harry'?" Another detective nearby says, "Ah, that's one thing about our Harry, doesn't play any favorites! Harry hates everybody," and he proceeds to utter a list of racial slurs for English, Irish, Arabic, Italian, African-American, Chinese, and generally "white" people, suggesting Harry hates them all and this hate is the source of his "dirtiness". Later, after working with Harry on the serial killer case and experiencing the difficulties of catching the culprit, Gonzalez says sympathetically, "No wonder they call him Dirty Harry. Always gets the shit-end of the stick." There are also a couple of consciously ironic "comic relief" moments in the film where Harry exhibits "peeping tom" behavior while on police stakeouts, hinting that he may be sexually "dirty" as well.

7. Other Hollywood and Bollywood films besides *Dirty Harry* that raise awareness of the coterminousness of external and excessive police violence with justice and necessity—and the concomitant indeterminacy of legality, morality and ethics—include *Insomnia* (Nolan 2002), *The Dark Knight* (Nolan 2008), *Cop Land* (Mangold 1997), *Ardh Satya* (Nihalani 1983), *Kurukshetra* (Manjrekar 2000), *Gangaajal* (Jha 2003), *Ab Tak Chappan* (Amin 2004), and *Sehar* (Kaushik 2005).

8. *Randwa* is a derogatory Hindi term for an elderly person (usually, though not necessarily, a male) who either has never married or has been widowed without begetting children—or, pointedly, without begetting sons as heirs. In some families with multiple brothers, only one brother will be allowed to marry and have children so as to avoid too much fragmentation of the family land when it is inherited by the next generation. But the remaining unmarried and childless brothers, who become stigmatized as *randwa*, still have a right to some of the land. As these bachelors age, they are increasingly in danger of being killed off by relatives who may want to grab their portion of the family land. This is apparently such a widespread problem that one of my interlocutors who was a district SSP in western UP actually started a special police watch list of elderly bachelors who could be potential *randwa pratha* victims, to try to protect them.

9. The only exception to this rule comes in IEA section 26, which allows a confession made to police in the presence of a magistrate; otherwise, a confession may only be recorded by a civil or judicial magistrate directly. It was not made clear to me by Yadav or any other CRT police whether the murder suspect in this case had made a recorded confession when he turned himself into the court.

10. In its entirety, the law says: "How much of information received from accused may be proved—Provided that, when any fact is deposed to as discovered in consequence of information received from a person accused of any offence, in the custody of a police officer, so much

of such information, whether it amounts to a confession or not, as relates distinctly to the fact thereby discovered, may be proved." Some legal experts have gone so far as to say that this IEA section 27 loophole is the primary reason that police in India regularly resort to torture in interrogations. The claim is that if they can use torture to extract information that leads to real and admissible evidence, then they can say that the suspect "volunteered" the information and that this led the police to the evidence (see Attokaran 2007). For further discussion of police interrogation in UP, see Jauregui 2013b and chapter 4.

11. In an interview with a retired IPS officer appointed to the recently formed (2002) UP Human Rights Commission, I am told that the Uttar Pradesh Human Rights Commission receives about nine hundred complaints per month on average (about thirty per day), most of which are against police, and the vast majority of which have to do with problems of police investigation—that is, not writing up reports, omitting or adding names to reports, inadequate attention, or not making an arrest quickly enough. This officer adds that "even the most honest cops with the best intentions, and doing everything according to the books, can often only get a 50 percent arrest or clearance rate that leads to prosecution, because witnesses become intimidated, or are wishy-washy, or there is just not enough evidence." The fact that it is a tough job made tougher by lack of resources, legal restrictions, and the power of politicians and others to influence and interfere in investigations and prosecutions should not be discounted any more than the fact that police often misuse their legal authority.

12. Besides erstwhile evidence, when police confiscate property and the owner from whom it was seized is too scared or otherwise disinclined to return to the *thana* to claim it, they auction it off as well to try to make some extra money to put into public coffers, with the stated intent of improving public services. See figs. 6 and 7.

13. The Bahujan Samaj Party (BSP) opposition, led by Mayawati, campaigned primarily on the claim that a reported decrease in crime in UP was completely false, and that the BSP was UP's only hope for the return of "law and order." The BSP won by a landslide in the 2007 General Assembly elections, and for the first time in more than fifteen years, a single party gained a majority and did not have to form a coalition government. To be clear, I would not support any claim that leaders of any one political party are more or less likely to give orders to keep reported numbers down by "any means necessary." My data collection occurred under specific historical circumstances in which certain individuals and groups happened to hold official positions; but it could have happened with a different ruling party in power, and with different individuals in particular offices.

14. The complexities of the policing and prosecution of gendered violence in India are beyond the scope of this analysis (see Vatuk 2006; Baxi 2010; Roychowdhury 2015; and, for a comparative perspective, see Corrigan 2013; Hautzinger 2016). But it is important to note how the umbrella term "domestic violence" is legally distinguished from other, sometimes overlapping, forms of gendered violence. While the fallout from the internationally infamous 2012 "Delhi gang rape" led to various Indian legal developments concerning sexual violence—such as the 2013 Criminal Law (Amendment) Act and the Sexual Harassment of Women at Workplace (Prevention, Prohibition, and Redressal) Act—domestic violence (and dowry) laws remained untouched.

15. For more on the strength of *dharma* as justification for violence, see chapter 4. For a broad overview of some of the active and passive threats against women in India, and the UPP's general (lack of) response as represented in popular media, see Jain 2014, Masih and Ghosh 2014, PTI 2014b.

16. IPC section 498-A "Punishment for subjecting a married woman to cruelty."

17. A *pradhan*, who would often negotiate with police on villagers' behalf, was usually a local man (or, occasionally, a woman) affiliated with the ruling political party and elected by the people. Pradhan would often make "casual visits" to meet the CRT SO to perform their power while also expressing the understanding that the station chief could dole out, withhold, and bring down the full force of the law when and if he chose to do so (Jauregui 2014b).

18. For a comparative historical case, see Marquis 1992 regarding moral policing of women in early twentieth-century Toronto, wherein certain women (e.g., married with children) were provided with help while others (e.g., unwed mothers of lower classes) were judged as unworthy of assistance.

Chapter Four

1. Many people also refer to it as Police Shaheed (Martyr) Diwas, and the Urdu word *shaheed* and English word "martyr" are also routinely used in written text and speeches to refer to police killed in action. See https://uppolice.gov.in/page.aspx?homage-to-martyres-of-up -police&cd=MQAyADcAMgA%3d, accessed October 31, 2015. The official UP state use of the Sanskrit-derived Hindi word *smriti* for "remembrance" rather than the Arabic-derived Urdu word *shaheed* for "martyr" is an explicitly political choice, likely intended to appeal to the Hindu majority population.

2. The word *jawan* derives from the Persian word for "youth," and in South Asia it is used most often to describe low-ranking soldiers, constables, warriors, literally translated as "able-bodied young men" (McGregor 2002).

3. For an edited clip of the 2014 iteration of the ceremony with Mulayam's son, Akhilesh Yadav, who became UP chief minister for the first time in 2012, see YouTube 2014.

4. The number of BSF KIAs counted in 2005–6 was 101. The police force in Jammu and Kashmir, in which violent conflict has raged for decades between Indian military and police forces against allegedly Pakistani and Chinese government backed insurgents, counted "only" seventy-one police constable KIAs that same year; and the next highest reported numbers of dead came from the states of West Bengal and Andhra Pradesh, both known for heated Naxalite (Maoist) insurgent activity, which tied for a total of twenty-six police KIAs each.

5. The rapid deconstruction of the set is visible in fig. 15, which was taken immediately following the ceremony.

6. The family compensation rate for UPP KIA in 2014 was Rs. 2 million, or approximately $30,000. Regarding other compensatory benefits, see chapter 4, note 22.

7. See chapter 4, note 1.

8. The reported number of UPP dead on Police Commemoration Day 2015 was 108 out of a total of 434 across the country, so almost 25 percent of the national total and "nearly eleven times higher than that of Maharashtra, [India's] second most populous state." (ENS 2015b).

9. http://icasualties.org/, accessed October 30, 2015.

10. Cf. Visvanathan and Sethi (1998) discussion of corruption as prosaic "work" cited in chapter 2.

11. For comparative arguments regarding "popular justice" in various African countries, including Ghana, South Africa and Nigeria, see Cooper-Knock 2014, Cooper-Knock and Owen 2015, Hornberger 2013, Tankebe 2013. See also Spencer 2007 on the state as a resource.

12. For a discussion of the inconsistencies in reported national statistics on the incidence and prevalence of encounter killings, see Jauregui 2015.

13. Julia Eckert (2005, 196) quotes a business person in Bombay saying, "Encounter killings are a good thing. But people who are innocent are killed. But it is necessary."

14. Eckert (2005, 195) also cites a novel by Indian Police Service officer Yogesh Pratap Singh, *Carnage by Angels* (the title arguably says it all), which asserts that "corruption is the force of evil, the true killer in society and true violator of human rights . . . you have to be brutal—brutality and corruption here are opposites" (cf. Chandra 2006; Mehta 2004).

15. I thank Umesh Jois for assistance with translating the Sanskrit.

16. Krishna is an avatar of Vishnu, the god of preservation, in contrast to the god of creation, Brahma, and the god of destruction, Shiva. This appeal to divine preservation of order is important to keep in mind when applying deified figures and energies to the Hindu-majority police in India.

17. The soldier motif is often applied to police in popular discourse. Moreover, the words "sepoy" and *jawan* (chapter 4, note 2), which are generally used to refer to military soldiers, are also routinely applied to police constables in northern India, especially the former term, which is also transliterated as "sepahi". But this linguistic convergence does not mean that police are generally conceived as isomorphic with soldiers of the national army (Jauregui 2010a and 2010b). While army soldiers fight wars against "foreign" others, there is a widely shared sense that "the enemy" the police are fighting may be something beyond individual criminal persons, terrorists, or enemy combatants. It is something more like evil incarnate, howsoever that may be defined.

18. Notably, *Ardh Satya* is an "art house" Hindi language film produced in a "gritty realism" vein rather than a Bollywood film with spectacular song sequences, mass distribution, and popular appeal, like *Kurukshetra*. The audience who has seen the former film is therefore probably much smaller in size and perhaps (though not necessarily) more likely to have come from relatively well-educated and "urbane" social classes. Even so, the allusions and metaphors *Ardh Satya* deploys permeate widely and are thus relevant to an analysis of how police imaginaries may be constructed and shared among a vast swath of the Indian public.

19. The city of Ayodhya is located in central Uttar Pradesh in Faizabad district, and has seen intense controversy and communal violence around a disputed site where a mosque, the Babri Masjid, was demolished in 1992 by Hindu activists who claimed it had been built over a temple marking the birthplace of Ram. This incited religious riots and pogroms against Muslims, which continue to flare up occasionally across the state around various issues, including rumors of persons handling, selling, or consuming beef. Police in UP and other areas of India are notorious for siding with the general caste Hindu social majority when crowd violence erupts, either by passively allowing attacks on Muslim, low-caste, or Dalit persons (and places) or even by actively abetting or participating in such attacks (van der Veer 1994; Nussbaum 2009; Rai 1998; Brass 1997; Engineer and Narang 2006; Hansen 2001). See chapter 1, note 17.

20. Viewing this latter structural dilemma of ideally "controlled" police violence with more emphasis on the legal angle, in an admittedly different historical context, Nasser Hussain (2003) analyzes the convoluted and often vague laws regarding police use of force in colonial South Asia as evincing the impossibility of "hitting the precise line," or meting out just the "right" quality and quantity of violence, at the "right" times, upon the "right" people according to law.

21. Foucault conceived the historical rise of biopower as a shift away from the sovereign power to "make die, let live" and toward the institutionalized capability to "make live, let die" in ways that discriminate among and against different populations or (sub)species of persons.

22. Each state government has its own standard ex gratia rates compensating families of police killed or permanently disabled while on the job, though the chief minister may decide under

certain conditions to grant an amount different from this rate. Recent reports indicate that families of UPP constables killed in the line of duty may receive a one time payment of Rs. 20 lakhs as well as a pension earned up to that point (see chap. 4, note 6). There is also a provision reserving a job with the police for one family member of each officer killed in the line of duty, though as evidenced by the complaints of police widows following the Police Commemoration Day ceremony, there may not always be follow through on this rule in the immediate or long term. Several police at CRT noted that sometimes such delay results from fellow police suspecting familial "foul play" in having their police relative killed in order to claim compensation, analogous to the *randwa pratha* phenomenon. See chapter 3, note 8.

23. For example, while I conducted fieldwork in March 2013, the killing of UP Deputy Superintendent of Police Zia ul Haq—allegedly on orders from an infamous "criminal politician" named Raghuraj Pratap Singh, a.k.a. "Raja Bhaiya"—made national and even international headlines for months until the latter was officially exonerated by the Indian Central Bureau of Investigation in August of that year.

24. The remaining 126 or 17 percent of police deaths were attributed to "anti-terrorist/extremist operations" or "other criminals," and 8 or 1.1 percent happened during unspecified "border duties."

25. Death rates were pretty evenly spread across age ranges, though the largest proportion of police who died while on duty, 276 or 37.3 percent, were over forty-five years old. Another 3,723 police reportedly sustained injuries on the job.

26. The latter category of "incidents of police firing" presumably includes many incidents that may also be categorized as "encounters," though no clear link with or listing of these types of police killings is made in the reports.

27. See chapter 1, note 35.

28. The *ardh kumbh mela* is part of the world's largest recurring religious pilgrimage during which tens of millions of Hindus gather periodically to bathe and purify themselves. This festival happens every twelve years in Allahabad (which is also, recall, the site of the UPP Headquarters), the sole site of the *sangam* (confluence) of three sacred rivers: the Ganges, the Yamuna, and the "invisible" underground Saraswati. Policing this festival involves mass scale temporary infrastructure to accommodate the enormous crowds, and an estimated seventy million people attended the 2007 *mela*.

29. Their accommodations were similar to those depicted in figs. 20–21.

30. Police subjection to threat is also apparent in the official reporting of 684 incidents of police firing in 2013 (NCRB 2013, 155).

Chapter Five

1. Elections in UP occur in phases over several weeks. During the 2007 state legislative assembly election, the number of external police assigned to election duty significantly outsized that of UP state police doing the same. UPP officers were allowed to operate only along the margins of polling booths, not to come inside.

2. I refrain from naming the district to maintain confidentiality. See chapter 1, note 6.

3. Sometimes transfer orders also come as mobile phone text messages.

4. As indicated in chapter 1, Yadav and others speculated that there could be many reasons for his relatively long tenure as CRT station chief, among them: (1) CRT is not a major *earning thana* (i.e., not a big black money maker), so there is less competition for the job of SO there than at some other stations; (2) the string of district SSPs who had been his bosses did not demand

bribes to keep the post (which may have been a function of it being a less desirable post), with one exception, a person who Yadav said was transferred out of the district chief post himself before he could "punish" Yadav with a transfer out of the CRT SO post for not paying the demanded bribe; and (3) he has a reputation for being a relatively honest officer who is tough on criminals, and does his job well enough that the locals do not complain about him (which is another common reason SOs are transferred—the people complain to local politicians, who then work to realize the needs and wants of their constituents). I say "relatively honest" because various sources, including Yadav himself, revealed that as CRT SO he could usually gather somewhere in the range of Rs. 50,000–60,000 (US\$1250–1,500 at the then exchange rate of approximately Rs.40/US\$1) in black money earnings per month. This is a relatively modest sum when compared with the amounts of *kaalaa daan* earnings reported to be possible in some other district stations.

5. See chap. 1, note 18, and also chap. 2 and chap. 6, regarding how inter-caste and communal competition and conflict configures electoral politics and access to state resources in UP, especially through the system of reservations.

6. The phrase "political interference" among police and other bureaucrats tends to serve as a vague catch all attribution of some outside or unofficial force—usually though not necessarily associated with the influence of elected officials or political party machinations—shaping official decisions and actions in undesirable ways. For an example of how the problem not only permeates public discourse on governance, but also may be enshrined in law, see Johari 2014.

7. The annual report on basic police data across India (BPRD 2014, 152) has one list of "State/UT-wise number of police officers transferred within less than one and two years" (in which UP, as usual, reflects a superlative high compared with other states); but this is a very limited data set, only listing district SSP and range DIG senior level numbers, an infinitesimal fraction of the whole. See also Malhotra 2008. Other than these sources, to my knowledge no one has tried to comprehensively calculate rates and types of transfers among all police, nationally or in a single state. I would encourage anyone with the resources and stamina to try to map these movements.

8. For an in-depth anthropological analysis of "red tape" in India, see Gupta 2012, not least the paperback cover, which uses an image drawn from the insightful photo series "Bureaucratics" by Jan Banning. http://blogchucuto.wordpress.com/2011/05/17/jan-banning-bureaucratics/, accessed October 30, 2015.

9. That said, at the time of writing, there is a link on the UPP website listing some transfer orders. Like the BPRD list (chap. 5, note 7) this list includes mostly transfers of gazetted officers (appendix). But it also includes some lists of transfers of non-gazetted officers dating back to 2013. See https://uppolice.gov.in/frmOrderDetails.aspx?slugName=dgphq&cd=NgA1ADAA, accessed October 30, 2015.

10. On my purposeful use of the terms "official" and "unofficial" over "formal" and "informal," see chapter 1, note 9.

11. Notably, IPS officers would often complain about the colonial inheritance of what is known as the "dual system" of public order governance, wherein Indian Administrative Service (IAS) officers would have more power and perks, and be favored by elected officials over police of analogous ranks. For example, while the district magistrate or DM (an IAS officer) and district senior superintendent of police or SSP (an IPS officer) are analogous in rank, the DM will often trump the SSP in making certain decisions related to "public order," such as use of police force in controlling a crowd. This generates a lot of resentment and competition between what are known as the two main pillars of the "steel frame" of the governance in each state, the police service and the civil service. For more discussion of this tension, and its history and outgrowths, see Verma 2005. For a critical and candid discussion of the politicization

of bureaucratic transfers from the perspective of a former chief secretary, an IAS officer, see Subramaniam 2004, esp. chap. 15, "Lucknow: Chief Secretary, After the Elections," pp. 271–91.

12. The rule actually says "inspector general" (IG) rather than "director general" (DGP) because the office of DGP was not created in UP until 1980. Prior to that, the top police official in the state was an IG. For other micro-details of the official transfer process in UP, see Kabir 2005, 245–47.

13. The UPP rules and regulations (Kabir 2005, 246) say, "Officers above the rank of constable should ordinarily not be allowed to serve in districts in which they reside or have landed property. . . . Sub-inspectors and head constables should not be allowed to stay in a particular district for more than six years and ten years respectively and in a particular police station not more than three years and five years respectively."

14. The stated reason is often that police under the chief's leadership provided an inefficient or insufficient response. But sometimes, even if the response is quick and reasonable, a chief will be transferred anyway for "allowing" the crime or conflict to happen in the first place.

15. For more on what police and others call the "VIP problem" and the way in which it siphons off vast amounts of state resources—not least, police protection—for a few elites while leaving little to nothing for the masses, see Jauregui 2014a.

16. I am not listing the specific divisions to which Anand was assigned, because I feel it is less important to know the specificities of his work and more important to know his rank in the official hierarchy as DIG, which means that he is still a relatively "junior" IPS officer, but steadily climbing the ladder. See appendix and chapter 1, note 6, regarding my purposeful "strategic imprecision."

17. See figs. 6 and 7 for images of "evidence" rotting in the yard surrounding CRT.

18. I have decided not to name the specific state ministry in the interest of confidentiality. Again, see chapter 1, note 6.

19. "Success" in riot control may mean different things to different actors and organizations, such as aversion of a riot altogether, or minimization of death and injury in general, or minimization of harm coming to a certain (perhaps social majority, or social minority) community.

20. For an example of how this played out in the post 2014 parliamentary election favoring the BJP at the national level, see Jha 2014.

21. The same may have been true for several of his colleagues in the UPP who also asked favors of me, like helping their children gain admission to prestigious schools in India and the US.

22. Many people would use the Persio-Arabic word *shatranj* for chess, though some, especially "general caste" Hindus, might use the more Sanskritic *chaturanga*, from which the former derives. I thank an anonymous reviewer of my manuscript for requesting that I clarify this point.

23. It is also not exactly the same as Ferdinand de Saussure's (1998) chess analogy for language, with *langue* as the structural rules of the game and *parole* as the actual moves people choose to make, though some productive comparisons could be drawn from putting these analogies into dialogue, especially if one takes what Saussure calls a diachronic approach to analyzing how the rules of the game change over time, which is a crucial component of my own analysis here.

Chapter Six

1. See chapter 3, note 5.

2. See chapter 1, note 8.

3. See Jauregui 2015; cf. Hornberger 2013 and Robb Larkins 2013 for comparable discussions regarding questions of police and popular justice in South Africa and Brazil, respectively. See also chapter 4, note 11.

4. Notably, Gandhi also spoke and wrote of the *satyagrahi* subject as being a "friend of the state":

> We are not to abolish gaols [jails] as an institution. Even under *Swaraj* [self-rule] we [Indians] would have our gaols. Our civil disobedience, therefore, must not be carried beyond the point of breaking *the unmoral laws of the country* . . . . A civil resister is, if one may be permitted such a claim for him, a philanthropist and a *friend of the state.* An anarchist is an enemy of the State and is, therefore, a misanthrope. *I have permitted myself to use the language of war because the so-called constitutional method has become so utterly ineffective.* (Gandhi 1951, 60, emphasis added.)

5. See chapter 4 note 20.

6. This act bans police personnel from (1) associating with "any trade unions, labour unions, or political associations"; (2) being a member of "any other society, institution, association or organization that is not recognized as part of the force . . . or is not [of] a purely social, recreational or religious nature"; (3) communicating with the press or publishing, "any book, letter or other document except which . . . is in *bona fide* discharge of his duties or is of a purely literary, artistic or scientific character or is of a prescribed nature" (Kabir 2005, 318). It was supposed to extend to the whole of India, but since power over policing and public order are also constitutionally reserved for state government (see chapter 1, note 15), each state had to ratify it separately, which is part of the reason why there is a wide variation in police union activity across the country. The UP state government did not ratify the act until March 28, 1973, following a surge of activity among a state-level police workers union, and preceding by less than two months one of the most violent police uprisings in the history of postcolonial India (see chapter 1, note 25).

7. At least fifteen large-scale police strikes occurred in various Indian states between 1951 and 1988, including a rash of protests across more than a dozen states in 1978 and 1979 (Ghosh 1981 and Chande 1997); and major police uprisings were also reported in Jammu and Kashmir in 1993 and Jharkand in 2003 (see again chapter 1, note 25). Many similar incidents and mobilizations of varying scales—including an ongoing movement at the time of writing by some constables in UP to have a union recognized and its demands for better working conditions met—remain underreported and understudied.

8. See chapter 4, note 19.

References

Abrahams, Ray. 2008. "Some Thoughts on the Comparative Study of Vigilantism." In *Global Vigilantes,* edited David Pratten and Atreyee Sen. London: Hurst and Company.

———. 1998. *Vigilant Citizens: Vigilantism and the State.* Cambridge: Cambridge University Press.

Abrams Philip. 1988. "Notes on the Difficulty of Studying the State." *Journal of Historical Sociology.* 1: 58–89.

Agamben, Giorgio. 1998 [1995]. *Homo Sacer: Sovereign Power and Bare Life.* Stanford, CA: Stanford University Press.

Aiyar, Swaminathan S. Anklesaria. 2010. "Success despite Government, Courtesy Jugaad." *Economic Times.* August 11.

Alavi, Seema. 1995. *The Sepoys and the Company: Tradition and Transition in Northern India, 1770–1830.* Oxford: Oxford University Press.

Amin, Shimit, dir. 2004. *Ab Tak Chhappan.* Varma Corporation, Mumbai.

Anderson, David M., and David Killingray. 1991. "Consent, Coercion and Colonial Control: Policing the Empire, 1830–1940." In *Policing the Empire: Government, Authority and Control, 1830–1940, edited by* David M. Anderson and David Killingray, eds. Manchester, UK: Manchester University Press: 1–15.

Anjaria, Jonathan Shapiro. 2011. "Ordinary States: Everyday Corruption and the Politics of Space in Mumbai." *American Ethnologist* 38 (1): 58–72.

Althusser, Louis. 1971. "Ideology and Ideological State Apparatuses." In *Lenin and Philosophy and other Essays,* edited by L. Althusser. New York: Monthly Review Press.

Arendt, Hannah. 1951. *The Origins of Totalitarianism.* New York: Meridian Books.

———. 1998. *The Human Condition.* Chicago: University of Chicago Press.

Arnold, David. 1985. *Bureaucratic Recruitment and Subordination in Colonial India: The Madras Constabulary, 1859–1947.* In *Subaltern Studies IV,* edited by Ranajit Guha. Oxford: Oxford University Press.

———. 1986. *Police Power and Colonial Rule: Madras 1859–1947.* Oxford: Oxford University Press.

Arora, Balveer, and Beryl Radin, eds. 2000. *The Changing Role of the All-India Services: An Assessment and Agenda for Future Research on Federalism and the All India Services.* New

Delhi: Center for the Advanced Study of India, University of Pennsylvania Institute for Advanced Study of India, Centre for Policy Research.

Arun, S. R. 1995. *U.P. Police ka udbhav evam vikaas tathaa: P.A.C. ka itihaas (The Origin and Development of the U.P. Police: A History of the PAC)*. UP PAC Director General.

———. 2000. *The Peace Keepers: India Police Service*. New Delhi: Manas Publications.

Attokaran, Ranjith Xavier. 2007. "Why Do Indian Police Resort to Torture?" Friday, October 12. http://indianlawyer.blogspot.com/2007_10_07_archive.html. Accessed February 15, 2015.

Austin, John. 1995 [1832]. *The Province of Jurisprudence Determined*. Cambridge: Cambridge University Press.

Bakhtin, Mikhail. 1981. "Forms of Time and of the Chronotope in the Novel: Notes toward a Historical Poetics." In *The Dialogic Imagination*. Austin: University of Texas Press.

Balko, Radley. 2014. *Rise of the Warrior Cop: The Militarization of America's Police Forces*. Public Affairs.

Banerjea, D. 2005. Criminal Justice India Series, vol. 15: *Jharkhand*. New Delhi: English Allied Publishers Private Limited.

Banerjee, Mukulika. 2014. *Why India Votes?* New York: Routledge.

Bardhan, Pranab. 1997. "Corruption and Development: A Review of Issues." *Journal of Economic Literature* 35 (3):1320–46.

Baxi, Pratiksha. 2010. "Justice Is a Secret: *Compromise* in Rape Trials." *Contributions to Indian Sociology* 44 (3): 207–33.

Baxi, Upendra. 1982. *The Crisis of the Indian Legal System*. Alternatives in Development Series: Law. New Delhi: Vikas Publishing House Pvt., Ltd.

Bayart, Jean-François, Stephen Ellis, and Béatrice Hibou. 1999. Introduction to *The Criminalization of the State in Africa*, xiii–xviii. Bloomington: Indiana University Press.

Beek, Jan. 2013. "Moving Police Officers: The Belief in Bureaucratic Order in the Ghanaian Police." Paper presented at workshop on "Reconsidering Policing in Africa," Oxford University, May 17.

Belur, Jyoti. 2010. *Permission to Shoot? Police Use of Deadly Force in Democracies*. London: Springer.

Benjamin, Walter. 1978 [1922]. "Critique of Violence." In *Reflections*, edited by Peter Demetz. New York: Schocken.

Ben-Porat, Guy. 2008. "Policing Multicultural States: Lessons from the Canadian Model." *Policing & Society* 18 (4): 411–25.

Berenschot, Ward. 2014. "Political Fixers in India's Patronage Democracy." In *Patronage as Politics in South Asia*, edited by Anastasia Piliavsky. Cambridge: Cambridge University Press.

Bhushan, Navneet. 2008. "Jugaad: The Way India Innovates." January 21. http://innovationcrafting.blogspot.com/2008/01/jugaad-way-india-innovates.html. Accessed August 19, 2012.

Biehl, Joao. 2005. *Vita: Life in a Zone of Abandonment*. Berkeley: University of California Press.

Birtchnell, Simon. 2011 "*Jugaad* as Systemic Risk and Disruptive Innovation in India." *Contemporary South Asia* 19 (4): 357–72.

Bittner, Egon. 1970. *The Functions of the Police in Modern Society*. Bethesda, MD: National Institute of Mental Health, Center for Studies of Crime and Delinquency.

———. 1990. *Aspects of Police Work*. Boston: Northeastern University Press.

Bottoms, Anthony, and Justice Tankebe. 2012. "Beyond Procedural Justice: A Dialogic Approach to Legitimacy in Criminal Justice." *Journal of Criminal Law and Criminology*. 102 (1): 101–52.

Bowling, Ben, and James W. E. Sheptycki. 2012. *Global Policing*. London: Sage.

Braithwaite, John. 2002. *Restorative Justice and Responsive Regulation.* Oxford: Oxford University Press.

Brass, Paul. 1997. *Theft of an Idol.* Princeton, NJ: Princeton University Press.

———. 2008. *Forms of Collective Violence: Riots, Pogroms and Genocide in Modern India.* Gurgaon: Three Essays Collectives.

———. 2010. "Leadership and the Power of Honor in a Corrupt System." In *Power and Influence in India: Bosses, Lords and Captains,* edited by Pamela Price and Arild Ruud. New Delhi: Routledge, 169–92.

Brodeur, Jean-Paul. 2010. *The Policing Web.* London: Oxford University Press.

Brown, Lorne and Caroline Brown. 1973. *An Unauthorized History of the RCMP.* James Lewis & Samuel.

Bureau of Police Research and Development (BPRD). 2014. "Data on Police Organizations in India." New Delhi. http://bprd.nic.in/showfile.asp?lid=1291. Accessed October 2, 2015.

Campion, David. 2003. "Authority, Accountability, and Representation: The United Provinces Police and Dilemmas of the Colonial Policeman in British India, 1902–1939." *Historical Research* (May) 76 (192): 217–37.

Cappelli, Peter, Harbir Singh, Jitendra Singh, and Michael Useem. 2010. *The India Way.* Boston: Harvard Business Press.

Chadha, Radhika. 2009. Indiagenous Ingenuity. *Hindu.* Business Line. May 14.

Chambliss, William J. 1988. *On the Take: From Petty Crooks to Presidents.* 2nd ed. Bloomington: Indiana University Press.

Chan, Janet. 1997. *Changing Police Culture: Policing in a Multicultural Society.* Cambridge: Cambridge University Press.

Chande, M. B. 1997. *The Police in India.* New Delhi: Atlantic Publishers and Distributors.

Chandra, Vikram. 2006. *Sacred Games.* New York: Harper Collins.

Chatterjee, Partha, ed. 2006. *The Politics of the Governed: Reflections on Popular Politics in Most of the World.* New York: Columbia University Press.

Chatterjee, Upamanyu. 2006. *English, August: An India Story.* New York: New York Review Books Classics.

Clifford, James. 1988. *The Predicament of Culture: Twentieth Century Ethnography, Literature and Art.* Cambridge, MA: Harvard University Press.

Code of Criminal Procedure (CrPC). 2005 [1973]. Lucknow: Eastern Book Company.

Cohn, Bernard. 1971. *India: The Social Anthropology of a Civilization.* Anthropology of Modern Societies Series. Englewood Cliffs, NJ: Prentice-Hall, Inc.

———. 1987 [1956]. "Some Notes on Law and Change in North India." In *An Anthropologist among the Historians and Other Essays.* Oxford: Oxford University Press.

———. 1987 [1965]. "Anthropological Notes on Law and Disputes in North India." In *An Anthropologist among the Historians and Other Essays.* Oxford: Oxford University Press.

———. 1987 [1966]. "The Recruitment and Training of British Civil Servants in India: 1600–1860." In *An Anthropologist among the Historians and Other Essays.* Oxford: Oxford University Press.

———. 1987 [1983]. "Representing Authority in Victorian India." In *An Anthropologist among the Historians and Other Essays.* Oxford: Oxford University Press.

———. 1996 [1989]. *Colonialism and Its Forms of Knowledge: The British in India.* Princeton, NJ: Princeton University Press.

Comaroff, Jean, and John L. Comaroff. 2006. *Law and Disorder in the Postcolony.* Chicago: University of Chicago Press.

Comaroff, John L. 2013. Foreword to *Policing and Contemporary Governance: The Anthropology of Police in Practice,* edited by William Garriott, xi–xxi. New York: Palgrave Macmillan.

Commonwealth Human Rights Initiative (CHRI). 2008. *Seven Steps to Police Reform.* December 10. http://www.humanrightsinitiative.org/programs/aj/police/india/initiatives/seven_steps _to_police_reform.pdf. Accessed February 16, 2015.

Cooper-Knock, Sarah Jane. 2014. "Policing in Intimate Crowds: Moving beyond 'the Mob' in South Africa." *African Affairs* 113 (453): 563–82.

Cooper-Knock, Sarah Jane, and Olly Owen. 2015. "Between Vigilantism and Bureaucracy: Improving Our Understanding of Police Work in Nigeria and South Africa." *Theoretical Criminology.* 19 (3): 355–75.

Corrigan, Rose. 2013. "The New Trial by Ordeal: Rape Kits, Police Practices, and the Unintended Effects of Policy Innovation." *Law and Social Inquiry* 38 (4): 920–49.

Daruwala, Reena. 2010. "Jugaad: Should We Be Proud of our Jugad-Ability?" http://reena-daruwalla .hubpages.com/hub/Jugaad-Should-we-be-Proud-of-our-Jugad-ability. Accessed August 19, 2012.

Das, Gurchuran. 2002. *The Elephant Paradigm: India Wrestles with Change.* New Delhi: Penguin.

Das, Veena. 2004 . "The Signature of the State: the Paradox of Illegibility." In *Anthropology in the Margins of the State,* edited by Veena Das and Deborah Poole. Santa Fe: School of American Research Press.

Das, Veena, and Deborah Poole. 2004. Introduction to *Anthropology in the Margins of the State,* edited by Veena Das and Deborah Poole. Santa Fe: School of American Research Press.

Dasgupta, Swapan. 2010. "Why Praise Jugaad? It's Bleeding Us." *Times of India.* August 29.

DeLord, Ron, John Burpo, Michael R. Shannon, and Jim Spearing. 2008. *Police Union Power, Politics and Confrontation in 21ˢᵗ Century.* Springfield, IL: Charles C. Thomas.

Derrida, Jacques. 2002. "Force of Law: The 'Mystical Foundation of Authority.'" In *Acts of Religion.* New York: Routledge.

De Saussure, Ferdinand. 1998. *Course in General Linguistics.* Chicago: Open Court Classics.

Dhillon, Kirpal. 1998. *Defenders of the Establishment: Ruler-Supportive Police Forces of South Asia.* New Delhi: Indian Institute of Advanced Study. In Association with Aryan Books International.

———. 2005. *Police and Politics in India: Colonial Concepts, Democratic Compulsions.* New Delhi: Manohar.

Dhuru, Arundhati, and Sandeep Pandey. 2007. "Mulayam Faces Uphill Battle in UP." *Rediff News.* April 4. http://in.rediff.com/news/2007/apr/04guest.htm. Accessed February 16, 2015.

Diphoorn, Tessa. 2015. *Twilight Policing: Private Security and Violence in Urban South Africa.* University of California Press.

Dubber, Markus D., and Mariana Valverde. 2006. *The New Police Science: The Police Power in Domestic and International Governance.* Stanford, CA: Stanford University Press.

Dumont, Louis. 1970. *Homo Hierarchicus: The Caste System and Its Implications.* Chicago: University of Chicago Press.

Eckert, Julia. 2005. "The *Trimurti* of the State: State Violence and the Promises of Order and Destruction." *Sociologus II*: 181–217.

Elliott, John. 2011. "India's 'Jugaad' Means Its Nuke Power Plans Should Be Dumped." *Independent.* March 15.

Engineer, Asghar Ali, and Amarjit Narang, eds. 2006. *Minorities and Police in India*. New Delhi: Manohar Press.

Erayil A. L., and Vadackumchery, James. 1984. *Public Relations at the Cutting Edge Level*. New Delhi: National Publishing House.

Express New Service (ENS). 2015a. "UP Govt Gives In, Appoints New DGP." *Indian Express*. February 1. Online ed. http://indianexpress.com/article/india/india-others/up-govt-gives -in-appoints-new-dgp/. Accessed September 30, 2015.

———. 2015b. "108 UP Cops, Most in Country, Killed in One Year." *Indian Express*. October 22. Online ed. http://indianexpress.com/article/cities/lucknow/108-up-cops-most-in-country -killed-in-one-year/. Accessed October 23, 2015.

Fassin, Didier. 2013. *Enforcing Order: An Ethnography of Urban Policing*. Cambridge: Polity.

Fogelson, Robert M. 1977. *Big-City Police: An Urban Institute Study*. Cambridge, MA: Harvard University Press.

Forbes, Duncan. 1866. *A Dictionary, Hindustani and English: Accompanied by a Reversed Dictionary*. London: William H. Allen.

Foucault, Michel. 1977. *Discipline and Punish*. New York: Vintage.

———. 1990 [1976]. *History of Sexuality*. Vol. 1. New York: Vintage.

———. 1991. "On Governmentality." In *The Foucault Effect*, edited by Graham Burchell, Colin Gordon, and Peter Miller. Chicago: University of Chicago Press.

———. 1998. *Ethics: Subjectivity and Truth*. Vol. 1. New York: New Press.

———. 2003[1976]. *Society Must Be Defended: Lectures at the Collège de France, 1975–1976*. New York: Picador.

———. 2009 [1977]. *Security, Territory, Population: Lectures at the Collège de France, 1977–1978*. New York: Picador.

Frankel, Francine. 2005. *India's Political Economy 1947–2004*. 2nd ed. Oxford: Oxford University Press.

Freitag, Sandria. 1989. *Collective Action and Community: Public Arenas and the Emergence of Communalism in North India*. Berkeley: University of California Press.

Gandhi, Mohandas K. 1951. *Non-Violent Resistance*. New York: Shocken.

Garriott, William. 2013. "Police in Practice: Policing and the Project of Contemporary Governance." In *Policing and Contemporary Governance: The Anthropology of Police in Practice*, edited by William Garriott, 1–15. New York: Palgrave Macmillan.

Geertz, Clifford. 1968. "Thinking as a Moral Act: Ethical Dimensions of Anthropological Fieldwork in the New States." *Antioch Review* 28 (2): 139–59.

———. 1977. *Interpretation of Cultures*. New York: Basic.

Geuss, Raymond. 2003. *Public Goods, Private Goods*. Princeton, NJ: Princeton University Press.

Ghosh, Gautam. 2007. *Police Accountability: At the Cutting Edge Level*. New Delhi: S. B. Nangia A. P. H. Publishing Corporation.

Ghosh, S. K. 1981. *Police in Ferment*. New Delhi: Light and Life Publishers.

Gidwani, Deepak. 2015. "Pay and Get Your Choice Posting in Uttar Pradesh Police." *Daily News and Analysis*. June 11. http://www.dnaindia.com/india/report-pay-and-get-your-choice-posting -in-uttar-padesh-police-2094347. Accessed October 2015.

Goldstein, Daniel. 2008. "Flexible Justice: Neoliberal Violence and 'Self-Help' Security in Bolivia." In *Global Vigilantes*, edited by David Pratten and Atreyee Sen. London: Hurst and Company.

Gramsci, Antonio. 1971. *Selections from the Prison Notebooks*. New York: International Publishers.

Guha, Ranajit. 1982. "On Some Aspects of the Historiography of Colonial India." In *Subaltern Studies I: Writings on South Asian History and Society*, edited by Ranajit Guha. Oxford: Oxford University Press.

———. 1983. *Elementary Aspects of Peasant Insurgency in Colonial India*. Oxford: Oxford University Press.

———. 1997. *Dominance Without Hegemony*. Cambridge, MA: Harvard University Press.

Gupta, Akhil. 1995. "Blurred Boundaries: The Discourse of Corruption, the Culture of Politics, and the Imagined State." *American Ethnologist* 22 (2):375–402.

———. 2005. "Narratives of Corruption: Anthropological and Fictional Accounts of the Indian State." *Ethnography* 6 (1): 5–34.

———. 2012. *Red Tape: Bureaucracy, Structure Violence and Poverty in India*. Durham, NC: Duke University Press.

Gupta, Akhil, and James Ferguson. 1997. "The Field as Site, Method and Location in Anthropology." In *Anthropological Locations*, ed. Akhil Gupta and James Ferguson, 1–46. Berkeley: University of California Press.

Gupta, Anandswarup. 1974. *Crime and Police in India Up to 1861*. Agra: Sahitya Bhawan.

———. 1979. *The Police in British India: 1861–1947*. New Delhi: Concept Publishing.

Gupta, Praveen. 2008. "Jugaad: The Way India Innovates." http://www.realinnovation.com/commentary/archive/global_innovation_part_ii.html#179. Accessed August 19, 2012.

Gurung, Shaurya Karanbir. 2011. "Sacked Cop Extorts Money from Couple." *Tribune India*, November 29.

Habermas, Jurgen. 1991 [1962]. *The Structural Transformation of the Public Sphere*. Cambridge, MA: MIT Press.

Hansen, Thomas Blom. 2001. *Wages of Violence: Naming and Identity in Postcolonial Bombay*. Princeton, NJ: Princeton University Press.

Hansen, Thomas Blom, and Finn Stepputat. 2006. "Sovereignty Revisited." *Annual Review of Anthropology* 35: 295–315.

———, eds. 2005. *Sovereign Bodies. Citizens, Migrants, and States in the Postcolonial World*. Princeton, NJ: Princeton University Press.

Hautzinger, Sarah. 2016. "Policing by and for Women in Brazil and Beyond." In *Handbook of Global Policing*, edited by Ben Bradford, Beatrice Jauregui, Ian Loader, and Jonny Steinberg. London: Sage.

Hawkins, Richard. 1991. "The 'Irish Model' and the Empire: A Case for Reassessment." In *Policing the Empire: Government, Authority and Control, 1830–1940*, edited by David M. Anderson and David Killingray, 18–32. Manchester, UK: Manchester University Press.

Henry, Francis, and Carol Tator. 2005. *The Colour of Democracy: Racism in Canadian Society*. Toronto: Nelson.

Herzfeld, Michael. 2005. *Cultural Intimacy: Social Poetics in the Nation-State*. New York: Routledge.

High, Holly. 2010. "Ethnographic Exposures: Motivations for Donations in the South of Laos." *American Ethnologist* 37 (2): 308–22.

Hindustan Times (HT). 2011. "Constable Held for Impersonating SI [Sub-Inspector]." Delhi ed. March 7.

Hobbes, Thomas. 1968 [1651]. *Leviathan*. London: Penguin.

Hobbs, Dick. 1988. *Doing the Business: Entrepreneurship, the Working Class, and Detectives in the East End of London*. Oxford: Oxford University Press.

Hornberger, Julia. 2013. "From General to Commissioner to General: On the Popular State of Policing in South Africa." *Law and Social Inquiry* 38 (3): 598–614.

———. Forthcoming. "On Complicity: Becoming Police." In *Writing the Worlds of Policing: The Difference Ethnography Makes*, edited by Didier Fassin. Chicago: University of Chicago Press.

Huggins, Martha K., ed. 1991. *Vigilantism and the State in Modern Latin America: Essays on Extralegal Violence*. New York: Praeger.

Hull, Matthew. 2012. *Government of Paper: The Materiality of Bureaucracy in Urban Pakistan*. University of California Press.

Human Rights Watch (HRW). 2009. *Broken System: Dysfunction, Abuse and Impunity in the Indian Police*. Human Rights Watch. 1-56432-518-0. August. http://www.hrw.org/sites/default /files/reports/india0809web.pdf. Accessed February 16, 2015.

Huntington, Samuel P. 1968. *Political Order in Changing Societies*. New Haven, CT: Yale University Press.

Hussain, Nasser. 2003. *Jurisprudence of Emergency: Colonialism and the Rule of Law*. Ann Arbor: University of Michigan Press.

Hussin, Iza. 2014. "Circulations of Law: Cosmopolitan Elites, Global Repertoires, Local Vernaculars." *Law and History Review* 32 (4): 773–95.

Jain, Mayank. 2014. "The Biggest Perpetrators of Sexual Assault on Women—Their Husbands." Scroll.in. November 4. http://scroll.in/article/685709/the-biggest-perpetrators-of-sexual -assault-on-indian-women-%E2%80%92-their-husbands&utm_source=newsletter&utm _medium=email&utm_campaign=newsletter. Accessed October 1, 2015.

Jauregui, Beatrice. 2010a. "Civilised Coercion, Militarised Law and Order: Security in Colonial South Asia and the Blue in Green Global Order." In *Blurring Military and Police Roles*, edited by Marleen Easton, Monica den Boer, Jelle Janssens, and Rene Moelker. The Hague: Eleven International Publishing.

———. 2010b. "Categories of Conflict and Coercion: The Blue in Green and the Other." In *Anthropology and Global Counterinsurgency*, edited by John D. Kelly, Beatrice Jauregui, Sean T. Mitchell, and Jeremy Walton. Chicago: University of Chicago Press

———. 2011. "Law and Order: Police Encounter Killings and Routinized Political Violence." In *A Companion to the Anthropology of India*, edited by Isabelle Clark-Deces. Hoboken, NJ: Wiley-Blackwell.

———. 2013a. "Beatings, Beacons, and Big Men: Police Disempowerment and Delegitimation in India." *Law and Social Inquiry* 38 (3): 643–69.

———. 2013b. "Dirty Anthropology: Epistemologies of Violence and Ethical Entanglements in Police Ethnography." In *Policing and Contemporary Governance: The Anthropology of Police in Practice*, edited by William Garriott. New York: Palgrave.

———. 2014a. "Provisional Agency in India: Jugaad and Legitimation of Corruption." *American Ethnologist* 41 (1): 76–91.

———. 2014b. "Police and Legal Patronage in Northern India." In *Patronage as Politics in South Asia*, edited by Anastasia Piliavsky. Cambridge: Cambridge University Press.

———. 2015. "Just Warriors: Police Vigilantism and Cosmologies of Justice in Northern India." *Conflict and Society* 1: 41–59.

———. Forthcoming. "Intimacy: Personal Policing, Ethnographic Kinship and Critical Empathy in Northern India." In *Writing the Worlds of Policing: The Difference Ethnography Makes*, edited by Didier Fassin. Chicago: University of Chicago Press.

Jeffrey, Craig. 2010. *Timepass: Youth, Class, and the Politics of Waiting.* Stanford, CA: Stanford University Press.

Jeffrey, Craig, and Stephen Young. 2014. "Jugaad: Youth and Enterprise in India." *Association of American Geographers* 104 (1): 182–95.

Jha, Dhirendra K. 2014. "Bureaucrats Rush to RSS Office to Prove Their Loyalty to Modi." Scroll.in. June 26. http://scroll.in/article/668169/bureaucrats-rush-to-rss-office-to-prove-their-loyalty-to-modi. Accessed October 2, 2015.

Jha, Prakash, dir. 2003. *Gangaajal.* Entertainment One Pvt. Ltd. & Prakash Jha Productions.

Johari, Aarefa. 2014. "How a New Bill Could Increase Political Interference in Maharashtra Police." Scroll.in. July 4. http://scroll.in/article/668989/How-a-new-bill-could-increase-political-interference-in-Maharashtra-police. Accessed October 2, 2015.

Kabir, Ali. 2005. *Commentaries on UP Police Regulations with Allied Laws.* Revised by Ram Nath Mishra. Allahabad: Hind Publishing House.

Kafka, Franz. 1925. *Before the Law.* http://records.viu.ca/~Johnstoi/Kafka/beforethelaw.htm.

Kakar, Sudhir. 1996. *The Colors of Violence: Cultural Identities, Religion, and Conflict.* Chicago: University of Chicago Press.

Kapur, Anandana, dir. 2009. *The Great India Jugaad.* A K Films.

Karpiak, Kevin. 2010. "Of Heroes and Polemics: 'The Policeman' in Urban Ethnography." *PoLAR: Political and Legal Anthropology Review* 33: 7–31.

Kaushik, Kabeer, dir. 2005. *Sehar.* Choice Films, Inc.

Khalidi, Omar. 2003. *Khaki and the Ethnic Violence in India.* New Delhi: Three Essays Collective.

Klockars, Carl B. 1980. "The Dirty Harry Problem." *Annals of the American Academy of Political and Social Science* 452: 33–47.

Kolff, Dirk H. A. 1990. *Naukar, Rajput and Sepoy: The Ethnohistory of the Military and Labour Market in Hindustan: 1450–1850.* Cambridge: Cambridge University Press.

Krishnan, Rishikesha T. 2010. *From Jugaad to Systemic Innovation: The Challenge for India.* New Delhi: Utprerka Foundation.

Kudaisya, Gyanesh. 2006. *Region, Nation, 'Heartland': Uttar Pradesh in India's Body Politic.* New Delhi: Sage.

Kumar, R. Anand, dir. 2009. *Jugaad.* Delhi: Promodome Films.

Kumar, Sumit, et al. 2008. *Pages from a Diary: Civil Lines Police Station, Raipur, Chhattisgarh.* New Delhi: Commonwealth Human Rights Initiative (CHRI).

Lévi-Strauss, Claude. 1962. *The Savage Mind.* Chicago: University of Chicago Press.

Loader, Ian, Ben Bradford, Beatrice Jauregui, and Jonny Steinberg. 2016. "Global Policing Studies: A Prospective Field." In *Handbook of Global Policing,* edited by Ben Bradford, Beatrice Jauregui, Ian Loader, and Jonny Steinberg. London: Sage.

Lorey, Isabell. 2015 [2012]. *State of Insecurity.* London: Verso.

Luce, Edward. 2006. *In Spite of the Gods: The Strange Rise of Modern India.* London: Little, Brown.

Machiavelli, Niccolò. 1966 [1513]. *The Prince.* New York: Bantam.

Mahagaonkar, Prashanth. 2008. "Corruption and Innovation: A Grease or Sand Relationship?" *Jena Economic Research Papers, 2008–17.* Jena, Germany: Friedrich Schiller University and Max Planck Institute of Economics.

Maheswari, S. 1978. "Unionism in Police: Redressal of Police Personnel Grievances." *Indian Journal of Public Administration* 24: 69.

Malhotra, Kritika. 2008. "Analysis of the Police Act, 2007." http://www.legalserviceindia.com /article/1253-Analysis-Of-The-Police-Act.html. Accessed February 15, 2015.

Mangold, James, dir. 1997. *Cop Land*. Miramax.

Manjrekar, Mahesh. 2000. *Kurukshetra*. Eros International.

Manning, Peter. 1997 [1977]. *Police Work: The Social Organization of Policing*. Prospect Heights, IL: Waveland.

Marcus, George E. 1997. "The Uses of Complicity in the Changing Mise-en-Scène of Anthropological Fieldwork." *Representations*. Special Issue: *The Fate of "Culture": Geertz and Beyond* 59 (Summer): 85–108.

Marks, Monique, and David Sklansky, eds. 2011. *Police Reform from the Bottom Up: Officers and their Unions as Agents of Change*. New York: Routledge.

Marquis, Greg. 1992. "The Police as a Social Service in Early 20th Century Toronto." *Social History* 50: 335–58.

Martin, Jeffrey. 2013. "Legitimate Force in a Particularistic Democracy: Street Police and Outlaw Legislators in the Republic of China on Taiwan." *Law and Social Inquiry* 38 (3):615–42.

Marx, Karl. 1978 [1852]. "The Eighteenth Brumaire of Louis Bonaparte." In *The Marx-Engels Reader*, edited by Robert C. Tucker. 2nd ed. New York: Norton.

———. 1990 [1867]. *Capital: A Critique of Political Economy*. Vol. 1. Translated by Ben Fowkes. New York: Penguin.

Masih, Niha, and Deepshikha Ghosh. 2014. 'Lack of Entertainment Options' Causes Rape, Say Uttar Pradesh Police." NDTV. October 30. http://www.ndtv.com/india-news/lack-of-entertainment -options-causes-rape-say-uttar-pradesh-police-686567. Accessed October 1, 2015.

Mastrofski, S., R. B. Parks, and R. E. Worden. 1998. *Community Policing in Action: Lessons from an observational study*. Albany: State University of New York Press.

Mathur, Nayanika. 2012. "Transparent-Making Documents and the Crisis of Implementation: A Rural Employment Law and Development Bureaucracy in India." *PoLAR: Political and Legal Anthropology Review* 35 (2):167–85.

McGregor, Ronald S. 2002. *The Oxford Hindi-English Dictionary*. Oxford: Oxford University Press.

Mehra, Ajay K. and René Levy. 2011. *The Police, State and Society: Perspectives from India and France*. New Delhi: Pearson Education in South Asia.

Mehta, Suketu. 2004. *Maximum City: Bombay Lost and Found*. New York: Vintage.

Méon, Pierre-Guillaume, and Khalid Sekkat. 2005. "Does Corruption Grease or Sand the Wheels of Growth?" *Public Choice* 122: 69–97.

Michelutti, Lucia. 2009. *The Vernacularisation of Democracy: Politics, Caste and Religion in India*. New Delhi: Routledge.

Mitchell, Timothy. 1999. "Society, Economy, and the State Effect." In *State/Culture: State-Formation after the Cultural Turn*, edited by George Steinmetz, 76–97. Ithaca, NY: Cornell University Press.

Mitra, Barun S. 2006. "Grassroots Capitalism Thrives in India." *Index of Economic Freedom: The Link between Economic Opportunity and Prosperity. Edited by Marc A. Miles, Kim R. Holmes, and Mary Anastasia O'Grady*, 39–47. Washington, DC: Heritage Foundation.

Molekhiet, Pankaj. 2010. "Wheels and Reels: Anandana Kapur as a Film Maker." *Economic Times*. September 5.

Muir, William Ker. 1977. *Police: Streetcorner Politicians*. Chicago: University of Chicago Press.

Murakawa, Naomi. 2014. *The First Civil Right: How Liberals Built Prison America*. Oxford; Oxford University Press.

Nader, Laura. 1972. "Up the Anthropologist: Perspectives Gained from Studying Up." In *Reinventing Anthropology*, edited by Dell Hymes, 284–311. New York: Pantheon.

Narasimha, Roddam. 2007. "Epistemology and Language in Indian Astronomy and Mathematics." *Journal of Indian Philosophy* 35 (5–6): 521–41.

Nath, Kamal. 2008. "India's Century: The Age of Entrepreneurship in the World's Biggest Democracy." New York: McGraw-Hill.

National Crime Records Bureau (NCRB). 2013. "Crime in India." http://ncrb.gov.in/CD-CII2013/Chapters.htm. Accessed February 16, 2015.

Navaro-Yashin, Yael. 2002. *Faces of the State: Secularism and Public Life in Turkey*. Princeton, NJ: Princeton University Press.

Nihalani, Govind, dir. 1983. *Ardh Satya*. Neo Films.

Nikelani, Nandan. 2010. *Imagining India: The Idea of a Renewed Nation*. New York: Penguin.

Nolan, Christopher, dir. 2002. *Insomnia*. Alcon Entertainment.

———. 2008. *The Dark Knight*. Warner Brothers.

Nuijten, Monique, and Gerhard Anders, eds. 2008. *Corruption and the Secret of Law: A Legal Anthropological Perspective*. London: Ashgate.

Nussbaum, Martha. 2009. *The Clash Within: Democracy, Religious Violence, and India's Future*. Cambridge, MA: Belknap Press at Harvard University Press.

Nye, Joseph S. 1967. "Corruption and Political Development: A Cost Benefit Analysis." *American Political Science Review* 61 (2): 417–27.

Ong, Aihwa, and Stephen J. Collier, eds. 2005. *Global Assemblages: Technology, Politics and Ethics as Anthropological Problems*. Malden, MA: Blackwell.

Ortner, Sherry. 1996. *Making Gender: The Politics and Erotics of Culture*. Boston: Beacon.

———. 2006. *Anthropology and Social Theory*. Durham, NC: Duke University Press.

Outlook India. 2011. "UP Tops 'Fake' Encounters List, Manipur Second: NHRC." August 7. http://news.outlookindia.com/items.aspx?artid=730444. Accessed February 16. 2015.

Owen, Olly. 2016. "Policing after Colonialism." In *Handbook of Global Policing*, edited by Ben Bradford, Beatrice Jauregui, Ian Loader, and Jonny Steinberg. London: Sage.

Oxford English Dictionary (OED). 2015. Online ed.

Parry, Jonathan. 2000. "The 'Crisis of Corruption' and 'The Idea of India': A Worm's Eye View." In *Morals of Legitimacy: Between Agency and System*, edited by Italo Pardo, 27–56. New York: Berghahn.

Pasquino, Pasquale. 1991. "Theatrum Politicum: The Genealogy of Capital: Police and the State of Prosperity." In *The Foucault Effect*, edited by Graham Burchell, Colin Gordon, and Peter Miller. Chicago: University of Chicago Press.

Pereira, Maxell. 2008. *The Other Side of Policing*. New Delhi: Vitasta.

Perry, Alex. 2003. "Urban Cowboys." *Time Magazine*. January 6.

Perry, Donna. 2009. "Fathers, Sons, and the State: Discipline and Punishment in a Wolof Hinterland." *Cultural Anthropology* 24 (1): 33–67.

Pestano, Andrew V. 2015. "Amnesty International Condemns Gang-Rape Sentence of Two Indian Women." United Press International. August 31. http://www.upi.com/Top_News/World-News/2015/08/31/Amnesty-International-condemns-gang-rape-sentence-of-two-Indian-women/8221441019846/. Accessed October 30, 2015.

Peterkin, Tom. 2008. "Bombay's Dirty Harry, Pradeep Sharma, Fired for Alleged Gangster Links." *Telegraph*. September 3. http://www.telegraph.co.uk/news/worldnews/asia/india/2672862 /Bombays-Dirty-Harry-Pradeep-Sharma-fired-for-alleged-gangster-links.html. Accessed February 16, 2015.

Philip, Kavita, Lilly Irani, and Paul Dourish. 2010. "Postcolonial Computing: A Tactical Survey." *Science, Technology and Human Values*, November 21: 1–27.

Pickles, Anthony. 2011. "Are Current Papua New Guinean Leaders Corrupt? Anthropological Ideologies of Gift and Debt versus the Moral-Money Landscape of Leadership in Goroka, Highland New Guinea." Paper presented at the conference "Debt: Interdisciplinary Considerations of an Enduring Human Passion," Cambridge, UK, May 13.

Piliavsky, Anastasia, ed. 2014. *Patronage as Politics in South Asia*. Cambridge: Cambridge University Press.

Prahalad, C. K., and R. A. Mashelkar. 2010. Innovation's Holy Grail. *Harvard Business Review* (July–August):133–41.

Pratten, David, and Atreyee Sen, eds. 2008. *Global Vigilantes*. New York: Columbia University Press.

Press Information Bureau (PIB). 2014. "Police Commemoration Day to Be Observed Tomorrow: Union Home Minister to Witness the Parade." Ministry of Home Affairs, Government of India. October 20. http://pib.nic.in/newsite/PrintRelease.aspx?relid=110729. Accessed October 2, 2015.

Press Trust of India (PTI). 2007. "Lawyers Clash with Police in UP." April 13. http://www.india abroad.com/news/2007/apr/13up.htm. Accessed October 1, 2015.

———. 2014a. "Handy Guns to Replace Outdated Rifles for UP Policemen." *Business Standard*. Lucknow ed. June 17. http://www.business-standard.com/article/pti-stories/handy-guns-to -replace-outdated-rifles-for-up-policemen-114061701206_1.html. Accessed September 30, 2015.

———. 2014b. "Mobiles, Western Culture, Indecent Dressing Reasons for Rape: UP Police." *Hindustan Times*. Lucknow ed. October 30. http://www.hindustantimes.com/india/mobiles-western -culture-indecent-dressing-reasons-for-rape-up-police/story-0Pw47YAB6QkRc5Epz8agmO .html. Accessed October 1, 2015.

Price, Pamela. 1999. "Cosmologies and Corruption in (South) India: Thinking Aloud." *Forum for Development Studies* 2: 315–27.

Radjou, Navi, Jaideep Prabhu, and Simone Ahuja. 2012. *Jugaad Innovation: Think Frugal, Be Flexible, Generate Breakthrough Growth*. San Francisco: Jossey-Bass.

Rai, Vibhuti Narain. 1998. *Combating Communal Conflicts: Perception of Police Neutrality during Hindu-Muslim Riots in India*. New Delhi: Renaissance Publishing House.

Raj, Pushkar and Shobha Sharma. 2007. "Culture of Encounters: Time to Fix Accountability on the Police." *Tribune*. November 6. http://www.humanrightsinitiative.org/new/2007/culture _of_encounters.jpg. Accessed February 16, 2015.

Ramnath, Nandini. 2014. "Uniform Change: How Hindi Film Cops Went from Zero to Superhero." Scroll.in. December 19. http://scroll.in/article/694871/uniform-change-how-hindi-film-cops -went-from-zero-to-superhero. Accessed October 2, 2015.

Rancière, Jacques. 2001. "Ten Thesis on Politics." *Theory & Event* 5 (3).

Rawlings, Philip. 2002. *Policing: A Short History*. Cullompton, UK: Willan.

Reiner, Robert. 2010. *The Politics of the Police*. 4th ed. Oxford: Oxford University Press.

Robb Larkins, Erika. 2013. "Performances of Police Legitimacy in Rio's Hyper Favela." *Law and Social Inquiry* 38 (3): 553–75.

Robben, Antonius C.G.M. . 1995. "The Politics of Truth and Emotion among Victims and Perpetrators of Violence." In *Fieldwork under Fire*, edited by Carolyn Nordstrom and Antonius C. G. M. Robben. Berkeley: University of California Press.

———. 1996. "Ethnographic Seduction, Transference, and Resistance in Dialogues about Terror and Violence in Argentina." *Ethos* 24 (1): 71–106.

Robbins, Joel. 2013. "Beyond the Suffering Subject: Toward an Anthropology of the Good." *Journal of the Royal Anthropological Institute*.

Roitman, Janet. 2005. "Fiscal Disobedience: An Anthropology of Economic Regulation in Central Africa." Princeton, NJ: Princeton University Press.

———. 2006. "The Ethics of Illegality in the Chad Basin." In *Law and Disorder in the Postcolony*, edited by Jean Comaroff and John L. Comaroff, 247–72. Chicago: University of Chicago Press.

Rosaldo, Renato. 1993. *Culture & truth: the remaking of social analysis.* Boston: Beacon Press.

Rose-Ackerman, Susan. 1999. *Corruption and Government: Causes, Consequences, and Reform.* Cambridge: Cambridge University Press.

Rotimi, Kemi. 2013. "The Malformation of the Nigerian Policeman and the Impediments to His Being an Agent of Reform." Paper presented at workshop on Reconsidering Policing in Africa. Oxford University, May 17.

Roy, Ramashray. 1974. "India 1973: A Year of Discontent." *Asian Survey* 14 (2) (February): 115–24.

Roychowdhury, Poulami. 2015. "Victims to Saviors: Governmentality and the Regendering of Citizenship in India." *Gender and Society* 29 (6): 792–816.

Rubinstein, Jonathan. 1973. *City Police.* New York: Farrar, Strauss and Giroux.

Ruud, Arild Engelsen. 2000. "Corruption as Everyday Practice: The Public-Private Divide in Local Indian Society." *Forum for Development Studies* 2: 271–94.

Scarry, Elaine. 1987. *The Body in Pain: The Making and Unmaking of the World.* Oxford: Oxford University Press.

Schwegler, Tara. 2012. "Navigating the Illegible State: The Political Labor of Government in Mexico." In *Governing Cultures Anthropological Perspectives on Political Labor, Power, and Government*, edited Kendra Coulter and William R. Schumann, 21–46. New York: Palgrave MacMillan.

Scott, James. 1972. *Comparative Political Corruption.* Englewood Cliffs, NJ: Prentice Hall.

———. 1987. *Weapons of the Weak.* New Haven, CT: Yale University Press.

———. 1999. *Seeing Like a State: How Certain Schemes to Improve the Human Condition Have Failed.* New Haven, CT: Yale University Press.

Seltzer, Mark. 1998. *Serial Killers: Death and Life in America's Wound Culture.* New York: Routledge.

Sharma, Aradhana, and Akhil Gupta, eds. 2006. *The Anthropology of the State: A Reader.* Malden, MA: Wiley-Blackwell.

Sharma, Supriya. 2014. "Why Uttar Pradesh Is in the Grip of an Epidemic of Bad Politics." Scroll.in. September 30. http://scroll.in/article/661661/why-uttar-pradesh-is-in-the-grip-of-an-epidemic-of-bad-politics. Accessed September 30, 2015.

Sherman, Lawrence, and Heather Strang. 2007. *Restorative Justice: The Evidence.* Smith Institute.

Silver, Alan. 1967. "The Demand for Order in Civil Society." In *The Police: Six Sociological Essays*, edited by D. J. Bordua, 1–24. Malden, MA: Wiley.

Simon, David, dir. 2004. *The Wire.* Season 3.

Singh, Sanjeet, Gagan Deep Sharma, and Mandeep Mahendru. 2011. "The Jugaad Technology (Indigenous Innovations) (A Caste Study of Indian Origin)." *Asia Pacific Journal of Research in Business Management* 2 (4) :1–15.

Singha, Radhika. 2000. *A Despotism of Law*. Oxford: Oxford University Press.

Sinha, Mithilesh Kumar. 1981. *In Father's Footsteps: A Policeman's Odyssey*. New Delhi: Vanity Books.

Sklansky, David. 2007. *Democracy and the Police*. Stanford, CA: Stanford University Press.

Skogan, Wesley G. 2003. *Community Policing: Can It Work?* Belmont, CA: Wadsworth Publishing.

Skolnick, J. H. 2011. *Justice without Trial: Law Enforcement in Democratic Society*. New Orleans: Quid Pro Books.

Skolnick, J. H., and Bayley, D. 1988. *Community Policing: Issues and Practices around the World*. Washington, DC: National Institute of Justice, Office of Communication and Research Utilization.

Sluka, Jeffrey. 1999. *Death Squad: The Anthropology of State Terror*. Philadelphia: University of Pennsylvania Press.

Smith, Daniel Jordan. 2001. "Kinship and Corruption in Nigeria." *Ethnos* 66 (3): 344–64.

———. 2007. *A Culture of Corruption: Everyday Deception and Popular Discontent in Nigeria*. Princeton, NJ: Princeton University Press.

Sontag, Susan. 2004. *Regarding the Pain of Others*. New York: Picador.

Spencer, Jonathan. 2007. *Anthropology, Politics, and the State: Democracy and Violence in South Asia*. Cambridge: Cambridge University Press.

Spivak, Gayatri Chakravorty. 1988. "Can the Subaltern Speak?" In *Marxism and the Interpretation of Culture*, edited by Cary Nelson and Lawrence Grossberg. Urbana-Champaign: University of Illinois Press.

Srivastava, Piyush. 2015. "Policemen Live in Fear in Akhilesh Yadav's Uttar Pradesh." *India Today*. March 11. http://indiatoday.intoday.in/story/uttar-pradesh-police-akhilesh-yadav-samajwadi-party-gonns-muzaffarnagar-basti/1/423171.html. Accessed October 1, 2015.

Srivastava, S. P., and Balraj Chauhan. 2002. *Criminal Justice India Series*. Vol. 3, *Uttar Pradesh, 2001*. New Delhi: Allied Publishers, Pvt., Ltd. and National University of Juridical Sciences.

Stalcup, Meg. 2013. "Interpol and the Emergence of Global Policing." In *Policing and Contemporary Governance: The Anthropology of Police in Practice*, edited by W. Garriott, 231–61. Basingstoke, UK: Palgrave Macmillan.

Strang, Heather, and John Braithwaite, eds. 2001. *Restorative Justice and Civil Society*. Cambridge: Cambridge University Press.

Subramaniam, T. S. R. 2004. *Journeys through Babudom and Netaland: Governance in India*. New Delhi: Rupa and Company.

Subramanian, K. S. 1988. "Police Unrest in India: Notes Towards an Understanding." *Occasional Papers on History and Society*. 2nd ser. No. 10. November.

———. 2007. *Political Violence and the Police in India*. New Delhi: Sage.

Sunshine, Jason, and Tom R. Tyler. 2003. "The Role of Procedural Justice and Legitimacy in Shaping Public Support for Policing." *Law & Society Review* 37: 513–47.

Taliaferro, Charles, and Paul J. Griffiths, eds. 2003. *Philosophy of Religion: An Anthology*. Hoboken, NJ: Wiley-Blackwell.

Thakur, Dinesh. 2013. "The India Way? No Way." *Hindu*. Opinion sec. June 12. http://www.thehindu.com/opinion/op-ed/the-indian-way-no-way/article4804513.ece. Accessed September 30, 2015.

Tillin, Louise. 2012. *Remapping India*. Oxford: Oxford University Press.

Tillin, Louise, K. K. Kailash, and Rajeshwari Deshpande. 2015. *Politics of Welfare: Comparisons across Indian States*. Oxford: Oxford University Press.

Times News Network (TNN). 2006a. "Cops Are Unsafe in State Capital." *Times of India*. Lucknow ed. April 24.

———. 2006b. "Goons Run Amuk, Cops Run for Cover." *Times of India*. Lucknow ed. July 19.

———. 2007. "Suspended Cop Held Impersonating as DSP." *Times of India*, January 6.

———. 2008. "DGP Orders Identification of Corrupt Cops." *Times of India*, June 20.

———. 2012. "Police Recruitment Scam: Charges Politically Motivated, Samajwadi Party Says." *Times of India*. May 24. http://timesofindia.indiatimes.com/city/lucknow/Police-recruitment-scam-Charges-politically-motivated-Samajwadi-Party-says/articleshow/13425770.cms. Accessed October 30, 2015.

Tribune News Service (TNS). 2004. "BJP, BSP Cry for Mulayam's Ouster Vajpayee for Caution on Lawyers-Cops Clash." September 4. http://www.tribuneindia.com/2004/20040905/nation.htm#1. Accessed October 30, 2015.

Tyler, Tom R. and Juen Huo. 2002. *Trust in the Law: Encouraging Public Cooperation with the Police and Courts*. New York: Russell Sage Foundation.

United News of India (UNI). 2011. "Inspector Impersonates as CBI [Central Bureau of Investigation], Indulges in Extortion." December 30.

Valverde, Mariana. 2003. *Law's Dream of a Common Knowledge*. Princeton, NJ: Princeton University Press.

———. 2015. *Chronotopes of Law: Jurisdiction, Scale and Legal Governance*. London: Routledge.

Van der Veer, Peter. 1994. *Religious Nationalism: Hindus and Muslims in India*. Berkeley: University of California Press.

Van Maanen, John. 1978. "The Asshole." In *Policing: A View from the Streets*, edited by John Van Maanen and Peter Manning, 221–38. New York: Random House.

Vatuk, Sylvia. 2006. "Domestic Violence and Marital Breakdown in India: A View from the Family Courts." In *Culture, Power, and Agency: Gender in India Ethnography*, edited by Lina Fruzzetti and Sirpa Tenhunen, 204–26. Calcutta: Stree.

Verma, Arvind. 2005. *The Indian Police: A Critical Evaluation*. New Delhi: Regency Publications.

Visvanathan, Shiv, and Harsh Sethi, eds. 1998. *Foul Play: Chronicles of Corruption, 1947–97*. New Delhi: Banyan.

Wade, Robert. 1982a. "Corruption: Where Does the Money Go?" *Economic and Political Weekly* 17 (40): 1606.

———. 1982b. "The System of Administrative and Political Corruption: Canal Irrigation in South India." *Journal of Development Studies* 18: 287–328.

———. 1985. "The Market for Public Office: Why the Indian State Is Not Better at Development." *World Development* 13 (4): 467–97.

Warner, Michael. 2002. *Publics and Counterpublics*. New York: Zone.

Webb, Martin. 2012. "Activating Citizens, Remaking Brokerage: Transparency Activism, Ethical Scenes, and the Urban Poor in Delhi." *PoLAR: Political and Legal Anthropology Review* 35 (2): 206–22.

Weber, Max. 1958a [1918]. "Politics as a Vocation." In *From Max Weber: Essays in Sociology*, edited and translated by Hans Gerth and C. Wright Mills. Oxford: Oxford University Press.

———. 1958b [1918]. "Bureaucracy." In *From Max Weber: Essays in Sociology*, edited and translated by Hans Gerth and C. Wright Mills. Oxford: Oxford University Press.

———. 1978 [1919]. *Economy and Society*, edited and translated by Guenther Roth and Claus Wittich. Berkeley: University of California Press.

Weldes, Jutta, Mark Laffey, Hugh Gusterson, and Raymond Duvall, eds. 1999. *Cultures of Insecurity: States, Communities and the Production of Danger*. Minneapolis: University of Minnesota Press.

Westley, W. A. 1970. *Violence and the Police: A Sociological Study of Law, Custom, and Morality*. Cambridge, MA: MIT Press.

Westmarland, Louise. 2001. "Blowing the Whistle on Police Violence." *British Journal of Criminology* 41: 523–35.

Witsoe, Jeffrey. 2011. "Corruption as Power: Caste and the Political Imagination of the Postcolonial State." *American Ethnologist* 38 (1): 73–85.

Wolf, Eric. 1990. "Facing Power: Old Insights, New Questions." *American Anthropologist* 92 (3): 586–96.

Wolfgang, Marvin. 1982. *The Subculture of Violence: Towards an Integrated Theory in Criminology*. New York: Routledge.

Yardley, Jim. 2010. "Games Official Angers India with Hygiene Comment." *New York Times*, September 25: A4.

YouTube.com. 2010a. "The Great Indian Jugaad Promo-2.mp4." Uploaded by Greenleaf Entertainment, April 29. http://www.youtube.com/watch?v=528cQkqN24U. Accessed October 30, 2015.

———. 2010b. "The Great Indian Jugaad Promo-3." Uploaded by Greenleaf Entertainment, April 29. http://www.youtube.com/watch?v=pghEkM1Aroo. Accessed October 30, 2015.

———. 2014. Police Smriti Diwas 2014 Lucknow Report by Senior Reporter Mr Roomi Siddiqui. ASIAN TV NEWS. October 21. https://www.youtube.com/watch?v=5b6pGVxWDOM , accessed October 30, 2015.

Zee Media Bureau (ZMB). 2013. "Police to People Ratio: 3 Cops for Every VIP but Just 1 for 761 Commoners." *Daily News and Analysis*. August 25. http://www.dnaindia.com/india/report-police-to-people-ratio-3-cops-for-every-vip-but-just-1-for-761-commoners-1879695. Accessed September 20, 2015.

Index

aachar sanhita, 113, 115. *See also* Central Election Commission (CEC); elections; politics; Yadav, Y. K.

aam aadmi, 94, 105, 152

Aam Aadmi Party (AAP), 57, 152. *See also* corruption; political parties; politics

Abhimanyu, 100, 103, 112. See also *Bhagavad Gita*; Hindu epic myth; *Mahabharata*

accountability, 10–11, 119, 149; democratic, 150; legitimacy and, 149; particularistic, 142, 150; transparency and, 10, 57, 129, 152, 157. *See also* ethics; governance; morality/moral; police

Aditya (sub-inspector cadet), 101–5, 111, 116, 154. *See also* duty; families; Moradabad; police; sacrifice; service; training; violence

Agamben, Giorgio, 104. See also *bali kaa bakra*; biopower; expendability; *homo sacer*; social theory; sovereignty

agency, 11–16, 37, 55, 136–37, 144, 158; and authority, 56, 136, 142; central government, 124; expressions of, 39; individual, 51; as intentionality, 47; *juga-adi*, 124–25, 132; moral, 64; Ortner concept of, 15–16, 47, 55, 58; provisional, 38–39, 51, 55–59, 142; and responsibility, 46. *See also* authority; *chalta hai*; corruption; *jugaad*; police; positionality/position; power; provisionality/provisional

Allahabad, 24, 109, 119, figs. 20–21

Althusser, Louis, 65. *See also* demand; Dirty Harry problem; order/orderly; social theory

Aman (constable), 51, 62, 90–91, 104, 111, 155. *See also* constable; dishonesty; *diwan*; expendability; violence

Anand, Manu (DIG), 125–29, 131, 133, 137, 158, 174n16, fig. 22. *See also* senior officer; transfers

Anjaria, Jonathan, 52, 56, 111, 167n14. *See also* anthropology; ethnography

anthropology, 1, 11, 26, 31, 37–39, 54, 132–34, 144, 158; dirty, 31; style of, 25. *See also* Anjaria, Jonathan; Eckert, Julia; ethnography; High, Holly; Jauregui, Beatrice; Jeffrey, Craig; Mathur, Nayanika; methodology; Nader, Laura; Navaro-Yashin, Yael; Roitman, Janet; Schwegler, Tara; Witsoe, Jeffrey

anti-corruption movement, 57, 152. *See also* bribes; corruption; Hazare, Anna; politics

ardh kumbh mela, 109, 111, figs. 20–21

Ardh Satya (Nihalani 1983), 97, 102, 171n18. *See also* Hindi film

Arjuna, 100, 103, 112. See also *Bhagavad Gita*; Hindu epic myth; Hinduism; Krishna; *Mahabharata*

assassination, 92. *See also* encounter killings; police; violence

authority, 2, 6–22, 56–59, 133, 136–37, 142, 146–57; abuse of, 10, 72; coercive, 8–13, 15, 145; expressions of, 15; field of, 13; as insecurity, 15, 147, 152–53, 156–58; legitimate, 137; negotiable, 15, 59; official, 143; position of, 39, 42, 136; provisional, 11–16, 26, 31–41, 51, 56–59, 104, 111, 115–19, 122–29, 132–37, 140–49, 155–58; provisional legal, 59, 63; rational, 11; social field of, 26; state, 11–12, 16, 32, 47, 57–58, 135, 150–57; theorization of police, 12; transmuting form of, 16; Weber's concept of, 14, 58. *See also* agency; governance; insecurity; police; positionality/position; power; provisionality/provisional; sovereignty

avatars, 103–4, 108, 112, 141, 171n16; encounter killing as the, 93; of police in public culture, 89, 98; soldier and servant, 104. *See also* Abhimanyu; Arjuna; *dharma*; duty; Eckert, Julia; expendability; Hanuman; police; public culture; sacrifice; violence

baanka, 69–70, 76, 81
badachlan, 77
Bahujan Samaj Party (BSP), 4, 18, 121, 131. *See also* Dalit; Mayawati; political parties; politics; Scheduled Castes/Scheduled Tribes (SC/ST)
bali kaa bakra, 103, 105. *See also* avatars; police; public; sacrifice
bekar aadmi, 123
Belur, Jyoti, 93, 95–96. *See also* encounter killings; social theory; violence
Benjamin, Walter, 12, 66, 144, 157. *See also* Benjaminian; social theory
Benjaminian, 71. *See also* Benjamin, Walter
Bhaaratha, 96. See also *Bhagavad Gita*
Bhagavad Gita, 96. *See also* Arjuna; *Bhaaratha*; Hindu epic myth; *Mahabharata*
Bharatiya Janata Party (BJP), 18. *See also* political parties; politics
Bhim Rao Ambedkar Police Academy, 23. *See also* police; training
bhrashtaachaar, 34, 55, 152. *See also* bribes; *crorepati*; corruption; *ghuus khaanaa*
Bihar, 56, 161n1. *See also* India
biopolitics, 153. *See also* Foucault, Michel; politics
biopower, 12, 104, 157, 171n21. *See also* Agamben, Giorgio; Foucault, Michel; power; sovereignty
Bittner, Egon, 8, 12, 15, 58–59, 65–66, 82, 141, 146, 162n12. *See also* authority; coercion; nonnegotiably coercive force; police; social theory
black money, 2, 48, 122, 130, 132, 136, 154. See also *kaalaa daan*; money laundering; organized crime; smuggling
Bollywood, 2, 96, 108, 171n18. *See also* Hindi film; police
Bombay, 18, 57, 95, 97. *See also* India; Maharashtra; Mumbai
Border Security Force (BSF), 85, 170n4
bribes, 2, 4, 12, 33, 38–42, 45–49, 57, 59, 133–35, 140–43, 154–55. *See also* corruption; dishonesty; ethics; *ghuus khaanaa*; *jugaad*; kingpin postings; morality/moral; police
British colonial administration, 19–21, 147, 164n29. *See also* bureaucracy; colonial expansion; India; Sepoy Rebellion; War of Independence
Buddhism, 149. *See also* religious minorities
bureaucracy, 38, 124–25, 132, 145–48; civil service, 131; disciplining force of, 147; legal, 11; Mexican development, 136; political economy of, 120–25; politics of, 134, 136; of the UPP, 24–25; Weberian, 118. *See also* bureaucrat; government; police; political interference; politics; transfers
bureaucrat, 23, 123–24, 127, 129, 131, 135–36, 143. *See also* bureaucracy; cynicism; government; Mathur, Nayanika; political interference; politician; politics; transfers

cadet, 23, 101–2. *See also* Aditya (sub-inspector cadet); police; training
capability, 15–16, 32, 99, 151; allocational, 54; coercive, 3; contingent, 55; ingenuity and, 51; institutionalized, 171n21; limited and variable, 16; provisional agency as a, 58; shifts in, 15; social expression of, 35; as a social good, 39; socio-material, 55; transformative, 55. *See also* agency; coercion; connectedness; ingenuity; *jugaad*
capital, 50–52, 166n3; Bombay the country's financial, 18; Lucknow the UP state, 2, 18–19, 22, 42, 123, 163n20, 164n29; monetary, 50; New Delhi the national, 113, 136; social and economic, 148; UP state, 2, 10, 18–19, 123, 164n29. *See also* connectedness; currency; *jugaad*
caste, 3–4, 7, 18–19, 51, 122, 131–33, 142, 149–50; conflict, 18; creamy layer, 51; lower, 51, 131; Yadav, 56. *See also* Bahujan Samaj Party (BSP); discrimination; inequality; Other Backward Classes (OBC); Samajwadi Party; Scheduled Caste/Scheduled Tribe (SC/ST); social difference; society; Yadav (caste)
Central Election Commission (CEC), 113–15, 121, 124. *See also* elections
Central Reserve Police Force, 83–84, 170n2. *See also* constable; *jawan*; police
Chakkar Rasta Thana (CRT), 1, 3–6, 25–30, 39–42, 48, 51–56, 60, 79, 102, 115–17, 126, 131–40, 153–54, figs. 5–9. *See also* chief station officer (SO); constable; Crime Register; police; *thana*; Yadav, Y. K.
chakravyuha, 97. *See also* Abhimanyu; *Ardh Satya*; *Bhagavad Gita*; Hindi film; Hindu epic myth; *Mahabharata*
chalta hai, 6–11, 52, 96, 103–4, 144, 148. *See also* authority; social dynamics
Chanakya (IPS officer), 113–14, 124, 131. *See also* district police chief; Indian Police Service (IPS); senior officer
chess analogy, 134–35
Chhattisgarh, 79
chief minister (CM), 22, 74, 84, 107, 111, 114, 119–21; as police commander-in-chief, 107. *See also* bureaucrat; government; Mayawati; police; Yadav, Mulayam Singh
chief station officer (SO), 1, 3–5, 20, 25–29, 39, 42–46, 56, 79, 114–16, 122–26, 131–37, 146, 154, 166n4. *See also* police; station house officer (SHO); *thana*; Yadav, Y. K.
children, 82–83, 168n8, 170n18; of police, 29, 75, 83, 102, 116, 136, 166n4, 174n21, fig. 9. *See also* families; society; women
chowki, 20, 86. *See also* police; *thana*
chowkidar, 20, 163n23, fig. 8. *See also* police
chronotope, 14, 146, 158. *See also* temporality

circle officer (CO), 4, 22, 117. *See also* deputy superintendent of police (DySP); police; Provincial Police Service (PPS); senior officer; transfers

civilian deaths, 5, 69, 108, 121. *See also* dowry death; murder; riot

class, 19, 93, 149; or caste, 51, 163n19; conflicts driven by, 105, 162n16; distinctions of, 21, 163n19; the governed or the subjected, 13; lower, 170n18; middle, 93, 166n3; of police, 137; political, 103; socioeconomic, 20; struggles, 105; well-educated social, 171n18. *See also* caste; inequality; Other Backward Classes (OBC); social mobility; society

CM. *See* chief minister

CO. *See* circle officer

coercion, 3, 8–12, 92–94, 41, 141, 143; and consent, 80; extra-legal, 66; failed, 58; as a form of police authority, 12–14; legal use of, 58, 162n10; police institutional ethos of, 94; provision and, 119, 157; servants of, 143; Weber's concept of, 162n10; of women, 168n2. *See also* authority; Bittner, Egon; power; social theory; state externality; violence

collective beneficence, 55, 141. *See also* exchange; good; *jugaad*; social dynamics

colonial expansion, 144. *See also* British colonial administration; India

command, 14–15, 58–59, 69, 85–86, 117; law as species of, 162n14; legalistic, 142; of the Leviathan, 157; obedience to, 14, 16, 56–58, 137; police chain of, 22, 26, 45, 64, 117, 137, 165n34; refusing police, 39–41, 58; sovereign, 146, 157–58; timing of, 59. *See also* authority; demand; police; provisionality/provisional; Weber, Max

community policing, 20, 127. *See also* police

compensation/compensate, 87, 141, 158; condemnation and, 101–5, 112, 143, 147, 151; familial "foul play" in order to claim, 172n22; family rate for police KIA of, 170n6, 172n22; of private laborers and drivers, 40–45, 61. *See also* condemnation; duty; ex gratia death compensation; expendability; police; sacrifice; working conditions

complicity, 145; with provisional authority, 133; public, 89; strategic, 31, 132. *See also* cutting-edge police; dirty anthropology; ethics; strategic complicity

conceptual framework, 12, 32, 144–45, 149. *See also* anthropology; ethnography

condemnation, 89, 94, 104, 158; and compensation, 101–6, 112, 143, 147, 151; moral-legal, 104; of police the world over, 89; social, 103. *See also* compensation/compensate; expendability

confessions, 65, 67, 69–71, 168n9, 169n10. *See also* legislation; police

confiscated property, 26–27, 169n12, figs. 5–7. *See also* Chakkar Rasta Thana (CRT)

Congress Party, 18, 116. *See also* political parties; politics; Yadav, Y. K.

connectedness, 26, 29, 48–50, 55, 142, 163n24; social, 50, 52. *See also* *jugaad*; nepotism; *pahunch*; Praveen; social connectedness; *yug/jug*; *yukti*

conscience, 91. *See also* ethics; morality/moral

constable, 1–6, 12, 20, 22–26, 29, 39–51, 62, 83–86, 106–9, 111, 122, 135, 137–42, 146–48, 153–55, 171n17, figs. 4, 13, appendix. *See also* Aman (constable); expendability; *jawan*; *nagar nigam* (municipal council) elections; police; Prithvi (constable); security; sepoy; Sharma (constable); Tiwari (constable); union, police; Vikram (constable)

contingency, 32, 45, 51, 59. *See also* insecurity; *jugaad*; provisionality/provisional

corruption, 4, 8, 23, 32–39, 45–47, 51–57, 94, 124, 142–45, 152–55; allegations of, 52; complexities of, 39; evaluations of, 56; legitimation of, 38; local understandings of, 54; in South Asia, 56. *See also* *bhrashtaachaar*; bribes; dishonesty; ethics; *ghuus khaanaa*; *jugaad*; kingpin postings; police; power; virtue/virtuosity

court, 5, 62, 69, 122, 137, 168n9; backlogs, 73; as an example of a collective subject giving a command, 15; evidence to the, 44, 58, 61–63, 68–71, 73; framing charges for criminal, 60, 167n1; inefficacy and inefficiency of the, 80, 95; of the people, 97; supreme, 15; UP High, 7, 164n29. *See also* criminal investigation; criminal justice; criminals; Indian Penal Code (IPC); *janata ki adaulat*; judges; law; lawyers; legality; legislation

Crime Register, 60, 77, 167n1. *See also* Chakkar Rasta Thana (CRT); police

criminal investigation, 22, 46, 54, 58, 124, 126. *See also* Crime Register; criminal justice; criminals; police

Criminal Investigation Division (CID), 123. *See also* criminal investigation; police

criminal justice, 20, 46. *See also* bureaucracy; criminal investigation; criminals; police

Criminal Procedural Code (CrPC), 61, 70, 75–76. *See also* criminal justice; law; legislation

criminals, 8, 73, 111. *See also* criminal investigation; criminal justice; murder; organized crime; violence

crorepati, 130. See also *bhrashtaachaar*; black money; bribes; corruption; *kaalaa daan*

CRT. *See* Chakkar Rasta Thana

cultural world, 133

currency, 50; material and relational, 45; social, 50. *See also* capital; economy; exchange; provisionality/provisional; social dynamics

cutting-edge, 21, 123, 141. *See also* cutting-edge police; ethnography; Geertz, Clifford; methodology; police; provisionality/provisional cutting-edge police, 21–32, 101, 107–9, 120, 125, 131–32, 138, 155–56, 168n5; accessing, 22–32. *See also* cutting-edge; police

cynicism, 127. *See also* Mathur, Nayanika; police

dacoity, 112

dalaal, 3, 50, 56, 81. *See also* fixer; *jugaad*

Dalit, 4, 18, 122. *See also* Bahujan Samaj Party (BSP); caste; Mayawati; poverty; Scheduled Caste/Scheduled Tribe (SC/ST)

darogha, 20. *See also* chief station officer (SO); sub-inspector (SI)

darshan, 3. *See also* Hinduism; temple

debt, 49. *See also* police

demand, 14–15, 40–42, 59, 82, 106, 142, 147–48, 162n12; changing, 150; conflicting, 30, 64, 145, 156–57; as distinct from command, 14–15, 146; excessive, 42, 143; by government leaders, 73, 81; moral-instrumental, 32; popular, 94–95, 143, 145, 151; social, 58, 151; unofficial, 26. *See also* authority; coercion; command; order/orderly; provisionality/provisional

democracy, 11, 16, 131, 149–50; liberal, 11, 152; world's largest, 13, 16, 152. *See also* economy; government; India; politics; society

depersonalization, 112, 129–30, 134. *See also* disempowerment; police

depoliticization, 147. *See also* bureaucracy; disempowerment; insecurity; union, police

deputy inspector general (DIG), 120, 125, 135, 137. *See also* Anand, Manu (DIG); Indian Police Service (IPS); police; senior officer; transfers

deputy superintendent of police (DySP), 6, 8, 117, 119, 134, appendix. *See also* circle officer (CO); police; Provincial Police Service (PPS); senior officer; transfers

developing countries, 53, 152. *See also* economy; India; poverty

DGP. *See* director general of police

dharma, 96, 144. *See also* avatars; duty; expendability; *nari-dharma*; police; women

DIG. *See* deputy inspector general

dimaag, 36. *See also jugaad*

director general of police (DGP), 19, 21–23, 84–85, 106, 113, 118–20, 125, 127, 130, 137, appendix; Headquarters, 24. *See also* Indian Police Service (IPS); Lucknow; police; senior officer; transfers

dirty anthropology, 31. *See also* complicity; ethics; ethnography; methodology; strategic complicity

Dirty Harry, 65–68. *See also* Sharma, Inspector Pradeep; violence

Dirty Harry problem, 65, 81, 94. *See also* ethics; Klockars, Carl; order/orderly; police; violence

discrimination, 50, 145, 151, 157; against minority groups, 23; reverse, 150; systemic, 151. *See also*

caste; inequality; police; religious minorities; social minorities; violence

disempowerment, 16, 147. *See also* bureaucracy; depersonalization; depoliticization; insecurity

dishonesty, 51, 62, 91, 155. *See also* Aman (constable); bribes; connectedness; corruption; ethics; instrumentality/instrumental; *jugaad*; morality/moral

district magistrate (DM), 115, 146

district police chief, 146. *See also* Chanakya (IPS officer); district senior superintendent of police (SSP); district superintendent of police; Indian Police Service (IPS); Lucknow; police; senior officer; superintendent of police; transfers

district senior superintendent of police (SSP), 7, 22. *See also* district police chief; district superintendent of police; Indian Police Service (IPS); Lucknow; police; senior officer; superintendent of police; transfers

district superintendent of police, 4. *See also* district police chief; district senior superintendent of police (SSP); Indian Police Service (IPS); Lucknow; police; senior officer; superintendent of police; transfers

diwan, 27, 90. *See also* Aman (constable); Chakkar Rasta Thana (CRT); Crime Register; *thana*

DM. *See* district magistrate

domestic violence, 75, 78, 91. *See also* dowry death; law; legislation; violence; women

domination, 13, 51, 150, 162n13. *See also* authority; coercion; hegemony; *Herrschaft*; police; violence; Weber, Max

dowry, 69, 77–79, 169n14. *See also* dowry death; women

dowry death, 69, 78. *See also* civilian deaths; domestic violence; dowry; violence

Dussehra, 98. *See also* Hinduism; *Kurukshetra*; Ramayana

duty, 42, 59, 64, 72, 81, 89, 109–11, 118, 121–22, 135–39, 156; election, 165n34, 172n1; first, 5; killed in the line of, 84, 87–88, 97, 101, 106–8, 172n22, 172n25, fig. 19; in Lucknow, 29, 39; moral, 96, 98; neglect of, 40, 74, 121; physically dangerous, 89; picket, 153; sentry, 48; specific police, 82, 103; violence as a, 95; woman's universal, 75. *See also* demand; *dharma*; ethics; killed-in-action (KIA); police; service; violence

DySP. *See* deputy superintendent of police

Eckert, Julia, 93–94, 171nn13–14. *See also* anthropology; avatars; encounter killings; ethnography; violence

economics, 18, 37, 45, 50, 54, 148, 157; depressed, 64; development, 37; global, 53; of growth, 122–23. *See also* developing countries; economy; politics; technology economy, 125; informal, 152; of police life, 105; political, 120–25; state, 18; street, 56. *See also* currency; economics; politics; society; technology

elections, 113–14, 116, 121–22, 143, 165n34, 169n13, 172n1; *nagar nigam* (municipal council), 47, 138, 153; parliamentary, 130, 174n20; UP state legislative assembly, 3; *Vidhan Sabha* (State Legislative Assembly), 73, 113, 121. See also *aachar sanhita*; Central Election Commission (CEC); Chanakya (IPS officer); chief minister (CM); Mayawati; *nagar nigam* (municipal council) elections; law; law and order; legislation; Lucknow; politics; transfers; *Vidhan Sabha* (legislative assembly); VIP; Yadav, Mulayam Singh

elites, 13, 20, 38, 94, 103, 134, 137, 163n18, 174n15. *See also* hegemony; patronage; politicians; politics; power; subaltern; transfers; VIP

emic and etic perspectives, 31. *See also* anthropology; ethics; ethnography

empathy, 98

encounter killings, 92–94, 111, 170n12, 171n13, 172n26. *See also* assassination; Belur, Jyoti; Eckert, Julia; encounter specialists; police; Sharma, Inspector Pradeep; violence

encounter specialists, 94–95, 97, 104. *See also* encounter killings; police; Sharma, Inspector Pradeep; violence

ethics, 31, 59, 95, 150; of ethnographic methods, 31, 132–34; Foucauldian concept of, 64; of illegality, 64; orderly, 32, 59, 64, 126, 134, 142. *See also* accountability; complicity; dirty anthropology; ethnography; Foucauldian; Foucault, Michel; Geertz, Clifford; morality/moral; order/orderly; Roitman, Janet; virtue/virtuosity

ethnography, 6, 11, 13, 22–31, 38, 45, 47, 51–52, 56, 111, 132, 136, 140–49, 158. *See also* anthropology; ethics; methodology

exchange, 42, 45, 50, 58; geography of, 45; of money, 50; resource, 15; system of, 41. *See also* connectivity; *jugaad;* patronage; provisionality/provisional; resources

ex gratia death compensation, 88, 106, 172n22. *See also* compensation/compensate; expendability; police

expendability, 32, 89, 105–12, 130, 133–34, 143, 156. *See also* avatars; compensation/compensate; condemnation; Hanuman; killed-in-action (KIA); *paavan smriti*; police; Police Remembrance Day; sacrifice; servants; service; violence

extrajudicial killings. *See also* encounter killings

extra-legality/extra-legal, 20, 66, 81, 93. *See also* encounter killings; law; law and order; law enforcement; legality; legislation; police

families, 29–30, 33, 50, 75, 78–79, 88, 101, 116, 124, 132–33, 138–39, 142, 145, 154, 167n9, 168n8, 170n6, 172n22. *See also* children; domestic violence; dowry; police; women

firearms, 1, 112, fig. 12. *See also* civilian deaths; encounter killings; police; violence

First Information Report (FIR), 30, 46, 77

fixer, 3, 50, 56, 81; of criminality, 73–81. See also *dalaal; jugaad*

Foucauldian, 58, 74, 147. *See also* Foucault, Michel

Foucault, Michel, 37, 104, 146–47, 157. *See also* biopower; Foucauldian; governance; governmentality; power

Gandhi, Mahatma, 145–46, 175n4. *See also* India; nonviolent resistance; *satyagraha*

Ganga, 18. *See also* Ganges; India

Ganges, 18, 172n28. *See also* Ganga; India

gang rape, 121, 169n14. *See also* rape; sexual assault; violence; women

Geertz, Clifford, 25, 133. *See also* anthropology; ethnography; methodology

ghuus khaanaa, 2. See also *bhrashtaachaar;* bribes; corruption; *jugaad*

global form, 144–45. *See also* anthropology; police

"glocal" discourse, 144

good, 4, 16, 35–36, 53, 67, 142, 145, 155; collective, 51; greater, 66, 95, 97; instrumental, 13; moral, 13, 51, 146; public, 8, 103, 117–20, 124, 131, 142–43, 158; social, 16, 36, 39, 63–64, 103; triumph of, 98. *See also* agency; ethics; expendability; instrumentality/instrumental; *janhit*, morality/moral; provisional/provisionality; public; resources; value/valuation; virtue/virtuosity

Gorakhpur, 121, 127, fig. 22

governance, 17, 153; good, 158; institutions of, 11; legal, 19; neoliberal global, 153; official, 10; state, 19. *See also* authority; democracy; government; state

government, 14, 23; accountability, 152; buildings, 151; employment, 49–50, 156; of individual states, 17; leaders, 143; money, 139; office, 8; officials, 26; property, 7; provisional, 14; state, 19, 45, 138, 147; transparency, 152. *See also* authority; connectedness; democracy; India; politics; state

governmentality, 12, 97. *See also* governance; power

grihastha, 49. *See also* Hinduism

Gujarat, 80

halka, 1. *See also* Chakkar Rasta Thana (CRT); patrol; police; Sharma (constable); Tiwari (constable)

hamraahi, 48, 166n4. *See also* constable; police; Prithvi (constable)

Hanuman, 98–100, 103, 112, figs. 17–18. *See also* avatars; Hindu deity; Hinduism; police; sacrifice

hawallat, 60. *See also* Chakkar Rasta Thana (CRT); police

Hazare, Anna, 57. *See also* Aam Aadmi Party (AAP); anti-corruption movement; corruption; politics

hegemony, 13. *See also* domination; elites

Herrschaft, 14, 55, 120, 162n13. *See also* Weber, Max

HG. *See* Home Guard

High, Holly, 134. *See also* anthropology; ethics; ethnography; methodology

Hindi, 2, 8, 34–35, 54, 78, 101, 127, 144, 165n32, fig. 22

Hindi film, 93, 97, 108, 171n18. See also *Ardh Satya*; Bollywood; *Kurukshetra*; police

Hindu deity, 98, 103. *See also* Hanuman; Hindu epic myth; Hinduism; Krishna; Ram; Sita; Sita-Ram

Hindu epic myth, 96–98, 108. See also *Bhagavad Gita*; Hanuman; *Mahabharata*; Ram; *Ramayana*; Sita; Sita-Ram

Hinduism, 3, 18, 49, 55, 98–99, 149, 171n16. *See also* Hindu deity; Hindu epic myth; Hindu temple

Hindustan Times, 93, fig.1. *See also* media; news media; public culture

Hindu temple, 3. *See also* Hindu deity; Hinduism

Home Guard (HG), 47–49, 154, 160, fig. 12, appendix. *See also* Praveen

human rights violations, 10, 109. *See also* violence

Human Rights Watch, 109, 111

IAS. *See* Indian Administrative Service

impersonation, 47–48, 58. *See also* misrepresentation; Praveen; uniform

indeterminacy/indeterminate, 10, 32, 64, 124, 135, 168n7; of law, 32, 71; multiplicity and, 15, 81–82, 143; of police roles, 15, 64, 119; of position, 64, 119; and provisionality, 68. *See also* ethics; law; legitimacy; multiplicity; order/orderly; provisionality/provisional; state; transfers

India, 6, 18, 32, 52–57, 141, 143, 146, 150–56, fig. 2; breakdown of law and order in, 8; chess in, 134; colonial, 162n16, 164n29, 173n11; ethnographic work in, 131; governance in, 135; independence of, 20, 148; international embarrassment of, 52; northern, 52, 144; police authority in, 11–22; police employment in, 153; postcolonial, 6, 130, 137, 140–44, 147, 149–50; social life in, 38. *See also* authority; British colonial administration; bureaucracy; caste; democracy; developing countries; economy; Gandhi, Mahatma; government; politics; postcolonial; society; South Asia; War of Independence

Indian Administrative Service (IAS), 6, 121

The Indian Express, 97. See also *janata ki adaulat*; *Kurukshetra*; media; news media; public culture

Indian Penal Code (IPC), 60, 62, 75, 170n16. *See also* India; legislation

Indian Police Service (IPS), 6, 20–24, 48, 94, 107, 113, 118–27, 132, 136, 171n14, fig. 4, appendix. *See also* Anand, Manu (DIG); Chanakya (IPS officer); deputy inspector general (DIG); director general of police (DGP); district police chief; district senior superintendent of police (SSP); district superintendent of police; inspector general (IG); police; senior officer

inequality, 31; historical, 149; power, 51; social, 20, 133, 148–49, 157; systemic sociocultural, 111. *See also* caste; discrimination; power; religious minorities; social difference; social minorities

ingenuity, 51, 54. *See also* agency; capability; connectedness; corruption; *jugaad*

innovation, 53, 56. *See also* ingenuity; *jugaad*; provisionality/provisional

insecurity, 138–58; collective, 15; extreme, 156; reproduction of, 153; site of, 152; sources of, 151; state of, 153, 158. *See also* authority; contingency; police; security

inspector general (IG), 120, appendix, 174n12. *See also* director general of police (DGP); Indian Police Service (IPS); senior officer

instrumentality/instrumental, 13–14, 16, 32, 35, 47, 58, 63–64, 88–89, 93, 95, 106, 119, 141–42, 145–46, 150, 152. *See also* agency; connectedness; exchange; good; *jugaad*; morality/moral; order/orderly; power; provision/provisionality; value/valuation

insurgency, 85, 112, 170n4. *See also* Mutiny; Sepoy Rebellion; union, police; violence; War of Independence

interdependence, 14, 32, 156. *See also* connectedness; contingency; exchange; *jugaad*; provisional/provisionality; sociality

intimate culture, 50, 63. *See also* connectedness; *jugaad*; sociality

investigating officer (IO), 60, 77. *See also* chief station officer (SO); police

IO. *See* investigating officer

IPC. *See* Indian Penal Code

IPS. *See* Indian Police Service

Islam. *See* Muslim; religious minorities; violence

janata ki adaulat, 97. *See also* court; Kurukshetra

janhit, 103, 117, 143–44. *See also* bureaucracy; bureaucrat; good; public; transfers

Jauregui, Beatrice, 24, 29–33, 45, 48, 63–68, 72–73, 83, 91, 93, 97, 99, 106, 130, 132, 135, 137, 142, 149–50, 165n32. *See also* anthropology

jawan, 83, 171n17. *See also* constable; sepoy

Jeffrey, Craig, 56. *See also* anthropology; fixer; *jugaad*

judges, 51, 60–62, 91, 120, 155; in khaki, 73–81; station chief as extra-legal, 20, 81. *See also* court; law; lawyers; legality

jugaad, 32–38, 46–47, 49–56, 58, 124, 129, 132, 134, 144, 154; attempts to define, 33–35; isomorphic with corruption, 59; opposed to corruption, 54, 59; praxis of, 54; vehicle, 34, fig. 10. *See also* Chakkar Rasta Thana (CRT); corruption; innovation; nepotism; Praveen; provisionality/provisional; Yadav, Y. K.

kaalaa daan, 2, 48, 122. *See also* black money; corruption; *crorepati*; kingpin postings; organized crime

khaki, 7, 39, 47, 60, 79, 111, 139. *See also* judges; police; uniform

KIA. *See* killed-in-action (KIA)

killed-in-action (KIA), 84–85, 87–88, 97, 101, 106–8, 170n1, 172n22, 172n25, fig. 19. *See also* compensation/compensate; ex gratia death compensation; expendability; martyr; *paavan smriti*; police; Police Remembrance Day; sacrifice; violence

kingpin postings, 122–23. *See also* bribes; chief station officer (SO); corruption; cutting-edge police; district police chief; district senior superintendent of police (SSP); district superintendent of police; *kaalaa daan*; transfers

Klockars, Carl, 65, 94. *See also* Dirty Harry problem; social theory

knowledge, 20, 58, 72, 133–34, 144, 165n33; flexible collage of, 167n1; fragmented, 105, 117; insider, 135; local, 119; partial, 30; public, 92, 117; shifts in, 15, 151; specialized, 13; strategic, 136; work of police, 150–51. *See also* agency; police; speculation

Krishna, 96. *See also* Arjuna; Hindu deity; Hinduism

Kurukshetra (Manjrekar 2000), 96, 171n18. *See also* Bollywood; encounter killings; *janata ki adaulat*; politics

lathi charge, 5, 7, 90. *See also* police; violence

law, 10, 19–20, 31, 64–65, 142, 144, 147, 149; contradictions inherent to the, 82; domestic violence, 75–76; indeterminacy of the, 32; letter of the, 46; originary violence of, 12, 66, 71–72, 144, 157; outside the, 40; provisionality of the, 64; spirit of the, 46; state, 137. *See also* authority; government; indeterminacy/indeterminate; law and order; law enforcement; lawyers; legality; legislation

law and order, 7–8, 10, 20, 22, 64. *See also* authority; elections; law; law enforcement; order/orderly; police

law enforcement, 144. *See also* law; legislation; police; violence

lawyers, 7–8, fig.1. *See also* court; judges; law

legality, 162n10; indeterminacy of, 82, 168n7; provisionality of, 63; questionable, 133; violations of, 66. *See also* extra-legality/extra-legal; law; legislation; provisionality/provisional

legislation, 141: Black Money (Undisclosed Foreign Income and Assets) and Imposition of Tax Act, 161n2; Criminal Law (Amendment) Act, 169n14; Domestic Violence Act, 75; Incitement to Disaffection Act, 147; Indian Evidence Act (IEA), 70; Indian Police Act, 19; Police Forces (Restriction of Rights) Act, 147; Sexual Harassment of Women at Workplace (Prevention, Prohibition, and Redressal) Act, 169n14. *See also* government; law; law enforcement; legality; legislative assembly; Member of Legislative Assembly (MLA); Member of Parliament (MP); police; politics; *Vidhan Sabha* (legislative assembly)

legislative assembly, 3–4, 22, 42, 73, 113–14, 172n1. *See also* elections; legislation; Lucknow; Member of Legislative Assembly (MLA); Member of Parliament (MP); police; politics; *Vidhan Sabha* (legislative assembly); VIP

legitimacy, 16, 34, 145, 158; indeterminacy of, 82; police, 149, 162n12; of violence, 94, 103, 146, 165n40. *See also* indeterminacy/indeterminate; legitimation

legitimate force, 145. *See also* legitimacy; violence

legitimation, 16, 37–38, 46, 104, 149, 162n10; *jugaadi*, 59, 63, 76, 81, 124–25, 132. *See also* authority; legitimacy; provisional/provisionality

Lucknow, 1–2, 7, 18–26, 29, 39, 47, 105, 111, 118–25, 133, 138, 140, 146, 153; district police of, 54; police-lawyer clashes in, 7–8, fig. 1. *See also* capital; Chakkar Rasta Thana (CRT); director general of police (DGP); district police chief; elections; elites; India; legislative assembly; Uttar Pradesh (UP); *Vidhan Sabha* (legislative assembly); VIP

Machiavelli, 65. *See also* Dirty Harry problem; ethics; politics; social theory; violence

Macht, 14, 37, 42, 55, 64. See also *Herrschaft*; power; Weber, Max

Mahabharata, 96. *See also* Arjuna; *Bhagavad Gita*; Hindu epic myth; Krishna

Maharashtra, 18, 96. *See also* Bombay; Mumbai

malik, 46

mandir, 3. *See also* temple

martyr, 97. *See also* killed-in-action (KIA), *paavan smriti*; police; Police Remembrance Day; sacrifice

Marx, Karl, 124, 139. *See also* social theory; value/valuation

Mathur, Nayanika, 127. *See also* anthropology; bureaucrat; cynicism
Mayawati, 121–22, 169n13. *See also* Bahujan Samaj
Party (BSP); chief minister (CM); Dalit; political interference; politicians; politics; Scheduled
Caste/Scheduled Tribe (SC/ST)
media, 4–5, 148. *See also* news media; public;
public culture
media mogul, 30. *See also* media
Member of Legislative Assembly (MLA), 4, 114–
15, 117. *See also* legislative assembly; Lucknow;
Member of Parliament (MP); politicians; politics; Uttar Pradesh (UP); *Vidhan Sabha* (legislative assembly); VIP
Member of Parliament (MP), 2, 18, 23, 74. *See also*
Central Election Commission (CEC); Member
of Legislative Assembly (MLA); politicians;
politics; VIP
methodology, 22–32. *See also* anthropology; cutting-
edge; ethnography
minority groups, 10, 13, 23, 92, 149, 151, 163n18. *See
also* religious minorities; social minorities;
society
miscommunication, 31
misrepresentation, 47, 58, 141. *See also* impersonation; Praveen; uniform
MLA. *See* Member of Legislative Assembly
money laundering, 2. *See also* black money; corruption; *kaalaa daan*; organized crime
Moradabad, 23, 101, 132, figs. 4, 19. *See also* Aditya
(sub-inspector cadet); training
moral ambivalence, 52, 94, 103–4, 106. *See also*
ethics; instrumentality/instrumental; *jugaad*;
morality/moral; power; virtue/virtuosity
morale, 41, 85, 124, 127, 132, 135, 141, 144
morality/moral, 8, 31–32, 36–39, 51–56, 58–59, 62–
68, 72, 90–91, 93–94, 96–98, 103, 126, 133–35, 152,
157, 170n18, 175n4; and instrumental value, 13–
14, 16, 35, 88–89, 105–6, 119, 141–42, 145–46, 150.
See also accountability; contingency; corruption; dirty anthropology; duty; ethics; good;
instrumentality/instrumental; provisionality/
provisional; value/valuation; virtue/virtuosity
MP. *See* Member of Parliament
Mughal Empire, 18, 20. *See also* India; Islam;
Muslim
mukhbir, 45
multiplicity, 14; and inconsistency, 14; and indeterminacy, 15, 81–82, 143; of moral-instrumental
demands, 32; of roles, 67, 81. *See also* indeter-
minacy/indeterminate
Mumbai, 57, 162n16, 167n14. *See also* Bombay;
India; Maharashtra
murder, 65, 69–71, 95–98, 121, 168n9. See also
baanka; civilian deaths; encounter killings;
randwa pratha; violence

Muslim, 18, 63, 103, 130, 149, 161n1, 171n19. *See
also* discrimination; Mughal Empire; religious
minorities; violence
Mutiny, 19. *See also* insurgency; Sepoy Rebellion;
uprising; War of Independence

Nader, Laura, 6. *See also* anthropology; ethnography
nagar nigam (municipal council) elections, 47,
138. *See also* constables; elections; government;
Lucknow; politics
nari-dharma, 75. See also *dharma*; domestic violence; dowry; dowry death; women
National Crime Records Bureau (NCRB), 24,
107, 109
nationalist movement, 147. *See also* British
colonial administration; colonial expansion;
uprising; War of Independence
Navaro-Yashin, Yael, 127. *See also* anthropology
Naxalite movement, 112. *See also* separatist movement
NCRB. *See* National Crime Records Bureau
nepotism, 50. *See also* connectedness; corruption;
jugaad; provisionality/provisional; sociality
New Delhi, 2, 6, 18, 22, 113, 121, 132, 136, 147; suburbs of, 122. *See also* India
news media, 7–10, 108, 118, fig. 1. *See also* media;
public culture
NGO. *See* nongovernmental organization
nongovernmental organization (NGO), 129
non-negotiably coercive force, 8, 15, 66, 141,
162n12. *See also* authority; Bittner, Egon; police;
violence
nonviolent resistance, 146. *See also* Gandhi, Mahatma; *satyagraha*

OBC. *See* Other Backward Classes
officer in charge (OIC), 30. *See also* Chakkar Rasta
Thana (CRT); chief station officer (SO); police
official, in relation to unofficial, 10, 12–13, 20–26,
31–32, 41–49, 51, 58, 61, 64, 72–74, 76–81, 97–99,
112, 114–15, 117–20, 122–29, 132–37, 139, 142–43,
146, 150, 162n9, 165n34, 166n1, 166n4, 166n7,
167n1, 173n6. *See also* indeterminacy/indeter-
minate; positionality/position; provisionality/
provisional; state official
OIC. *See* officer in charge
order/orderly, 8, 11, 32, 50, 65, 81, 101, 135, 144, 153–
57, 168nn3–5; ambivalent, 90–95; cosmic, 98,
171n16; enforce, 143; ethics, 32, 59, 60–82, 126,
134, 142; executing, 21, 106; follow, 4, 130; giving, 15, 39, 45, 69–70, 121, 169n13; good, 98–100;
juridical, 104; logistical, 86; official, 26, 64; of
provisional authority, 115–16, 136; public, 173n11,
175n6; shifting, 10, 105, 138; sociocultural, 13,
16–17, 46, 63; transfer, 119–20, 124, 137, 172n3,

173n9; unofficial, 74, 122. *See also dharma*;
   ethics; law and order; police; public; security;
   social order
orderly room, 21, 138, 168n5. *See also* constable;
   order/orderly; police; senior officer
organized crime, 45, 112. *See also* bribes; corruption; criminals; money laundering; murder;
   smuggling; violence
Ortner, Sherry, 47, 55, 57–58, 134, 144. *See also*
   agency; power; serious games; social theory
Other Backward Classes (OBC), 3–5, 51. *See also*
   caste; class; Samajwadi Party; Yadav (caste)

paavan smriti, 85, figs. 15–16. *See also* expendability; police; Police Remembrance Day; sacrifice
PAC. *See* Provincial Armed Constabulary
pahunch, 10, 48, 105, 122, 133, 135. *See also* connectedness; *jugaad*; patronage; provisionality/
   provisional
Pandey (sub-inspector), 69–73. *See also* sub-
   inspector
party bandi, 132, 174n20. *See also* bureaucracy;
   jugaad; political parties; politicians; politics;
   transfers
patrol (*gasht*), 24–25, 30, 39–40. *See also* police
patronage, 62–68; local relations of, 157; systems
   of, 68. *See also* connectedness; *pahunch*; police
performance/performativity, 38, 107, 121, 142; of
   collective beneficence, 141; didactic, 107; ritual
   public, 143. *See also* police; public
PHQ. *See* UPP Headquarters
police, 6–11, 19–20, 26, 36, 51, 144–48; academy,
   132; accountability of, 119, 149–50; ambivalence,
   90–95; armed, 24; as avatars, 89, 98, 103–4, 108,
   112; barracks, 27, 109; brutality, 5, 7, 13, 32, 108;
   bureaucracy, 143, 147; business, 27; chain of
   command, 26; civil, 24; classes of, 137; coercive
   authority of, 12, 40–41, 58; confessions to, 70;
   demographic composition of the, 149; *dharma*,
   95; discrimination, 149–51; duty, 42, 59, 64, 72,
   81–82, 89, 103, 109–11, 118, 121–22, 135–39, 156;
   encounters, 92–95, 97, 111, 172n26; expendable,
   32, 95–112, 134–35, 143, 156; expressions, 31; families, 27–29, 47–49, 98, 101–2, 154, fig. 9; filmic
   representations of, 96–98; fungibility, 143, 156;
   as a global form, 144; global problems of, 144–
   53; hierarchy, 4, 20, 23, 49, 129, 131; history, 23;
   housing, 154; hyper-empowerment of, 10; the
   image of the fat-bellied, 42; infrastructure, 108–
   9; injustice, 13; inquiry, 30; institution, 144–45,
   147–49; interactions, 149; investigation, 30;
   jobs, 47–49, 141; killed-in-action, 84–85, 87–88,
   97, 101, 106–8, 170n1, 172n22, 172n25, fig. 19;
   killings, 10, 92, 96, 172n26; knowledge, 150–51;
   legitimacy of, 149; life, 31, 88–90, 143, 148, 156–
   57; low-level, 48; as the muscle of governance,

143; non-negotiably coercive force of, 8, 15, 66,
   141, 162n12; officer, 4–6, 20, 31, 51, 132–33, 143–
   44, 147, 149–50, 153, 155; official, 57, 145, 155–56;
   orderlies, 65, 68, 82, 89, 103–5, 143; organization, 20, 147; poor image of, 5; poor working
   conditions, 109–11; practice, 11, 13–20, 25–26,
   31–32, 38, 133–38, 142–44, 152, 156–57; presence,
   138; pressures on, 32, 138, 141; protection, 151;
   public, 11–12, 148; recruitment, 20, 24, 48–49,
   135, 155, fig. 13; reform of, 10, 145; sacrifice, 134;
   as servants of coercion, 143; as servants of violence, 151; as social other, 89, 104; social role
   of, 12; state, 38, 148, 158; station, 20, 25–30, 100;
   subjectivity, 157; subjectivization, 32, 129; training of, 23; under-resourced, 40; universal authority of, 8; unofficial agreement with, 41, 46;
   uprising of, 148; as vigilante, 93, 95; vigilantism,
   93–94; welfare, 103, 141, 147, 156; widow, 106;
   work, 7, 25, 31, 59, 132, 136, 140–41, 156. *See also*
   accountability; authority; avatars; bureaucracy;
   Chakkar Rasta Thana (CRT); command;
   connectedness; constable; corruption; Crime
   Register; duty; families; Hanuman; insecurity;
   instrumentality/instrumental; *jugaad*; killed-
   in-action (KIA); martyr; morale; morality/
   moral; *pahunch*; patronage; performance/
   performativity; political interference; power;
   provisionality/provisional; sacrifice; security;
   servant; *thana*; transfers; violence; work; working conditions
Police Commemoration Day, 83. *See also* Police
   Remembrance Day
Police Remembrance Day. 83, 105–7, 143. *See also*
   expendability; killed-in-action (KIA); *paavan
   smriti*; police; Police Commemoration Day;
   Uttar Pradesh (UP)
political interference, 103, 105, 114, 118, 129, 173n6,
   fig. 22. *See also* bureaucracy; corruption;
   government; patronage; police; politicians;
   politics; transfers
political parties, 18–19, 56, 77, 90, 121–22, 143, 150,
   152. *See also* Aam Aadmi Party (AAP); Bahujan Samaj Party (BSP); Bharatiya Janata Party
   (BJP); Congress Party; politician; politics;
   Samajwadi Party
political society, 11. *See also* politics; society
politicians, 8, 10, 23, 25, 45, 131–32, 139, 141. *See also*
   elites; government; Lucknow; political parties;
   politics; VIP
politics, 11, 19, 150, 158; bureaucratic, 19, 150; of
   bureaucratic postings, 32; caste, 18–19, 56; democratic, 6, 16–17, 51; electoral, 23, 148, 150;
   electoral-cum-identity, 149; UP state, 18; volatile, 152. *See also* bureaucracy; bureaucrat;
   caste; class government; India; patronage; political interference; political parties; politician;

politics (*cont.*)
  power; religious minorities; social minorities;
    society; state; transfers; vendetta politics; VIP
positionality/position, 13–16, 32, 37, 48–49, 64, 96,
    103, 123, 146, 162n6, 164n30; of authority, 42, 132,
    135–36; contingent, 45; official, 58, 119, 169n13;
    shifts of, 119, 121, 133; social, 38–39, 48, 51, 56,
    141, 151, 155; strategic, 119, 122. *See also* agency;
    authority; power; provisionality/provisional;
    sovereignty
postcolonial, 6, 19–20, 94, 130, 137, 141–50, 163n18,
    163n25, 165n32, 175n6, fig. 3. *See also* India
poverty, 53, 166n7. *See also* Dalit; developing
    countries; economics; inequality; Other Back-
    ward Classes (OBC); urban slums
power, 6, 14–15, 37–39; 55, 157; corrupts, 48; Foucault's
    concept of, 58; global, 53, 152; international, 26;
    as *Macht*, 14, 37, 42, 55, 64; productive, 13; rela-
    tions, 10, 32; shifts in, 7; Wolf's concept of, 55. *See
    also* agency; authority; biopower; Foucauldian;
    Foucault, Michel; governance; governmentality;
    Macht; Ortner, Sherry; police; politics; violence;
    Wolf, Eric
PPS. *See* Provincial Police Service
pradhan, 20, 77–78, 170n17
Praveen, 26, 47–50, 54, 58, 133, 135, 154. *See also*
    Home Guard (HG); impersonation; *jugaad*;
    police, families; uniform
Prithvi (constable), 39–42, 45, 60–62, fig. 12. *See
    also baanka*; Chakkar Rasta Thana (CRT); con-
    stable; *hamraahi*; police; *tempo*; Yadav, Y. K.
Provincial Armed Constabulary (PAC), 24. *See
    also* police; uprising
Provincial Police Service (PPS), 20, 22, 48, 107,
    appendix. *See also* circle officer (CO); deputy
    superintendent of police; police; senior officer
provisionality/provisional, 30–32, 36–55, 58; of
    agency, 55, 57–58; of authority, 11–16, 26, 31–41,
    51, 56–59, 104, 111, 115–19, 122–29, 132–37, 140–49,
    155–58; exchanges of, 42; social, 46, 48, 52, 56–57;
    of sociocultural order, 13; of virtue, 57. *See also*
    agency; authority; contingency; cutting-edge;
    exchange; good; innovation; instrumentality/
    instrumental; *jugaad*; morality/moral; police;
    positionality/position; resources; temporality
public, 8, 11–12, 20–22, 143, 149–51, 157; account-
    ability to the, 11; demands for police discrimi-
    nation and violence, 32, 89, 93–95, 105, 143–45,
    151; employment, 52; everyday police interac-
    tions with the, 22; face of the police, 22; good,
    103, 117–20, 124, 131, 142–43, 158; misapprehen-
    sions, 5; office for private gain, 54; and private
    spheres, 37–38, 52, 120–25, 129–30; protest, 151;
    shame, 20; sphere, 11; welfare, 141. *See also* gov-
    ernment; *janhit*; media; news media; police;
    public culture

public culture, 112, 145–46. *See also* media; news
    media; public
public prosecutor, 7

raid (*dabish*), 40, 42. *See also* police
Rajasthan, 5, fig. 10. *See also* India
Ram, 98–100. *See also* Hanuman; Hindu epic
    myth; Hinduism; *Ramayana*; Ravana; Sita;
    Sita-Ram
Ramayana, 98. *See also* Dussehra; Hanuman;
    Hindu epic myth; Hinduism; Ram; Ravana;
    Sita; Sita-Ram
randwa pratha, 69, 168n8, 172n22. See also *baanka*;
    murder; violence
rape, 20, 65, 80, 168n2. *See also* domestic violence;
    gang rape; sexual assault; violence; women
Ravana, 98–100. *See also* Hanuman; Hindu
    epic myth; Hinduism; Ram; *Ramayana*;
    Sita-Ram
reform, 111, 148. *See also* social movement
religious minorities, 7, 19, 149–51. *See also* Bud-
    dhism; discrimination; Islam; Muslim; Sikh;
    social minorities; violence
resources, 32, 35, 39–40, 49, 51; scarce, 30, 34, 42.
    See also exchange; good; *jugaad*; police; provi-
    sionality/provisional
riot, 7–8, 121, 130, 162n7, 171n19, 174n19. *See also*
    civilian deaths; lawyers; religious minorities;
    violence
Roitman, Janet, 56, 64, 142. *See also* anthropology;
    ethics

sacrifice, 89, 99–101, 105–12, 134–35; difference be-
    tween service and, 101; of life, 84–85, 104, 106;
    the path of, 97; of self, 75; as separation from
    the good life, 103; soldierly, 97–98, 100–3, 111.
    See also Agamben, Giorgio; avatars; *bali kaa
    bakra*; biopower; duty; expendability; Hanu-
    man; *homo sacer*; killed-in-action (KIA);
    martyr; police; servant; service; social theory;
    sovereignty
samadhan, 80
Samajwadi Party, 2–4, 18, 22, 26, 121, 130–31, 133,
    137. *See also* Lucknow; political parties; politics;
    Yadav, Mulayam Singh
samjhana, 80
samjhauta karna, 80
sarkar, 19, 122
satyagraha, 146. *See also* Gandhi, Mahatma; non-
    violent resistance; truth
Scheduled Caste/Scheduled Tribe (SC/ST), 4,
    19. *See also* Bahujan Samaj Party (BSP); caste;
    Dalit; Mayawati
Schwegler, Tara, 136. *See also* anthropology;
    ethnography
SC/ST. *See* Scheduled Caste/Scheduled Tribe

security, 6, 16, 32, 122, 157, 165n33; global trends in hyper-, 94; job, 49, 156; for the public, 146; state, 66. *See also* authority; government; insecurity; law and order; order/orderly; police

senior officer, 10, 19, 21–25, 33, 48, 118, 125, 130–31, 139, 155, fig. 4. *See also* Indian Police Service (IPS); police; Provincial Police Service (PPS)

senior sub-inspector (SSI), 127, 137, fig. 22. *See also* police; sub-inspector (SI); transfers

senior superintendent of police (SSP), 24, 39–41, 121–23, 125, 127, 137, appendix. *See also* police; senior officer; superintendent of police

separatist movement, 112. *See also* Naxalite movement; social movement

sepoy, 19–20, 171n17. *See also* constable; *jawan*; Sepoy Rebellion

Sepoy Rebellion, 19. *See also* British colonial administration; India; sepoy; War of Independence

serious games, 57–58, 144. *See also* Ortner, Sherry

servant, 2, 65, 82; civil, 23; expendable, 32, 83–112. *See also* constable; duty; expendability; order/ orderly; police; service; violence

service, 56, 72. *See also* duty; ethics; police; servant; work

sexual assault, 121, 169n14. *See also* gang rape; rape; violence; women

Sharma (constable), 1–6, 25, 30, 40–41, 45, 49, 103, 117, 140. *See also* Chakkar Rasta Thana (CRT); constable; police; Tiwari (constable); Yadav, Y. K.

Sharma, Inspector Pradeep, 94–95. *See also* Bombay; Dirty Harry; encounter killings; encounter specialist; Mumbai; violence

shatranj, 134

shikshan, 39

shishtaachar, 111

shloka, 96–97

SHO. *See* chief station officer (SO); station house officer (SHO)

shoshan, 111

SI. *See* sub-inspector

Sikh, 149. *See also* religious minorities

Sita, 99–100. *See also* Hindu epic myth; Hinduism; Ram; *Ramayana*; Sita-Ram

Sita-Ram, 99–100, 104. *See also* Hindu epic myth; Hinduism; Ram; *Ramayana*; Sita

smuggling, 48, 132. *See also* black money; *kaalaa daan*; organized crime

SO. *See* chief station officer; Yadav, Y. K.

social capital, 148. *See also* social mobility

social change, 11. *See also* social justice

social connectedness, 50, 52. See also *jugaad*; Praveen; *yug/jug*; *yukti*

social critics, 8

social difference, 151. *See also* caste; class; discrimination; inequality; positionality/position

social dynamics, 144. *See also* *chalta hai*; collective beneficence; currency; *jugaad*

social good, 16. *See also* good; *jugaad*

sociality, 49–50, 54. *See also* connectedness; *jugaad*; nepotism

social justice, 145. *See also* social change

social minorities, 10, 13, 23, 149. *See also* discrimination; religious minorities; social difference

social mobility, 21, 54, 141, 148, 156. *See also* social capital

social movement, 21, 163n25; anti-corruption, 57, 152. *See also* Naxalite movement; reform; separatist movement; police; union, police

social order, 6, 10, 12–13, 16–17, 32, 46, 63; Durkheimian, 57, 64. *See also* agency; authority; morality/moral; instrumentality/instrumental; official, in relation to unofficial; order/orderly; society

social theory, 12, 66. *See also* Agamben, Giorgio; Althusser, Louis; Belur, Jyoti; Benjamin, Walter; Bittner, Egon; Eckert, Julia; Foucauldian; Foucault, Michel; Klockars, Carl; Machiavelli; Marx, Karl; Ortner, Sherry; Weber, Max; Wolf, Eric

social world, 141. *See also* society

society, 11–16, 143–46, 151–53. *See also* caste; children; class; democracy; politics; social order; state; women

South Asia, 13, 45, 56, 96, 170n2, 171n20; postcolonial, 19. *See also* ethnography; India

sovereignty, 12, 104, 157; anthropological conceptions of, 162n14; command, 146, 158; concept of, 157, 171n21; decision, 104, 150. *See also* authority; government; politics; positionality/ position; power

speculation, 117, 133, 134–37. *See also* indeterminacy/indeterminate; knowledge; social order; transfers

SSI. *See* Senior Sub-Inspector

state, 11, 22, 152–53, 156–58; authority of the, 153; externality of the, 11–12, 16; liberal democratic, 152; monopoly, 157; police as figures of the, 153; violence the monopoly of the, 12. *See also* anthropology; authority; democracy; governance; government; governmentality; politics; power; society; sovereignty; state externality; state office; state officials

state externality, 11–12, 16, 143, 145, 157, 162n8. *See also* state

state office, 147, 155. *See also* state; state officials

state officials, 6–7. 14–15, 22, 26, 38, 40, 42, 48–49, 51–52, 57–59, 83, 88–89, 92, 106, 109, 111, 115, 117–22, 124, 127, 129, 132, 136–37, 145–46, 150– 51, 155–56, 161n3, 162n9, 166n3, 169n13, 173n11, 174n12. *See also* bureaucracy; bureaucrat; official, in relation to unofficial; politicians;

state officials (cont.)
   politics; positionality/position; servant; state;
      state office
station. See thana
station house officer (SHO). See chief station officer (SO); police; thana
station officer (SO). See chief station officer (SO);
   police; thana
strategic complicity, 31, 132. See also anthropology;
   complicity; dirty anthropology; ethnography;
   methodology
studying up, 6. See also anthropology; ethnography; methodology; Nader, Laura
subaltern, 22, 38, 49, 147, 156. See also Subaltern
   Studies collective
Subaltern Studies collective, 147
sub-inspector (SI), 4, 20–22, 29, 33, 39–41, 46, 97, 101,
   131–33, 139–40, 146, fig. 8, appendix. See also Pandey; police; senior sub-inspector; Yadav, Y. K.
subjectivity, 16, 32, 64, 82, 125, 129, 143, 146–47, 151–
   53, 157; political, 104. See also agency; ethics;
   expendability; Foucault, Michel; order/orderly;
   positionality/position; power; sacrifice; servant; transfers
superintendent of police, 6–7, 39, 76, 117, 134, 164n30.
   See also district police chief; district superintendent of police; Indian Police Service (IPS); police;
   senior superintendent of police (SSP)
survival, 47, 56. See also police; sacrifice
swadeshi, 146

technology, 37, 53. See also economics; economy;
   jugaad
temple, 1, 3. See also darshan; Hanuman; Hinduism; mandir
tempo, 39–42, 58
temporality, 14, 36, 54–55, 59, 126, 162n12. See also
   chronotope; jugaad; provisionality/provisional
thana, 21–24, 26–30, 39, 41, 125, fig. 5. See also
   Chakkar Rasta Thana
Times of India, 87. See also media; news media;
   public culture
Tiwari (constable), 1–6, 12, 25, 40–42, 45, 49, 103,
   117, 140, 142. See also Chakkar Rasta Thana
   (CRT); constable; police; Sharma (constable);
   Yadav, Y. K.
training, 21–23, 39, 62, 101, 123, 126, 132, 136, 140,
   154–55, 164n28, fig. 4. See also Aditya (sub-
   inspector cadet); Bhim Rao Ambedkar Police
   Academy; Moradabad; police
transfers, 3–4, 45, 60, 74, 102, 112, 113–37; 143;
   kingpin postings, 122–23; transfer industry, 131,
   134. See also bureaucracy; bureaucrat; official,
   in relation to unofficial; police; positionality/
   position

trees, illegal cutting down of, 42–44, figs. 11–12
truth, 55, 64, 69, 71, 76, 97–98, 133, 145–46. See also
   Ardh Satya; ethics; Gandhi, Mahatma; order/
   orderly; satyagraha; value/valuation; virtue;
   yug/jug

uniform, 7, 39, 47, 79, 83, 111, 138–39; mismatch-
   ing, 127; paying out of pocket for, 47. See also
   impersonation; jugaad; police; Praveen
union, police, 21, 175n7. See also police; social
   movement; uprising; working conditions
union territories (UT), 16–17
UP. See Uttar Pradesh
UPP. See Uttar Pradesh Police
UPP Headquarters (PHQ), 24, 119. See also Allahabad; police; Uttar Pradesh Police (UPP)
uprising, 21, 147–48; police, 175n6. See also insurgency; Mutiny; union, police
urban slums, 111. See also caste; class; inequality;
   poverty; social minorities
Urdu, 7, 165n32, 170n1
Uttar Pradesh (UP), 2, 13, 17–18, 38, 51, 56, 149, 152,
   158, fig. 2; state government, 42. See also India;
   Lucknow
Uttar Pradesh Police (UPP), 1, 8–10, 23, 33, 50, 53,
   60, 138–40, 147, 149, 153, figs. 3, 17; rules and
   regulations of, 29, 119. See also police; UPP
   Headquarters (PHQ); Uttar Pradesh (UP)

value/valuation, 13, 47, 119, 153; of collective provision, 50; cultural, 54; devaluation, 105, 111–12,
   129, 141; devaluation via transfer, 113–37; exchange, 124; instrumental, 16, 35, 88; moral, 134;
   of police life, 143, 157; political, 130; resource,
   156; semiotic, 54. See also expendability; good;
   instrumentality/instrumental; jugaad; moral-
   ity/moral; virtue/virtuosity
vendetta politics, 122, 131. See also politics
Vidhan Sabha (legislative assembly), 22–23, 42;
   elections, 73, 113, 121. See also elections; elites;
   legislation; Lucknow; politics; VIP
vigilantism, police, 93–94. See also police
Vikram (constable), 153–55. See also black money;
   bribes; Chakkar Rasta Thana (CRT); constable;
   corruption; duty; families; kaalaa daan; order/
   orderly; police; poverty; Yadav, Y. K.
violence, 7–8, 32, 112, 133, 143–51, 157; coercion by,
   12–13; communal, 121; control of, 146; crowd, 5;
   disciplined, 146; ethnoreligious, 18; mass, 112,
   151; ordinary, 91; originary, 12, 144; police, 4–5,
   10, 102–4, 111; political, 18, 90; potential or actual, 143, 145; public demands for, 145; religious,
   18, 101, 151, 171n19; as a service, 145; slow, 157;
   social, 91; social reproduction of, 146; state
   monopoly on, 12, 31, 145–46; structures of, 111,

148; (sub)culture of, 91; thrill and sensuality of, 145; against women, 121. *See also* Aman (constable); *baanka*; discrimination; dowry death; encounter killings; encounter specialists; gang rape; human rights violations; insurgency; killed-in-action (KIA); *lathi* charge; legitimate force; murder; organized crime; police; *randwa pratha*; rape; religious minorities; riot; sexual assault

VIP, 20, 29, 48, 103, 111, 122–23, 146, 165n38, 174n15. *See also* authority; elites; Lucknow; patronage; politicians; politics; power

virtue/virtuosity, 32, 35–37, 47, 51–55, 57, 106, 152, 157. *See also* domestic violence; ethics; good; *jugaad*; morality/moral; instrumentality/instrumental; value/valuation

voice, 147; political, 147

Wade, Robert, 45

War of Independence, 19. *See also* British colonial administration; Gandhi, Mahatma; Sepoy Rebellion

Weber, Max, 12, 14, 16, 55, 58, 118, 165n40; concept of authority of, 16, 58; concept of bureaucracy of, 118; concept of monopoly on violence of, 12. *See also* authority; bureaucracy; coercion; command; *Herrschaft*; legitimacy; *Macht*; power; social theory

welfare, 103, 141, 147, 156. *See also* Aditya (constable); constable; expendability; good; police; sacrifice; servant; union, police; working conditions

Witsoe, Jeffrey, 56, 131, 141, 150. *See also* anthropology; Bihar; caste; ethnography; politics; Yadav (caste)

Wolf, Eric, 55. *See also* power; social theory

women, 5, 149. *See also* domestic violence; dowry; dowry death; families; gang rape; *nari-dharma*; rape; violence

work, 5, 11, 30–31, 40, 45, 56, 64, 66, 89, 122, 126–27, 143–44, 156–57; of cutting-edge police, 22, 101; of everyday police, 7, 26–27, 67–68, 105, 132, 140; of global demands of police, 59; of official police, 25, 81, 136; in tandem, 52, 73. *See also* duty; ethics; order/orderly; police; servant; service

working conditions, 64, 111, 148, 175n7. *See also* police; union, police; welfare

Yadav (caste), 18. *See also* caste; Other Backward Classes (OBC); Samajwadi Party

Yadav, Mulayam Singh, 84, 121–22, 170n3. *See also* bureaucrat; chief minister (CM); Other Backward Classes (OBC); Samajwadi Party; vendetta politics

Yadav, Y. K., 3–4, 25–26, 39, 42–46, 121–22, 126, 131, 133, 135, 154. *See also* authority; Central Election Commission (CEC); Chakkar Rasta Thana (CRT); chief station officer (SO); ethics; *jugaad*; order/orderly; Other Backward Classes (OBC); political parties; politics; provisionality/provision; Samajwadi Party; transfers; Yadav (caste)

yug/jug, 54–55, 71

yukti, 54, 71